Library of
Davidson College

SOCIOLOGY OF LEISURE

SOCIOLOGY OF LEISURE

Joffre Dumazedier
Professor of Social Sciences in the Department of Education
Université-René Descartes, Paris

Translated from the French
by Marea A. McKenzie

 Elsevier

AMSTERDAM — OXFORD — NEW YORK 1974

ELSEVIER SCIENTIFIC PUBLISHING COMPANY
335 JAN VAN GALENSTRAAT
P.O. BOX 211, AMSTERDAM, THE NETHERLANDS

and

52 VANDERBILT AVENUE
NEW YORK, N.Y. 10017

Library of Congress Card Number: 74—77580
ISBN 0-444-41226-3

Copyright © 1974 Elsevier Scientific Publishing Company, Amsterdam

All rights reserved. No part of this publication may be reproduced, stored in a retriev
system, or transmitted in any form or by any means, electronic, mechanical, photo-
copying, recording, or otherwise, without the prior written permission of the publish
Elsevier Scientific Publishing Company, Jan van Galenstraat 335, Amsterdam,
The Netherlands.

Printed in The Netherlands

Contents

Introduction 1

I Sociology of Leisure 9

II The Dynamics Generating Leisure 13
   1. Origins 13
   2. Soviet Society. The Evolution of Leisure, 1924–1967 43
   3. French Society. A Hypothesis Covering the Period 1955–1965 . 53

III The Quarrel over Definitions 67
   1. Definitions 67
   2. Classification Problems 77
   3. Implications 84
   4. Leisure and the Third Age 92

IV Work – Leisure – Time – Space 107
   1. Relations between Work and Leisure 108
   2. Relationships between Work and Leisure 122
   3. Can the Duration of Work be Reduced? 125
   4. Leisure and Space: The Need for a Policy of Cultural Development as Part of Town and Country Planning 138
   5. Some Conclusions 145

V Frames of Reference and Methods 153
   1. Cultural Development: Concepts and Dimensions 153
   2. Adult Education: an Operation for Cultural Development . . 173
   3. Towards an Active Sociology: Social Determinants, Forecasting, Decision-making 181
   4. Forecasting, Decision-making. The Comparative Method . . . 187

Conclusion 207

References 217

Author Index 227

Subject Index 230

Introduction

Prophecies of doom greeted the approach of the year One Thousand: the end of the world was alleged to be at hand. As the year Two Thousand draws near, our prophets are rather less than unanimous. Under cover of ideological critiques, of futurology, of utopian speculations, of science fiction or even of "sociology," forecasts are ventured, ranging from the rosy to the bleak. However, bleakness tends to prevail and, as a result, scientific observation, exploration and forecasting lose out.

This attitude has impinged on the study of leisure, which may well be peculiarly vulnerable to the delusions of prophesying. The indefiniteness of its scope, the heterogeneousness of its forms, the elusiveness of its far-reaching implications, the emotional undertones conjured up by some of its current or unusual, lawful or forbidden practices, prompt either enthusiasm or spite — which are equally incompatible with rigorous study. In addition, epistemological difficulties slowing down the development and dissemination of scientific knowledge spring from the overt or hidden resistance of the old ideologies centering on work or study, on family duties or political commitment, to the distrusted values embodied in leisure.

From the complex and changing reality of leisure, each observer abstracts the aspects in which he happens to be interested, assigns primacy to it and overlooks all others. The approach to leisure tends to be manichean rather than dialectical. While some authors see it as a widespread phenomenon in the emerging society of tomorrow, others denounce leisure as an ideologically induced delusion. According to some, it offers freedom for self-expression, while to others it conceals the manipulation or the repression of individual preferences. Leisure is either described as a future substitute for alienated work or is increasingly downgraded by the reform of the work situation to the status of a more or less uninteresting pastime. Some argue that it will be devoted to continuous and voluntary adult education in order to make up for the inadequate instruction forcibly dispensed by a crisis-torn school system. Others, however, feel that it will be reduced to the provision of entertainment by the expansion and reform of formal education. To some, leisure is outside the sphere of "necessity" and hence constitutes an autonomous basis for a theory of freedom. To others, it is far too dependent to underpin any theory. It has been praised as the best means of enhancing self-expression and blamed as the artificial epiphenomenon of a sick society, incapable of generating any new civilisation.

These contradictory views are witness to the likely importance of the problems raised by leisure in advanced industrial societies, faced with the uncertainties of post-industrial change. Despite the differences between them, they all share a common characteristic; they all dispense — albeit to varying degrees — with the painstaking and tedious observation of facts, systematically carried out. When data is used, it is selected to substantiate a case by providing appropriate examples. It is hardly ever chosen so as to cover the whole dynamic range of positive or negative facts relevant to a clearly delineated problem. Yet it seems imperative to outline the different types of facts and their diverse manifest or latent mutual relationships, unearthed by empirical sociology at various times.

Such facts are known to vary according to the questions asked and questions to be always related to a meta-sociological stance. Yet, whatever its limitations, factual data provides landmarks without which sociological analysis — whether concerned with practical change or with the progress of theory — will reduce to mere speculation. Any sociological theory exhibits the following three characteristics:

(1) It is deduced from a more general theory.
(2) It possesses logico-deductive coherence.
(3) It shows that no important fact is incompatible with it. Al-

though it is always an exciting exercise to blend into a coherent whole the ideas deduced from a more general theory, how is theory to be distinguished from speculation unless theoretical thought yields to the discipline of induction? The time is not yet ripe to devise a sociological theory of leisure, despite the interest afforded by attempts at theorising. However, in this complex and troubled time in which certainties are questioned everywhere, analysing the endeavours and the findings of empirical sociology appears to be the most useful way of liberating theoretical thought from the delusions of dogmatism and of guiding practical action away from the powerlessness of mere practicality.

Sociologists of leisure are characterised by a particularly self-critical attitude. Both Girod (1972) and Lanfant (1972) stress this feature. Thus I shall be true to type in failing to conceal the difficulties which any scientific study in our field is bound to encounter.

Far from hiding such difficulties, I shall bring them to light and shall endeavour to show how I have tackled them. If my attempt proves successful, this study covering a chapter in the history of our discipline ranging from 1953 to 1973 will perhaps be considered as a contribution to the knowledge of a *scientific strategy*. I realize that such a task can be hazardous and that I am in danger of succumbing to all the illusions to which the authors of testimonials, memoirs or diaries, even so-called "scientific" ones, are prone. How can this sort of professional self-analysis avoid attitudes of exaggerated self-praise or self-blame, patterns reconstructed after the event in a search for coherence, and, last but not least, glaring prejudice? Yet how is one to approach sociological problems without adopting a standpoint? Since information about the conditions and the origins of my work exists, I believe it ought to be given. Thus I shall state the *conscious* motivation of the scientific choices I am making.

I shall not hesitate to tackle the double task which reflects the dual nature of any sociology, corresponding on the one hand to the problems it proposes and, on the other, to the results it imposes.

With regard to actual statements, I shall first attempt to rely on systematic observations, made as far as possible according to the rules of representativeness and probability. I willingly accept this constraint of scientific discipline, although it has been challenged and despite the restrictions it may impose on the scope of my arguments. Even the most brilliant method of illustrating ideas by confirmatory evidence or the most coherent theoretical reasoning can only transcend this limitation at the cost of frequent confusion between the unscientific and the scientific. This is a confusion I shall endeavour to avoid. Bachelard (1957) in his study of the history of science shows how general ideas, while useful *at a given time* as an incentive to formulating new hypotheses, later turn out to be the major obstacle to their corroboration. On the other hand, I shall not exclude emotion from my treatment of problems and hypotheses. I shall not dress it up as pure theory, although I acknowledge that the rationalisation without proof known as "theory" is of limited and provisional, but undeniable, utility. "Emotion" strikes me as a necessary component in the outline of sociological problems with which the sociologist who formulates them must be emotionally involved, even if no one else is. It is the spice of the social sciences. Without it empirical sociology might be reduced to a cold and costly reckoning of frequencies and correlations, often all too obvious. In the dispute between Bachelard and Scheler about the relationship between science and culture, I agree with Bachelard's refusal to exclude the former from the latter, as if science were only concerned with rationality and culture with personality. For him, the scientist who is most exacting about standards of evidence, is emotionally committed as a person when challenging ignorance or the mistaken views of public opinion. Since science deals with man, how could it exclude the emotions by which men are swayed? Scientism can only be naive or dishonest.

I claim the right to express the axiological preferences (which some would call ideological) fundamental to the epistemological and methodological choices made in approaching problems in all the areas covered by my work. The following questions must therefore be raised.

1. Any sociological work runs the risk of concentrating on problems already tackled and of seeking results already known, unless it is integrated not only in research teams, but with the kind of workshop, both real and fictional, made up of the main special-

ists in the field, even if they dwell thousands of miles apart. How did this problem strike me in the fifties and how have I endeavoured to solve it in the context of the national and international condition and prospects of the sociology of leisure?

2. It would be superfluous to show that scientific resources are somewhat scarce, especially in relation to the almost unlimited needs for information on a new subject (which became fashionable only between 1955 and 1965), within a young discipline. Why was I led to seek knowledge of the conditions in which spare time and leisure originated and developed in industrial societies and of inequalities in this development? Why did a diachronic sociology increasingly impose itself in this work, despite the often insurmountable difficulties which it forced me to face?

3. The problems of synchronic sociology are often linked in our field with those which diachronic sociology can (or cannot) solve. To define the object of sociology has been a constant issue from the very beginnings of this discipline. However, in the study of leisure, arguments about definitions are connected both with situational and with axiological problems. It is difficult to solve the former in relation to stages of the economic, social and cultural development of pre-industrial, industrial or post-industrial societies, but the latter are, in my view, virtually impossible to resolve in the current state of our subject matter. They are bound up with competing doctrines which shape human behaviour and which assess quite differently the role pertaining to work, to family responsibilities and to socio-spiritual or socio-political obligations as distinct from leisure, in a context of social stratification and of social mobility.

I shall try to explicitly state my conceptual and dimensional options, as well as the scientific *and* non-scientific reasons underlying them. I shall show their implications in the objective analysis of activities which are usually located in other frameworks, although they are mainly hidden aspects of a phenomenon which I call "leisure".

4. I shall seek to explain why the level of *values* currently seems the most important of those on which leisure can be analysed (and which roughly correspond to what Georges Gurvitch would have termed "levels in depth"). Manifest or hidden implications of

values held strike me as having a major impact on leisure, while interacting with the determining influence of unequal conditions in work, housing and culture. At present, on the brink of the crises which will change industrial societies into societies of another type, a one-sided study of leisure as a dependant variable, under the exclusive influence of the independent variables of the given society, might fail to highlight the impact of leisure values on time and space, on the living culture of all social classes. I shall attempt to formulate a new set of problems to cover these facts which, if they remained unexplored, might undermine systems of cultural policy in all advanced industrial societies.

5. Which will be the best frame of reference for this work, the best fitted to the study of the quantitative and qualitative problems concerning the content of leisure for the various social groups? Are the categories used for the analysis of mass culture most appropriate for investigating the kinds and levels of content of leisure as differently practiced by the different social classes, as well as the conditions and processes of their improvement according to explicit criteria? In outlining a sociology of cultural development, I shall seek to show how an adequate scientific conceptualisation of the frame of reference compels one to transcend the schism which, in the 19th century split humanistic culture from anthropological culture. Lastly, in order to devise this necessary cultural frame of reference, I must confront the rules of sociological method which currently delineate the relations between knowledge and action, between statements of fact and value judgements, according to the dominant trend of sociology. These rules posit a complete separation between two worlds, so that the vast sphere of future action eludes scientific knowledge. Yet relations between knowledge and action, as outlined by the so-called "critical" school of sociology and by the various interpretations of historical praxis, are ambiguous. They have the merit of repudiating a fictional dichotomisation of ideology and science, but they lead to a *confusion* between the proven and the non-proven, the subjective and the objective. Is there not a risk of thus destroying the very conditions on which science rests? I shall endeavour to avoid both pitfalls.

These issues provide the major axes of my analysis. I might have attempted an analysis in depth of the intellectual process from which originate both a scientific quest for the integration of problems of action and an active step towards the integration of scientific results. However such a design exceeds my present capacity. I shall limit myself therefore to dealing with the main aspects of the five issues described here, using as starting points the hypotheses and the facts which I am about to present.

I Sociology of Leisure

Some of the problems investigated here can only be grasped after gaining a preliminary understanding of the development of the sociology of leisure, at least in its main aspects. Thought about spare time has a long tradition, it is probably as ancient as work itself. Andrée (1966) has recently devoted a lengthy study to *otium* and *neg-otium* in the ruling class of Roman society. Is "otium" leisure in the sense which the gradual reduction of work-time for the majority of the labour-force during a century has entailed? I shall say later why I believe this not to be the case. It is from the advent of industrial society that 19th century social thinkers foresaw the importance of leisure or rather of the *time made free* by the reduction of factory work. However, after more than a century and a half, sociologists have failed to reach agreement either on the dynamics, or on the specific properties of "leisure" as a phenomenon, or on its main implications. In some writings, Karl Marx considered work in itself as the prime need of man. Elsewhere he stated that only the collective ownership of machines will enable mankind to gain free time, hence "space for human development", and thereby to humanize labour. Time thus liberated from work should, according to Marx, permit the present antinomy of labour and leisure to be transcended and the fulfilment of the Whole Man to be achieved. Naville (1967) has developed this thesis in an interesting way. As is well known, Comte and Proudhon differed from Marx in their concept of the future society, but all three gave the same importance to the acquisition of leisure as a result of technical progress and social emancipation. All three linked the development of leisure with progress in the intellectual culture of workers and with an increase in their participation in public affairs. "Thanks to leisure and to the means given to all, the reduction of the necessary social work to a minimum will favour the artistic and scientific development of everyone" (Marx, 1963).

Leisure as a fact in the 20th century proved more complex and ambiguous, as shown by the observations of sociologists in industrial societies, whether they be dominated by private or by collective ownership. It is in Europe that a militant socialist, Lafargue (1965), wrote in 1883 the first pamphlet advocating leisure for the workers and attacking the mystique of work. This started a debate among socialists which is still on-going: is work an end or a means? However, it is in the United States that the sociology of leisure was founded. I do not refer to Veblen's *Theory of the Leisure Class* (1899) which deals rather with the idleness of the various idle categories of the bourgeoisie than with the workers' leisure. Idleness negates work, leisure implies the existence of it. Veblen stressed mostly the conspicuous spending to which the quest for social prestige leads the ruling classes. It is only in the 1920's that the first empirical sociological studies of leisure proper appeared, both in Europe and the United States. The advent of the eight-hour day stimulated the hope and also the concern of social reformers: will spare time be used to fulfill or to degrade the personality of the working man? In the USSR a policy of organized leisure was accompanied by a campaign of enquiries into time-budgets, at the instigation of Strumilin (1964). The International Labour Office in Geneva organized in 1920 the first international congress on workers' spare time; three hundred members from eighteen countries attended. The need for organized leisure was perceived as a corollary of the reduction in working hours. Enquiries were launched in the United States. In *Middletown* the Lynds devoted much attention to traditional, modern and organized leisure. In 1934 appeared the first major enquiry centering on leisure, conducted by Lundberg and Komarovsky. It defined leisure by contrasting it with activities "considered in high degree obligatory or necessary to the maintenance of life and which are on the whole instrumental to other ends rather than ends in themselves" (Lundberg, 1934). This work is in my view the starting point of an empirical sociology of leisure. After the Second World War, the development of this sociology gave it a new sense and a new dimension. The United States faced the problems of "mass society", characterised by the massification of consumption, culture and leisure. In this new setting, the ambiguousness of leisure prompted numerous studies. In 1948 appeared David Riesman's *The Lonely Crowd*, whose impact proved worldwide and which sold over a million copies (Riesman et al, 1950). According to this author, modern man experienced only two "revolutions". The first was ushered in by the Renaissance: by becoming urbanized, man ceased to be "tradition directed," but was increasingly ruled by the norms and values of the restricted family. He became "inner directed." The second revolution started towards the middle of the 19th century in countries where mass consumption, mass culture and mass leisure appeared. Man is motivated by norms and values transmitted by the mass media and by peer groups. He becomes "other directed." From this standpoint, the development and the impact of mass leisure are central areas of study. In 1958 appeared the first book of readings on this theme, *Mass Leisure*, edited by E. Larrabee and R. Meyersohn, followed a year later by *Mass Culture* (A. Rosenberg and L. White, 1957). Decisive progress in the empirical validation of these new ideas on the relations between leisure and culture in mass societies was made by the Kansas City study team led by Havighurst (Havighurst and Feigenbaum, 1959) and especially by the Detroit study conducted by Wilensky (1964).

During the same period, the sociology of leisure experienced a parallel growth in Europe. Georges Friedmann in France attributed a privileged role to the meaning of leisure for the "reinsertion of man" in a technical civilisation where work is inhuman for a majority (Friedmann, 1946, 1950, 1956). In England, Rowntree started a series of studies and social surveys whose impact abroad, particularly in the Netherlands, was to prove considerable. (Rowntree and Lovers, 1951). Large-scale opinion surveys on youth leisure in 1954 led to an active equipment and training policy in Britain. In socialist industrial societies, studies on leisure (or spare time) also underwent a new development. In the Soviet Union, the gradual passage from an eight-hour to a seven-hour day between 1956 and 1962 stimulated new enquiries on time-budgets and leisure activities. In the tradition of Strumilin, there were publications by Prudensky (1964), Petrosjan (1965), Patrushev (1966), Grushin (1967) and Gordon (1969). It is in Yugoslavia that the first leisure survey using the most modern empirical methods was made (Ahtick, 1960). It was followed by many other surveys, especially those conducted by Mihovilovitch between 1967 and 1972 (Mihovilovitch 1968, 1969, 1971). The empirical sociology of leisure and of mass culture experienced also a considerable development in Poland since 1956, with the work of Zygulski, Skorzynski and Olzewska (Zygulski 1972; Skorzynski 1962, 1965), as well as in Czechoslovakia, mainly under the auspices of a team led by Filipcova (Filipcova, 1966).

The vitality of the sociology of leisure as a discipline has resulted in a multiplicity of approaches to problems. The same author may adopt several in turn, but one tends to prevail in his work. Leisure has been studied in its relationship to work, as by Filipcova, Friedmann, Parker, Prudensky, Riesman (Parker, 1971), to the family (Scheuch, 1960), to the status of women (Govaerts, 1969), to youth (Villadary, 1968), to religion (Pieper, 1958; Cox 1971), to politics (Lipset 1960), and to culture, as by Bosserman, Kaplan and Wilensky (Bosserman and Kaplan, 1971). It is treated as a time framework by Prudensky, Petrosjan, and Szalai (Szalai et al., 1973), in the context of daily life by Lefebvre (1972) and Busch (1973), as a pattern of activities by Littunen (1960) or as a value system by de Grazia (1962), or in connection with ideology by Lanfant (1972), etc. . . . Equal diversity prevails at the level of methodology. The sociology of leisure is not characterised by a specific method, but relies on many. It is historical from Veblen to Riesman or de Grazia; empirical in a majority of cases; comparative in some instances. The survey on spare time in time budgets (1967) deals with a national sample out of twelve countries: Austria, Belgium, Federal Germany, France, Hungary, Poland and the Soviet Union. It is conducted by A. Szalai (Hungary) under the auspices of the European Centre of Documentation in the Social Sciences in Vienna (1972). It is the most important international sociological study of spare time, based on observation and on a minimum number of explicit hypotheses.

II The Dynamics Generating Leisure

II.1. Origins

The advent of leisure raises such a problem that some have wondered, as has already been mentioned, whether it actually exists or whether it is a mere fiction. The laws of its development remain a subject of controversy among sociologists and historians alike. Can the holidays and feast-days of traditional society be described as leisure? Or is leisure a specific product of industrial society? What are the dynamics of its creation and of its development? What future may we foresee for it in the societies to which our advanced industrial societies are giving birth? Despite a prolific literature on this fashionable theme, no clear image of the future emerges and the forecasts made by researchers tend to contradict each other.

Some feel that leisure has existed at all times, in all civilisations. This is not my view, but it is asserted, e.g. by Sebastian de Grazia (1962). While spare time, in other words time off work, must obviously be as old as work itself, leisure has distinct characteristics, specific to the civilizations born of the industrial revolution.

In ancient societies, work and play were integrated in the feasts through which man shared in the world of his ancestors (Cazeneuve, 1961). Both activities, though differing in their practical ends, had similar meanings for the basic life of the community. The feast covered both work and play. Moreover the two were often interconnected. Contrast between them was either insignificant or non-existent. Nor would it be accurate to consider the category of shamans or sorcerers exempted from ordinary labour, as the forerunners of a "leisure class" in Veblen's sense, since their magic or religious functions were essential for the community. Leisure as a concept is ill fitted to ancient times.

In historical pre-industrial societies (Varagnac 1948) leisure did not exist either. Work followed the natural cycle of seasons and days: it was intense during the good season, slower during the winter. Its rhythm was natural, interrupted by breaks, by songs, by games and ceremonies. It tended to coincide with the pattern of the day, from sunrise to sunset. There was no clearcut division between work and rest. In our temperate climates, during the long winter months the pace of work slowed down and the struggle for survival was often hard in those periods of reduced activity. Cold was a killer, famines frequently added to the ill-effects of epidemics. To be inactive at such times was a necessity rather than a choice. A number of misfortunes often accompanied this condition, which clearly failed to possess the attributes of modern leisure.

Natural cycles were punctuated by a sequence of Sundays and holidays. Sundays were devoted to religious cult. Holidays often gave rise to a great expenditure of food and energy; they were the obverse of everyday life or its negation. Feasting was inseparable from ceremonies and generally closer to religious ritual than to leisure. Thus, although there were more than one hundred and fifty-five workless days per year, I do not feel that the concept of leisure is applicable to their analysis. To take France as an example, Vauban (1707) distinguished feast days, often imposed by the Church against the peasants' and artisans' will, in order to ensure the performance of religious obligations, and non-work days. In La Fontaine's fables the poor man complains that his parish priest is "forever adding some new saint to his sermon". In early 18th century France there were 84 such saint's days, to which should be added some 80 days a year when work was impossible (due to sickness, frost etc.). Peasants and artisans, who made up approximately 95% of the French labour force, were idle, according to Vauban, for 164 days per year, mostly because of religious observances or lack of work. In contemporary pre-industrial societies, many workers are deprived of jobs or reduced to irregular short-term employment by technological underdevelopment. I shall not call this free time, let alone leisure, but idle time.

Some researchers, such as de Grazia, have traced leisure back to the life style of the aristocratic classes in traditional civilisations. However, I am not convinced that the *idleness* of philosophers in ancient Greece or of sixteenth century gentlemen can be described as leisure. Such privileged individuals, whether cultivated or not, achieved idleness at the expense of their working slaves, peasants or servants. Therefore this idleness cannot be defined in relation to work, since it was neither a complement to, nor a compensation for it, but merely a substitute. This pattern of aristocratic idleness has undeniably contributed much to the refinement of culture. The Greek philosophers associated it with wisdom; the development of the whole man, both in body and mind, was the ideal of this life without work. Aristotle justified the rejection of servile labour by reference to higher values; the word "Schole" meant both idleness and school. In post-medieval European courts gentlemen discovered or praised the ideal of the humanist and of the "honnête homme". The idleness of the nobility was always linked with the most exalted values of civilisation, even when it was accompanied by mediocrity or baseness in real life. The concept of leisure is unsuited to the activities of these idle castes. Leisure is not synonymous with idleness; it does not abolish, but implies work, since it corresponds to a periodical release from employment at the end of the day, the week, the year or the active life.

Two preliminary conditions had to be met in social life in order to make it possible for the majority of workers to gain leisure:

a) Activities in society are no longer regulated as a whole by ritual obligations prescribed by the community. At least some of them, such as work and leisure, are not covered by collective rituals. Individuals are free to decide how to use their free time, although their choice is socially determined.

b) Remunerated work is demarcated from other activities. Its delineation is arbitrary rather than regulated by nature. Its specific organisation clearly separates it from free time or makes such a separation possible.

These two conditions exist in conjunction only in industrial and post-industrial societies. They make the concept of leisure inapplicable to ancient and pre-industrial ones. When leisure appears in modern rural communities, it is because work in the countryside tends to pattern itself on industrial work and life on its urban counterparts (Mendras, 1967). Similar comments apply to the agrarian societies of the Third World which are attempting to become pre-industrial.

II.1.1. Free time in the future

Does the undeniable increase in free time observed since the advent of industrial society until the last twenty years have implications for the future? Is this extension a mere delusion for many workers of all categories, from the wealthiest and most responsible managers to the poorest and most dependent unskilled immigrants? Not only has the scope of this increase been challenged, but it has been argued that free time has reached a peak which does not foretell the future of industrial society and already reflects its past. Two major theses are advanced in this connection.

Kahn and Wiener predict that in the year 2000 a humanitarian capitalism with high production rates will result in shorter worktime in American society; people might work only seven and a half hours a day for three days a week (Kahn and Wiener 1968). The weekend would extend over four days, from Friday to Monday inclusive, and the holidays currently enjoyed by the teaching profession i.e. thirteen weeks a year, might be common to most workers. Within a future post-industrial socialist society, Mandel envisages a twenty to twenty-four hour week, with five or six working hours per day provided outputs increase by 5% a year (which is a plausible assumption) within an economy effectively planned in relation to genuine needs and divested of its enormous military burdens (Heilbronner and Fords 1971). The long-term comments made by Fourastie on "tertiary societies" are analogous, but less specific and less committal since their target is beyond the year 2000. In about 2100 our distant successors would only work 1,200 hours a year (instead of 2,000 to 2,200 as in today's advanced industrial societies) divided into forty weeks of thirty hours each, over a thirty year working life (as against fifty years at present).

Other prophets take an entirely different view and do not

anticipate increased leisure in the future of industrial and post-industrial societies. The most recent and most outspoken exponent of this thesis is Galbraith. "During the last quarter of a century the average working week in industry has increased slightly (40.6 hours in 1941 to 41 hours in 1965). As their income rises, men spend more time at work and ask for less leisure. The concept of a new era of much expanded leisure is a mere conversational commonplace which will be in less and less frequent use" (Galbraith 1968).

Forecasts often rely on overemphasising one aspect of the present. Instead let us begin by observing the various facts without putting special stress on any. Any thesis or theory may be illustrated by selecting the cases which support it either in the past or the present. Thus it is all too often forgotten that to corroborate a hypothesis one should (1) collate all pertinent facts; (2) confront those which substantiate it and those which invalidate it, without making any omission or repetition; (3) observe the relationships which obtain between facts, so as to know which have the greatest impact on others; (4) observe the evolution of all facts, in order to ascertain which are increasing and which are decreasing. Whenever possible, I shall endeavour to use sets of representative facts obtained from censuses or surveys on which generalisations can be based by reference to probability.

I am aware both of the difficulties involved in this task and of the limitations inherent in this approach. I know that facts are always culled from answers to questions which depend on the person asking them as much as on the situation. I realise also that any truly sociological knowledge implies a concordance between a coherent theory and facts elaborated by a method whose scope and whose limits are known. In the current state of the sociological method in our field where prophecy all too often replaces probability calculations and where so-called "theoretical" speculations disregard any objective system of proof, this inductive approach, though limited, strikes me as providing the best way to avoid gratuitous statements. Induction ought to enable one to detect pertinent variables in the production of free time and, later, of leisure time in industrial societies. I expect it to point towards: (a) the different types of evolution undergone by free time and, later, by leisure according to the categories of workers; and

(b) the various components which can account for these types.

At this stage I shall not offer any definition of leisure; the approximate notion suffices for the first outline given here. The reader already familiar with the definition which I derived in 1955 from the results of a national survey on the representation of leisure in a sample of 819 French workers and employees, is requested to forget it. The issue of definitions will be tackled again later after this sketch of historical sociology. My comments will not be based only on surveys of French society, but will utilise data from America and from some other societies; the reasons for this approach will be given later. I shall attempt to find out whether despite differences in socio-economic and socio-political organisation, the hypothesis of convergence between industrial and post-industrial societies with respect to the dynamics generating leisure is tenable.

Post-industrial societies have been differently characterised by various authors (Dumazedier and Samuel, 1969; Kahn and Wiener, 1968; Richta, 1969; Touraine, 1969). They have been named scientifico-technical, cybernetic, neo-technical, programmed, or electronic; they have been identified with mass consumption, mass education, the sexual revolution, generational conflicts etc. It is to be hoped that the results of comparative study on cultural changes linked with increased leisure, which is currently conducted in seven countries, will permit the choice of an adequate definition. In the meantime, this type of society will be characterised by reference to the interaction between two interconnected sets of socio-economic variables.

a) The advanced stage of development of the forces of production (machines, organisations, skilled manpower) allows the highest levels of production.

b) These levels of production are due to an active population whose majority is no longer employed either in the agricultural or in the industrial sector, but in *services*, i.e. in the so-called post-industrial sector.[1]

The first empirical studies of this new type of society show that industrialisation remains the mainspring of the economy and that social relationships are still conflictual (between classes, sexes and generations). However, these relations and these conflicts are no longer the same. Societal and cultural changes occur which alter not only the content of social relationships, but the connection between obligations and options, between social duties and individual rights, between individual and collective value systems. Such changes appear to usher in the main transformations in the meaning of leisure and in its relations with basic civic duties.

Be that as it may, the trend towards a reduction in the duration of the working week in France has been resumed since the collective conventions of Grenelle, negotiated between unions, employers and the government in 1968. The average duration in the non-agricultural sector was 46 hours in 1967; it went down to 45 in 1969 and the Planning Authority ("Commissariat au Plan") forecasts that in 1975 it will decrease by an hour and a half to 44 or 43 hours. During this period (1968—71) the five-day week has become widespread. It is currently claimed by a growing number of workers. The working year has also shrunk, as the twelve days of paid holidays granted in 1936 were extended first to three weeks, then after 1968 to a month for most wage-earners. Outlooks keep changing. Thus a national survey conducted in 1963 by the French Institute of Public Opinion (IFOP) showed that about one third of manual workers preferred a reduction in working hours to an increase in wages, while the remaining two thirds favoured the opposite alternative (IFOP, 1964). Yet in the meantime the reduction of the working week (leaving the whole Saturday free) and earlier retirement have become more popular. In a recent survey conducted at the Renault factories, 65% of the staff at the Boulogne works and 80% at the Le Mans works expressed a preference for a reduction in working hours as against an increase in income (Faure and Bracke, 1971); it was voiced by 43.7% of the unskilled workers at Boulogne and 78.4% at Le Mans, and by 55.4% of those working in teams at Boulogne and 87.9% at Le Mans. It is not certain, however, whether these results could be generalised to the working class as a whole.

Some writers have challenged the general trend towards a reduction of work-time in the context of American society. For instance Wilensky used fragmentary data concerning some categories of manual workers, including observations on their working-week and their working-life (Wilensky, 1961). Since he drew up his calculations on this incomplete basis, two exhaustive studies have been published by Henle and by Clawson which give a more accurate picture of actual trends. Henle's study covers the evolution between 1948 and 1966 and enables one to sum it up (Henle, 1966). It shows two patterns: firstly, it is true that the number of non-agricultural wage-earners working over 48 hours a week has nearly doubled in seventeen years, passing from 7.8 to 9.4 million, i.e. from 12.9% to 19.7%. Such workers are mainly top-level managers or, at the other end of the scale, workers with few skills, domestic servants or small shopkeepers. However, it should be remembered that those who work 40 hours or less have passed from 56.6% to 64.5% during the same period and that they are a large majority of the working population. In the last five years the trend towards a decrease has been more marked, with a rapid growth in part-time employment especially for female workers whose share of the employment market has increased.[2] Not only has the four-day week (with 9—10 hours a day) been spreading, the trend towards longer holidays is recent and widespread. According to a recent report of the Bureau of Statistics, most wage-earners enjoy three weeks holiday, although the relevant legislation is less progressive than its French counterpart.

There are no studies in France on the basis of which the argument that the overall duration of the working life cancels out or reduces the evolution towards more free time, could be assessed. However, Clawson has studied time-budgets in American society between 1900 and 1950 and has drawn up forecasts for the year 2000 (Clawson and Knetsch, 1966). Despite the necessarily approximate nature of such a macro-economic and macro-sociological study, the orders of magnitude of the free-time enjoyed by the active population during the investigated period differ sufficiently from the present to leave no doubt about the general trend of time-budgeting in that post-industrial society. It is quite true that the global time worked by the active population has been steadily rising: from 86 million hours in 1950, it then passed to 132 million in 1970 and, according to probability studies, it will reach 206 billion in 2000. Yet such figures are more indicative of population growth and longer life expectancy[3] than of increases in work-times in daily life. Moreover it is often overlooked that the share of work in the nation's time budget has been decreasing, from 13% in 1900 to 10% in 1950 and an estimated 5% in 2000, whereas that of free time has been growing from 137 billion hours (i.e. 27%) in 1900 to 453 billion hours (i.e. 34%) in 1950 and an estimated 113 billion hours (i.e. 38%) in 2000. In addition, global increases in work-time and free time are distinctly unequal. Between 1950 and 2000, the former will be multiplied by three, the latter by six.

If "work as a value" is considered as representing an incentive for change, facts must be faced: even in an advanced industrial society like the USSR, which has done more than any other to propagate such values, a survey of workers aged between 18 and 30 in twenty-three works in Leningrad has shown in 1966 that only 7.7% were dominated by an "orientation towards productive work" (Zdravomyslov et al., 1967).

The following assertions can be made in the light of all these facts. Firstly, despite the increased availability of free time, the post-industrial or scientific and technical society will not be characterised by free time for all. Some of the workers will face working days, weeks, and years as long as in present-day society, either because they consider work as a source of cultural creation or of social responsibility, or because consumption needs prevail with them, or because spare-time activities fail to interest them. To overlook these facts when discussing present and probable future trends is to falsify reality, to put forward an ideology of free time or leisure. However, such remarks are only applicable to minorities.

For the majority of workers in advanced industrial societies, the overall trend seems to be towards more free-time even under socialist regimes. To consider only the duration of the working week during a given period or the overall evolution of working hours in our life-span, without assessing it *in relation* to the trend of free time within the global time-budget is to truncate reality. Such distortions of the relevant facts result in changing time-budgets. Those who make generalisations to that effect are prompted by the *wish* to see work become "the first need of man" rather than by scientific thought about the changing relations between work and free time in all types of advanced industrial societies.[4]

Under the influence of scientific and technical progress applied to production, of some producers' economic action, of mass consumption and of the unions' social action, the increase of free-time in relation to work time for a majority will be likely to represent the main problem of post-industrial societies before the end of the century. By that time, children who are now entering primary school will not have reached half their life-span.

II.1.2 Moonlighting

To what kind of activity is time freed from work devoted? It is not absorbed by leisure. In 1957, Swados, a social essayist guided by the collective comments of a militant unionists' group on the use of spare time generated by the advent of the thirty-two hour week in Akron's rubber factories, published an article under the striking title "Less Work, Less Leisure" (Meyersohn, 1958). This title became famous, as did some remarkable facts, e.g., that 40% of the workers to whom the new schedule applied allegedly took on additional jobs and 17% a second occupation. An impressive number of sociological works and social essays quoted these instances. The explicit or implicit comment usually derived from them was to cast doubt on the utility of reducing work times if another kind of work, moonlighting, took over. Does this not provide evidence of men's inability to master free-time, especially leisure, and show that work is the first of human needs (Grazia, 1962)? Georges Friedmann sums up this view when he asserts that spare time is experienced as a vacuum and filled with paid jobs or a second employment, not only because of economic needs, but also to fill the void (Friedmann, 1970).

Some recent surveys by empirical sociologists will be used in an attempt to clarify the situation. Firstly, in ascertaining the conditions under which Swados found his facts, it appeared that his assessment was founded on the testimony of militant unionists attempting to denounce the practice of overtime in factories, rather than on an empirical investigation. In systematic enquiries it is of course, difficult to rely on the figures stated by the respondents themselves. It is therefore necessary to resort to the estimates of those who can observe actual behaviour, but, in order to avoid arbitrary and biased statement, it seems advisable to start from empirical investigations in the first instance and then to endeavour to correct them by the critical observation of behaviour. The official statistics of the American Federal Bureau of

Labour (1968) show that 5% of workers practice moonlighting. In France the same percentage was revealed by a recent survey of one hundred and twenty workers in Toulouse, selected by quota according to an experimental plan (Larrue, 1965). Both the American and the French authors make similar reservations about the percentage given, but do not possess the data required to amend it. In a survey conducted at Annecy, a representative sample of the town's workers (1 in 20) and participant observation over several years (1955–70) resulted in an assessment based on cross-cutting testimonies whereby about 25% of wage-earners in the working class are moonlighters.

Two recent empirical investigations carried out in the Soviet Union and one in the United States have provided direct and indirect replies to questions about uses made of free time. In the first, factory workers were asked "if the working day was reduced and your spare time increased, how would you use it?" 16.9% replied "I'd do extra work", as a rule, "in order to earn more" (Zdravomyslov et al., 1967). In the second, conducted by Grushin with nearly 2000 workers in Moscow, 28.7% of respondents had worked in their spare time (Grushin, 1966). On the other hand, in the United States, a questionnaire was sent to all the 700 workers employed by an (unrepresentative) sample of factories which had adopted the three-day weekend in 1970. The first 148 replies were retained for rapid processing; they originated from 80% of the workers. Among them 4% admitted to "moonlighting" at the time of two-day weekends. With three-day weekends the proportion rose to 17% and the group who assessed the actual number of workers involved thought that it may have corresponded to about a quarter of the whole (de Riva Poor, 1970).

It is very difficult to provide a conclusion which eludes criticism. However, after analysing all these systematic observations and the critical assessments made in connection with some of them, I think one could venture to estimate moonlighters of all kinds (from those who only "potter for cash" to those who hold a second job) in most industrial societies, whether under capitalism or socialism, at about 25% on average, with considerable variations. If this is the likeliest assumption, the three-quarters of workers use their spare time for other activities, which do not include remunerated work.

On the other hand, managers are often described as lacking in leisure, or threatened by heart failure due to overwork, etc. There are no large-scale investigations to rely on. Medical enquiries show that some big business managers work up to 50 or 60 hours a week, that they take work home and that their leisure is eaten up by "social and professional commitments" (Bize, 1961). However, many systematic surveys have shown that it is among managerial workers that the highest percentages of amateur skiers, riders, sailors, golf or tennis players, theatre or concert goers, book readers, holiday travellers and safari enthusiasts are found. In a city like New York, it is difficult to find a manager in his office on Friday afternoon. How can such contradictory observations be reconciled? In my view it is the top managers, whose responsibilities are heaviest or whose lust for power is greatest, who are deprived of spare time, but participant observation shows them to be in the minority. The majority appear to be privileged with regard to leisure, according to all surveys on leisure conducted in the United States, in France or in other advanced industrial societies. They may be considered in a sense as the heirs of the "leisure class" studied at the end of the 19th century (Veblen, 1899). An enquiry conducted in 1962 under the auspices of the Harvard Business Review with a sample of about 5000 industrial and administrative managers showed that they work on average 43 hours a week at the office and 7 additional hours at home. They have 41.3 hours of semi-professional leisure a week, but it still leaves 30 hours for their personal leisure. In the American study of the changes brought about by the three-day weekend, 80% of workers, employees and managers "use their free time for leisure activities rather than to earn added income" (de Riva Poor, 1970). In the Leningrad enquiry (in which 16.9% of workers would have opted for additional work, had they been given the spare time) from 40.3 to 78.7% of respondents selected ten spare-time activities, seven of which were leisure-time pursuits (cinema, literature, theatre, exhibitions, spectator sports, sport and/or TV). It is likely that a *majority* of workers in all categories devote the time freed from work to non-remunerated activities and in particular to leisure.

Thus, two conclusions may be derived from recent survey data: 1) To fail to mention the quarter of workers for whom work-time has increased in the United States and the quarter (often made up of the same people as the former category) who use free time for moonlighting, is to take an ideological view of the situation, to conceal social inequalities and to ignore the heavy burden of work for underprivileged or exaggeratedly active minorities. 2) However, to overstress these facts, to leave aside others (which apply to the majority of workers), to negate or minimise — for the sake of work as a value — the historical trend towards more free time, which gives added value to time spent away from work, is also to construct an ideology of work. It is to take a metaphysical view of labour, to confuse the wish with the facts, to adhere to an anachronistic outlook born out of 19th century situations, and to cast aside observations on the actual behaviour of a majority of workers belonging to all categories in advanced industrial societies, both under capitalism and under socialism. (We should recall the sociologists of labour who, whilst recognising that the logic of industrial labour is to produce non-labour, state a priori that those activities of non-labour stem from the sociology of labour: "the sociology of labour thus extends to include its very negation — non-labour — within the sphere of free activities" (Naville, "From Alienation to Enjoyment"). Without denying the obvious importance of the relationship between, for example, work and leisure, one does not quite see how sociology of labour could find its concepts and specific dimensions in any other field than its own.)

II.1.3. The ambiguousness of "family pursuits"

Do "family pursuits" absorb most of the time freed by the reduction in working hours for both male and female workers?

This is the view advanced by Anderson and by many sociologists of the family. For some, leisure is a less useful concept than the "recreational function of the family."

Undoubtedly time freed from work was first taken up to a large extent by family pursuits. Scheuch has shown in a study of the Cologne population that leisure or semi-leisure is mainly family-centred and contributes to an increase in family cohesion, due to the generalisation of motoring, televiewing, holidays, weekends, etc. The development of three-day weekends in the United States has led in 23% of cases to a further increase in the time devoted to family duties. Thus travel to visit relations is mentioned by approximately one in two respondents and the growth rate of this activity reaches 121% (de Riva Poor, 1970). If these patterns spread, it could be argued that increases in free time will benefit the extended family. In a socialist advanced industrial society (USSR) a time-budget study conducted in an industrial concern (Kirovsky) has shown that 96.4% of spare time is spent within the family, either as leisure or as a duty, (Beljaev and Vodzinskaya, 1961). In the enquiry conducted among young adults, in Leningrad, family-centered values were dominant for 41.6% of respondents (whereas only 7.7% were mainly oriented towards productive work, as already mentioned).

Whenever time-budget studies have been made for female workers who have no domestic help and work at home as well as in a firm, housework is added to their other employment, resulting in weeks of up to 80 hours. It is a well-known fact that the *working woman* is much less free than the *working man,* even in the socialist societies which have made great political efforts to emancipate women. Thus in the Soviet Union the male urban worker has on average 5.10 hours of spare time, while the woman has only 3.20 hours, i.e. about *two hours less.* (Beljaev and Vodzinskaya, 1961). According to the International Survey of Time-Budgets, there are no greater differentials in other countries. Yet differentials exist everywhere; it is only their magnitude which varies.

This situation will lead up to a decrease in working hours if women organise themselves as a pressure group. In his investigation of discrepancies between the schedules of firms in the Paris area, Grossin has shown that reductions in the number of hours worked are determined by the pressures of female workers rather than the intervention of unions or the type of work (Grossin, 1969). It is the double load borne by women who work both in and out of the home, which has prompted the trade unions (G.G.T. and C.F.D.T.) to revise their views on equality between the sexes in relation to employment and to require better provision for part-time work, with appropriate safeguards.

However, the conjunction between scientific progress and Women's Liberation, as well as youth protest, induced a change in the concept of "family pursuits". The expression is intrinsically ambiguous. What does it cover? Which of these activities are necessary, which are optional? Some are implicit in the functions of a household, whether a bachelor's, a couple's or a collective establishment, but others may perhaps be described as forms of leisure or semi-leisure.

A recent enquiry conducted in 1970 by Evelyne Sullerot on a representative sample shows that in all classes a "decomposition" of house work formerly considered as an unavoidable necessity and a duty has occurred to a varying degree. This type of work is now split into a number of occupations, differentiated by their degree of necessity; thus making preserves or tidying wardrobes is not on the same level as cleaning or washing up (Sullerot, 1971). Consequently such jobs can no longer be covered by the generic label "house work". Some of the former household chores made superfluous by mechanisation or mass production have become a kind of leisure or semi-leisure to be chosen from among other leisure pursuits after a certain level of consumption and of income has been reached. The education of children after infancy no longer requires constant presence as a pedagogic necessity. Parents have been partly superseded by physicians, teachers and the peer group (Riesman, 1950). Aside from their school or family responsibilities, the young claim earlier and earlier the autonomous use of their time and their cash; their activities can no longer be described as "child play"; they are a parallel way of life, with the same characteristics as adult existence, and represent a kind of leisure. In American society, where according to a recent survey two-thirds of the age group between 15 and 25 hold vocational, educational and family ideals analogous to their parents', almost all the young claim an increasing degree of autonomy with regard to leisure (Yankelovich, 1969). The mother's educational role includes upbringing proper, which may be more necessary than ever, and leisure or semi-leisure activities shared with children in outings, holidays and weekends. The requirements of bringing up a family are increasingly intermingled with personal leisure (Chombart de Lauwe, 1963). In each case, the necessary emotional commitment and the additional emotional involvement may be demarcated.

Finally, the woman's conjugal role (especially in the form of "conjugal duty") has undergone a basic change. The discovery of methods which affect the process of procreation is the scientific cause of this transformation, and operates in conjunction with changes in the values held. How do conjugal obligations affect the partners' leisure?

In the United States, the Kinsey Report has shown that in 85% of cases the sexual life of male and female Americans no longer reflects the ideal type defined by the dominant ethical system (Kinsey, 1948). The discovery of the pill has increased and accelerated the dissociation between maternity and sexuality. A Swedish enquiry on a representative sample (unlike the Kinsey Reports) of the urban population has proved that in the month during which it was conducted, sexual intercourse resulted in birth only in one case out of 1000, the overwhelming majority of cases being protected against any risk of procreation (Zetterberg, 1971). Sexual relations are now dissociated from the necessity of perpetuating the species, except in a small minority of instances. For the overwhelming majority their primary purpose is the pursuit of pleasure with the partner of one's choice, whether spouse, lover or friend. The Movement for Women's Liberation claims the right for women no longer to be passive with regard to their conjugal duties. Women aspire to the right to a sexual life expressing their true self. Sexuality freed from maternity becomes in Sullerot's words, "an individual and cultural fact", a "dimension of human freedom" (Jeannière et al, 1963). The terms are clear, but may not be well chosen. Conjugal policy is also a "cultural fact" and a "dimension of human freedom". It would be better to say that a range of activities formerly regulated by the laws of the species and by institutional duty is becoming part of the sphere aiming at the fulfilment of the human being for his own sake. Time freed from housework, the upbringing of children, the perpetuation of the species or the requirements of marriage as an institution, becomes spare time and may, despite inequalities, time-lags and oppositions, become leisure or semi-leisure time for women.

Do the habits and attitudes of today's men and women permit such a liberation? Let us consider the data quoted above. In large American cities men work on average 6.3 hours a day and women who are wage-earners 4.7 hours. The former devote on average 3.3 hours to family and household duties (including personal care), as against 5.7 hours in the case of the latter, so that men's daily spare time amounts to 5.6 hours and women's to 5 hours. In France men work 6.6 hours a day and women wage-earners 5.5 hours. Leaving work-time aside, men devote 4.1 hours to family and household duties and women 6.4 hours, so that the former have on average 4.3 hours of free time per day and the latter 3.3 hours. Has this inequality been reduced by the socialist ethic of an advanced industrial society? We have seen that this is not the case. In the Soviet Union, men work on average 6.2 hours a day and women 5.7 hours. The former devote only 3 hours of their time to family or household duties and the latter 5.7 hours. Thus the time which is not taken up by either type of work amounts to 5.7 hours for men and to 3.8 hours only for women.

In history the right to leisure has been defined in relation to the right to work and has been claimed by men. The right to be idle is the demand of men protesting against the reduction of workers to the role of producers. For women working in the house, the time was not yet ripe. They barely had the right to claim the rest required to restore the strength spent in serving their household, their children, their man. Until a recent date, "women's activities were performed in an atmosphere of moral obligation while their leisure was often spent in a state of quasi-guilt" (Sullerot, 1971). The time they granted to themselves would seem stolen from their children, their husband, their family.

Today, with the progress in household technology and in birth control techniques, with the development of new women's liberation and youth liberation movements, this right to leisure is explicitly claimed, as a substitute for some of the former household, conjugal and family duties. For many the time when a poet could write "the duty of a wife is to appear happy" (Destouches) seems remote. Part of the services which were recently performed by all women have become a servitude rejected by a growing number of people. Attitudes to personal life which used to be called "selfishness" in the recent past are now considered as a form of "dignity". Consequently leisure must be revalued in relation both to occupational and to household work and for both sexes.

Thus time freed from work outside the home may be absorbed in one of two ways in relation to household, conjugal and family obligations. In one case, it is partly allocated to an increase in the time devoted to institutional duties towards the child, the spouse, the home. In the other, part of yesterday's institutional commitments are converted into leisure, either within or outside the family group.

Those who claim that the new cultural values bound up with leisure (especially in the young generations) supersede family duties and usher in a crisis, or even the dissolution of the family, forget or arbitrarily underestimate the first category of facts mentioned above. Their "theory" is only the expression of an aprioristic and abstract ideology, more or less nihilistic, anarchistic or hedonistic.

By contrast, those for whom increases in free time contribute to strengthening "family life" forget or cast aside all the facts which show that while some family duties become semi-leisure pursuits for all its members, others are replaced by leisure outside the family for individual members, men, women and children.

An anachronistic ideology of the family as a self-contained unit conceals the meaning of women's liberation and youth protest movements against the authoritarian, or even the totalitarian, interpretation of family duties. These conflicts are not aimed at the abolition, but at the limitation of such duties and of the control exercised by the family as an institution over the personal life of each human being. This outlook is spreading, particularly among the educated young.

II.1.4. Increase and limitation in socio-occupational and socio-political duties

The problem raised by socio-spiritual and socio-political activities is that both undeniably take place in free time, but may or may not be classified as leisure. Some authors consider spiritual activities "such as contemplation" as a form of leisure (Pieper, 1958), while most Soviet sociologists do so in the case of socio-political activities (Prudenski, 1964). Such is not our own view. It seems that to treat such activities as distinct is to raise three problems of major importance for the understanding of leisure as a phenomenon.

1) Has the increase in free time benefited mainly socio-spiri-

tual and socio-political activities or mainly leisure?

2) In the time freed from occupational and family obligations, has it not been the regression of some forms of socio-spiritual, even socio-political activities which led to the development of a new leisure component?

3) In that case, what would be the possible new relationship between leisure activities and activities of socio-spiritual and socio-political involvement?

These questions are basic to a grasp of the true dimensions assumed by leisure in advanced industrial societies, and also of the *concrete* conditions under which socio-spiritual and socio-political commitments are fulfilled.

To begin with the former commitment, have the reduction in work time and the limitation of family responsibilities allowed for an extension of religious practices? I am not aware of any historico-empirical work on this issue, but observation shows that some minorities, particularly devout female pensioners and religious youth organisers, have devoted this spare time to religious activities. For instance at Annecy 300 Sunday school teachers have completely rethought the religious education of the Catholic children. In the American survey of the three-day weekend, some of the workers stated that their religious practices had increased since they had three spare days instead of two; however the numbers involved were very small: 14 cases out of 138 instead of 9 out of 118 as in the past. Among young American, Dutch or French students and employees who limit or temporarily discontinue their education or their work in order to centre their lives on their free time, there has been an undeniable development of religious or para-religious group activities, under Eastern or African influences (Tyriakian, 1970). However, as in the past, at least since the Renaissance, this remains the prerogative of small minorities within minority groups. In the past, they have proved marginal. Their ideas became fashionable, then a new fashion superseded them; will it be otherwise this time? (Morin, 1970, Reich, 1970).

At present in all advanced industrial societies, the extension of free time has undeniably coincided for the great majority of the population with a regression of the time devoted to activities controlled by religious authorities. Even in societies where religious practice remained particularly widespread over a long period, its rate has decreased over the last five years: in Canada, those who practise a religion more or less regularly have dwindled from 40 to 30% of the population. In the United States, the nation wide youth survey already mentioned showed that 64% of the age group who do not attend university consider religion "very important", but that this view is held by only 38% of students. In France, more or less regular attendance at mass characterises only 20% of the population (Luccini).

This trend can be traced back over a long period. Students of traditional French society have shown that games and fetes sponsored by religious authorities have gradually receded over the last hundred and fifty years to give way to leisure activities (dances, sport and TV) (Varagnac, 1948). Leisure is no longer controlled by these authorities. After the Second Vatican Council (1962–65) a left-over of this traditional patronage has recently vanished: the clergy's domination over children's clubs and youth movements was abolished as a result of growing protest within the Church. Undoubtedly, an important share of the time formerly taken up by religious activities, games or fetes sponsored by the religious authorities in the local community, is now allocated to leisure pursuits chosen by the individual himself.

Though institutional control over the leisure of the faithful has receded, recreational and cultural activities have developed instead, sometimes on Church premises, for a public which is not limited to the congregation; these include jazz and classical concerts, exhibitions, tourist trips etc. The use made of Church buildings and organisations for reasons connected with leisure may be ambiguous in terms of faith. Many theologians, priests and members of the congregation feel it to be the case. An American humourist wrote that in the United States the Lord's day has become barbecue day for the majority, that fishing or hunting tend to supersede prayer and that prayer tends to become an occupation of the same kind as other leisure pursuits practised on Sunday. Leisure thus results in part from the secularisation of some collective celebrations and from the regression of the religious or para-religious obligations imposed by the community.

Thus many sociologists with a secular outlook forget the impact made by the reduction of socio-religious obligations on the dynamics which generate leisure, and concentrate exclusively on the influence of the scientific and technical revolution at work. They distort these dynamics and, at the same time, they forget or conceal the fact that, for some active minorities, part of the time freed from occupational duties is devoted to the development of traditional or new socio-spiritual activities.

On the other hand, those who a priori identify the modern, secular concept of leisure with the traditional and spiritual concept of contemplation (Pieper, 1958) may preclude thereby an analysis of the specific features exhibited by leisure as a phenomenon distinct from contemplation, merely because they accept an ideology of socio-spiritual commitment.[5] This applies also to the authors who categorise leisure under "community development". They often rely on anachronistic traditional concepts (fetes, brotherhood, community) ill-fitted to the analysis of gatherings or groups, whether made up of sportsmen, fishermen, cinema fans or whatever. They usually forego the concept of leisure, overlooking its specific characteristics as a phenomenon, its hidden dimensions, and its dialectical relations with socio-spiritual commitments in crisis-torn industrial societies. They live under the delusion or with the nostalgia of community as it may have existed in an earlier age.

By socio-political activities will be meant the part of spare time devoted to activities intended to serve society in all its political and social forms. Epistemological difficulties are such that this issue is even more complex than the previous one. For most intellectuals, whether they be revolutionaries, reformists or conservatives, emotional involvement reduces this problem to ready-made views. The situation in socialist advanced industrial societies such as the USSR or Czechoslovakia will not be discussed, as empirical sociological data is lacking. Engels foresaw that shorter working days would enable workers to more actively participate in civic affairs. Today many of his disciples are less optimistic than the Master, when confronted with facts. Since they would like to witness an increase in the political activity of "liberated" workers, they fear leisure as a possible factor of depoliticisation, as a new "opium of the people" (Dommanget's Introduction to Lafargue, 1966; Naville, 1967). This is a genuine danger. Unless social and political participation is encouraged, its decline may be caused by the development of leisure pursuits.

Other sociologists consider that, broadly speaking, the opposition between left and right is no longer as radical as a century ago. Some have even announced the end of ideology (Bell, 1960). Abstract ideologies would be superseded by criteria for action, derived from widespread values and dictated by a greater awareness of probability in relation to available resources in a given situation. Leisure activities would be valuable substitutes for some political activities which are in fact purely verbal.

Leaving temporarily aside these two conflicting views, I shall attempt to tackle the three questions asked at the beginning of this chapter and review the results of historical and empirical research in an endeavour to produce replies to them. The task is far from simple and the meaning of the replies may vary with the criteria and the indicators selected.

Rates of abstention in political elections may be considered as indicators. How have they evolved? Can a decrease of interest in elections be imputed to the impact of leisure activities or values? The study made by Lancelot of abstentions in legislative elections in France since the beginning of the last century shows this increase to be a myth (Lancelot, 1968). In fact, there has been a marked consistency in rates which have varied between 20 and 40% depending on periods and circumstances.

Another criterion is the interest in political information and training. Results concerning various countries converge: they show that political news and debates have a much wider audience than before the age of television (Cazeneuve, 1970). Yet the meaning of this phenomenon is ambiguous: the information received does not so much prompt involvement as turn political events into shows. It does not so much stimulate the study of political programmes as make politicians into attractive or unattractive star turns. Active concern for morality tends to give way to the passive collection of anecdotes (Riesman, 1950). Among the 60% of Americans who have engaged in adult education in their spare time in the past and among the 20% who are still so engaged, those who are studying with a leisure activity in mind are five times as numerous as students of socio-political problems (Johnstone and Rivera, 1965). Yankelovich's national survey of the 15 to 25 age group has shown that American young workers consider patriotism very important, but that only 35% of young university people do so (Yankelovich, 1969). At Annecy in 1956 20% of respondents would have accepted a year's study leave with pay during their life, had the opportunity existed, but only 1% would have devoted such studies to socio-political subjects. Even in socialist advanced industrial societies, despite widespread information and intense propaganda to increase the citizens' socio-political involement, political studies have lagged behind others, have stagnated or even declined. In Czechoslovakia, between 1950 and 1968 lectures and seminars on political training at the Socialist Academy have trebled according to the Academy's published statistics, whereas the teaching of sport and leisure pursuits was multiplied by five. In the USSR, the time-budget studies conducted by Strumilin at twenty-five years interval (1924–59) have shown that the time devoted by urban workers to study, including that of politics, has remained quasi constant, whereas the number of hours spent on spectator sports has quadrupled (Strumilin, 1964).

Voluntary work may also be considered as an indicator. In France, the number of participants in the activities of political parties, including the Communist Party, has fallen by half between 1948 and 1971 (from one million to 500,000).[6] By contrast, the development of voluntary organisations in the social and the cultural spheres over the last 50 years has been striking (Hausknecht, 1962). At Annecy, while the town's population trebled in that period, the number of these organisations passed from about thirty in 1900 to over 300 in 1960, with a membership of 40% of all heads of households. A growing number of groups are involved in political activities, but these tend to be more fragmented, more practical and more independent from party politics than was formerly the case.[7]

Those who were granted an additional free day at the weekend by American employers have become involved in political activities at the rate of 4% instead of the previous 2% (de Riva Poor, 1970), but the main increase has been in voluntary work connected with leisure pursuits (Dunn, 1971).

In Soviet society, even before TV became widespread, i.e. in 1959, the number of hours devoted to socio-political work in the yearly time-budget had shrunk from 109 to 17 over the 25 years studied by Strumilin, (Strumilin, 1964). According to a more recent Leningrad survey, in the event of a reduction in the duration of the working day, only 12.9% of individuals choose to do voluntary work locally; this corresponds roughly to the percentage (12.3) of respondents whose values are dominated by a commitment to "social work", including political activity. Such data prompted Richta to make what I consider a very important comment: "Unless new forms of participation are developed over time, a political vacuum appears, even in the context of a socialist society" (Richta, 1969).

The small share of socio-political activities in the free time of workers is shown by the time-budgets from all industrial societies studied by Szalai's team (Szalai, 1973). A worker has on average from 4.7 hours of spare time a day (in Bulgaria) to 5.7 (in the US). The whole time he devotes to participation in organisations of all kinds (spiritual, social or political) covers on average 0.1 to 0.3 hours per day (0.2 to 0.7 hours per day, including voluntary participation in adult education), i.e. about fifty times less than he devotes to leisure.

What conclusions may be drawn about the relationships between socio-political activities and leisure? Firstly, while citizen participation in shaping the future and managing the affairs of the community is a basic requirement of democracy in society and hence a duty freely accepted by conscious citizens, it cannot in my view be equated with leisure activities primarily aimed at individual gratification. A clear distinction should be made between political commitment and leisure. Even if the two kinds of activity impinge on each other, the study of their comparative evolution and of their dialectical relationships requires unambiguous sociological distinctions to be drawn between their respective characteristics.

Part of the time freed from work has certainly served to facilitate political activities, as Engels had wished. Within minorities, greater leisure has not led to lesser political participation; between minorities, ideological struggles have remained intense. Political life thus remains active and the end of ideology is not imminent, even though the actual provisions adopted by governments, whether of the left or of the right, are increasingly similar. However, in advanced industrial societies, the majority have not devoted spare time to political activities, as Engels expected, but to leisure pursuits, and this is equally true of all social classes (Goldthorpe and Lockwood, 1969). In this new context political activists can no longer disregard the specific problems of leisure. In 1934, William Reich had already foreseen the impact of these new problems on class consciousness, especially among the young: "working among the young teaches one that, contrary to what political parties generally assert, the understanding of his class situation is as a rule, very superficial and unstable in the teenager. The position of apprentice generates apathy and indifference rather than a revolutionary attitude. It could only become positive in connection with other specific factors of the class situation, such as the need for better leisure" (Reich, 1971).

Is political control over leisure no different from political control in general? All attempts by political authorities to take over and to organise leisure have met with temporary successes in advanced industrial societies, but have then run into permanent difficulties and resulted in many failures, at all political levels, whether national or local. During the last five years there have been many clashes in France between municipal authorities and the leaders of cultural centres (*Maisons de la Culture*), youth clubs (*Maisons des Jeunes*) or socio-cultural associations, who have always pleaded freedom of expression, of information and of education in intellectual, artistic and social leisure activities. Even in the socialist advanced industrial societies, a trend towards the autonomy of culture from the economic and political sphere has emerged.

This trend has been emphasised by Richta in the collective work entitled *Civilisation at the Crossroads* (Richta, 1969). A cultural policy is developing in a dialectical relationship of cooperation and tension with the economic and political powers. On the one hand, political parties tend to organise more fetes, outings, trips and shows, in order to adapt to patterns of leisure. On the other, control by political and ideological organisations over the sporting or artistic leisure time pursuits of the population is increasingly resented, as the social and cultural effects of advanced industrialisation develop. Political involvement must be distinguished from involvement with political parties. At Annecy, between 1955 and 1971 the latter receded in the cultural sphere, whereas the former increased (Dumazedier and Ripert, 1966).

To sum up, this investigation of survey results shows that time freed by shorter work schedules is taken up, for minorities, by moonlighting, by household and family responsibilities, and by activities deriving from spiritual and socio-political commitment, but, for the majority of working people, predominantly by leisure pursuits, which have increased *most*.

II.1.5. *The social dynamics of leisure*

As has been argued, the dynamics generating leisure in the most advanced stage of industrial society are probably more complex than the so-called "laws of history" or prophecies for the future announce. What do they consist of?

Firstly, the production of free time, into which leisure is inserted, is obviously the outcome of higher outputs, due to the implementation of scientific and technical discoveries: all economists, from Marx to Keynes, agree on this point. This scientific and technical progress is supplemented by a double intervention: that of the trade unions which press occasionally simultaneous and generally alternate claims for increased wages and reduced working hours and that of the businessmen who need an extension of the time devoted to consumption in order to sell their products (Henle, 1966). All these facts do not always make for harmony. Therefore, as has been observed in American society since the advent of mass consumption, there may be longer strikes, more extensive social conflicts which involve old age pensioners, housewives etc., as well as factory workers. Yet *all* these forces converge towards claims for increased free time, not only by a reduction in occupational, but also in household and family responsibilities.

It should be stressed that the scientific and technical component interacting with social movements affects not only the reduction of professional working hours but also the reduction of working hours in the home. This fact is often overlooked by analysts of the technical and economic dynamics which generate leisure.

Fourastié has highlighted the difference in the time devoted to household chores due to inequalities in the technical equipment of homes (Fourastié 1962). Szalai's study of time-budgets has shown the economies of time made by the American housewife as against her counterparts of the same social class in other, less affluent countries, where houses are not so well equipped in consumer durables.

Yet the technological and economic component does not account for everything. It does not enable one to understand why the time free from work has mainly become leisure time. An ethnic and social component must also be taken into account. Indeed my hypothesis is that the production of leisure is the result of two simultaneous trends: a) scientific and technical progress accompanied by social pressures frees a certain amount of time from work and household duties; b) the reduction of social control by the basic institutions of society (the family, the socio-spiritual and socio-political agencies) allows this time to be mainly devoted to leisure pursuits. This reduction in institutional controls is linked with women's liberation and youth protest movements which have challenged the pervasiveness of family and/or conjugal obligations, with the laity's claims for bigger responsibilities in guilds and clubs formerly managed by the church and in other sectors of parish life, and with citizens' resistance to political totalitarian threats to freedom and to the so-called "private life" of individuals, which includes leisure.

A new problem arises, since these economic and social dynamics are, so to speak, negative. Time is being freed from former constraints, from former duties imposed by mediating institutions which make up society. Is this time to be confronted only with a vacuum? So strong an attraction for a vacuum would be hard to grasp. Is there not in all advanced industrial societies, whether capitalist or socialist, a *positive* force which orientates towards leisure most of the time freed from work? What might be the main source of this increasing attraction towards leisure in industrial societies evolving towards the post-industrial stage? This will be the last question tackled in the present chapter.

At first glance, it is very difficult to detect this central attraction, since apparently heterogeneous activities abound. Can unity be assumed within this growing diversity, which technical discoveries or the whims of fashion alter time and again? This heterogeneity has led some to deny the validity of leisure as an operational concept on which a branch of sociology could be based (Busch, 1973). By contrast, others, including myself, maintain that an underlying reality is probably common to all these activities and must be brought to light. The concept of leisure, its limits, its internal structure and its external relationships should be analysed in an attempt to grasp this underlying reality.

What is the basis of the central *attraction* of this phenomenon, whatever its forms: holidays, rest, entertainment, weekends, walks, sport, shows, cafés, conversations, pleasure trips, TV, theatre, music, dances, adult education, gambling, card games, love play and even light drugs, etc.? I would argue that the attraction shared by these manifold activities rests on a new *social* need for the individual to be his own master and to please himself, to enjoy the time formerly taken up by activities which were in part imposed by the firm, the family, and socio-spiritual or socio-political institutions. As lengthy working days are less necessary, and as the control of social institutions is less pervasive, marginal time is freed. Its *raison d'être* is no longer the operation of an institution, but the self-fulfilment of the individual. As stated by Richta, in the leisure society "the subjectivity of the individual has become a social value in itself."

Although this new social need is deeply felt by a growing number of individuals, it is difficult to express as a scientific concept. It is rooted in a conflict with the ethical standards and the structure of the previous age.[8] It may be reduced to nearly nothing by lack of money and time among the underprivileged. It may be distorted by becoming a source of "escape", of maladjustment, of social delinquency. It may provide an opportunity for ideological mystifications of all kinds. It may come under new economic controls, more insidious and better adapted than the institutional controls whose repression permitted its birth and its growth (Baudrillart, 1968).[9]

However, the specific characteristics of this phenomenon in the dynamics of industrial societies should be understood before it is criticised. Otherwise social criticism would fail to reach its target, but would aim at a myth made to order; it would denounce flaws, delusions, suspect ideologies associated with leisure in our society, without approaching the subject itself, without taking account of leisure as such. Under the influence of the sociologists of "real" life (industry, the family, politics, religion, education) leisure tends as a rule to be made conceptually respectable by being incorporated into a social ideology which conceals some of its aspects under reassuring conceptual labels. Are people frightened of leisure as a possible source of delinquency or anarchism?

On the other hand, sociological observation shows that leisure does not only correspond to the genuine needs of the individual. These needs constantly interact with the subjective and objective conditions which favour or counteract them. Market imperatives standardise them, ethnic traditions censor or channel them, policies attempt to manipulate them, for ends which are often alien to aspirations towards self-expression and communication. Such observations contradict the over-simplified, sketchy views which either equate leisure with absolute freedom or crush it under the weight of social determination. Obviously leisure cannot abolish social conditioning or promote complete liberty in some miraculous way, but freedom of choice in leisure time is a fact, even though it is limited and part illusory. The child does not fail to distinguish between play and schoolwork, nor does the adult between leisure and occupational or household duties, even if he enjoys them. Yet any freedom is always limited, conditioned.

It is under these actual conditions, which are complex, dialectic or conflictual, that the new historical possibilities for personality fulfilment through leisure develop. The individual gradually gains the right and some power (time) to choose activities primarily aimed at disinterested ends, at the fulfilment of personal or social needs, without a direct social purpose, at the expression, the creation or the re-creation of his personality. The high valuation of play, mainly associated with childhood in the previous period, increasingly extends to adult life. With respect to leisure, the demarcation between the norms regulating the activities of the various age groups becomes increasingly vague (Mead, 1971). Under present standards leisure time is no longer exclusively intended for rest and recuperation, though many overtired workers treat it as such; this has become a period in which activities valued for their own sake are conducted. Some individuals who used to live in order to work now dare to work in order to "live" or at least dream of doing so.

It is as if this revaluing of individual rights in and through leisure was a new stage in the historical achievements of the human personality. On the borderline of history and psychology,

Meyerson has shown how what appear to be attributes specific to the individual (a way of feeling, of thinking, of acting) are in fact deeply affected by the history of society, which transforms earlier states of equilibrium (Meyerson, 1948). This applies also to individual rights to leisure. The ethics of leisure appear to be related to other ethics, of work, of family duties, of social service, etc. These ethical systems limit and condition them, as well as being affected by them. Social and personal ethics have changed. What used to be called idleness when confronted with the requirements of the firm is now described as dignity; what used to be called selfishness when confronted with the requirements of the family is now perceived as respect for the personality of one of its members. Part of what was considered sinful by religious institutions is now recognized as the art of living. Some have referred to the ethics of hedonism. This is ambiguous: the ethics of leisure are not those of idleness rejecting work, or of licence disregarding duties, but are based on a new equilibrium between the utilitarian requirements of society and the disinterested requirements of the individual. If history validates this orientation, leisure will not be so much a compensation for, or a complement to work and household duties, but rather the cause and the outcome of a new individual aspiration linked with a new stage of technological society. The need for shorter production times in order to free additional time in which producers can become better consumers, would be a corollary of this historical change, which each system of production and consumption will attempt to turn to advantage, without, however, having created it.

We may be experiencing a new stage in the liberation of the human personality from the totalitarianism of social institutions, whether brutal or insidious, manifest or hidden. During the Renaissance, following a long protest movement which culminated in the Reformation, the Catholic Church began a process of change leading up to the abolition of trials for sorcery, for atheism, for heterodoxy. Thus men gained the right to choose their God or to have none. Two centuries later, as a result of social movements against absolutism, the arbitrariness of the sovereign and his discretionary powers were checked; the Habeas Corpus came into being. Thus the King's subjects became freer citizens. A century later, the powers of the corporation over the workers were abolished. The Le Chapelier law of 1791 left the workers unprotected from their employers, but stopped them being tied to the enterprise. As the workers became aware of their specific interests, the class struggle was organised, despite a repressive legislation, and wage-earners gained the right to defend their dignity, at the outcome of a harsh struggle. Now it is the family itself which relaxes its controls over its members, even when it remains an efficient framework for functional and affective exchanges. The all-powerful control exercised by the head of the family on its members' leisure becomes less rigid, negotiable. Everyone's right to choose or reject leisure within the family group under the aegis of the family as an institution increases; the right to dispose of one's leisure time in the company of one's choice begins at an earlier age. Riesman has shown the change in individual values in modern societies (Riesman, 1954). His thesis is that the individualism initiated by the Renaissance no longer meets the need to break out of the social isolation characteristic of large anonymous cities. This is confirmed by their inhabitants' search for more natural neighbourhood units in which individuals are closer to each other (Gans, 1962, 1967). Yet in connection with leisure, individualistic values are also being reappraised in opposite ways: games, travel, affective relationships or personal studies, considered by many in the recent past as a waste of time, a doubtful form of entertainment or an infringement on family and social duties, now tend to become personality requisites, within conditions which fluctuate and vary with each situation. Within the leisure time prescribed by this new social norm, it is neither technical efficiency nor social utility, nor spiritual or political commitment which is the end of the individual, but his own fulfilment and self-expression. This is my central hypothesis.

II.2. Soviet Society. The Evolution of Leisure, 1924–1967

This general hypothesis has been much challenged. Its corroboration would require long-term studies to be conducted jointly by the sociologists and historians who endorse it. Such work, as will be shown, is not only difficult to carry out, but even to undertake. Criticisms have therefore to be met with other counter-arguments. This evolution of industrial society towards a leisure society is not only challenged by neo-liberal thinkers, like Galbraith, but by many thinkers of Marxist leanings. Their thoughts are well worth considering. To them leisure and consumption are twin aspects of one reality which is not the product of advanced industrial society, but of the capitalist mode of production, distribution and consumption. I am convinced that this uncontrolled system, geared to the search for maximum profit, despite the existence of certain protected sectors, results in producing some types of goods and services for comfort or leisure, whose aim is to serve the interests of their producers rather than to fit personality requirements among consumers. This has already been said and will be repeated. It is a crucial problem for the social and cultural content of mass leisure.

Still, if leisure as such, regardless of its content, were *produced* (and not merely influenced) by the capitalist system, it should be impossible to observe a similar evolution in both capitalist and socialist advanced industrial societies. To ascertain the facts, it is possible to observe the evolution of a comparatively advanced industrial society with a socialist regime over a period of half a century, namely that of the USSR.

It is not by coincidence that I have already referred to some results derived from observation by empirical sociologists in the USSR. It seems useful to become better acquainted with the evolution of that society from the angle of leisure in its *relationships* with other problems, especially those of work.

Therefore I have searched for comparable observations made in the oldest of socialist industrial societies at sufficiently long intervals. I have been able to use (Dumazedier, 1970) fairly comparable materials on the Soviet factory worker's way of life at thirty-five year intervals. It has clearly not been possible to test all the hypotheses outlined above on the historical dynamics of leisure. Yet I have been able to note, despite obvious differences, some common trends which seem attributable to the evolution of work and workers in advanced industrial societies. To be better understood, some preliminary comments should be made about the evolution of social research in Soviet society.

1) *The problems studied have evolved.* The recent publication of an empirical study on spare time highlights the change under-

gone both by Soviet society and by the social or sociological research it inspired.[10]

In the history of sociological research on time-budgets in the USSR, three periods may be demarcated. They reflect both the stage of economic development reached by the Soviet Union and the dominant socio-political concerns of the time.

The first period corresponds to the 1920s and extends until the suppression of social investigations in the thirties. It coincided with an upsurge of research just after the revolution and consisted mainly in team-work by statisticians, economists and sociologists led by Strumilin (Strumilin, 1964). Their work dealt with the impact of the revolution on all spheres of economic, political and cultural life. Research on time-budgets in general (and on free time in particular) was mainly prompted by a practical concern. It was meant to help solve a number of problems connected with the planning of manpower resources, with social welfare, town planning, the provision of cultural amenities etc.

The second period began with the tentative emergence of sociological research in the post-Stalinist period (see the bibliography in Kolpakov and Volgov, 1968, and Dumazedier and Guinchat, 1969). All the studies conducted in those years were closely linked with work problems and with increases in output. The main questions asked were: "How to recuperate the billions of hours spent on dull housework to devote them to productive work first, and then to leisure?" Three names were representative of this type of research: Maslov, Pisarev and Prudenski (Maslov and Pisarev, 1965).

It is only in the 1960s that sociologists initiated research wholly devoted to leisure, to its structure, and to the conditions under which the individual gains free time, defined by deducting work time and the time spent on family and social daily commitments.[11] This work attempts to empirically assess socialist practice and ideology after fifty years of socialist construction. For the first time since 1920, Grushin's enquiry provides information on life in the Soviet Union after work, on the cultural and material practices, and on the wishes of the population.

It should be remembered that a certain continuity exists between the three periods. The Marxist concept of "relationship" between work and free time remains the basis of any Soviet research, even when interest in the problems of non-work time, of leisure, is growing. The second shared concern is the elaboration of a research method for the investigation of free time. The concentration on industrialisation and urbanisation since the 1930s has been reflected in this research. While Strumilin in 1923 and also in 1932 gave a full picture of the time-budgets of Kolkhoz members and of other peasants, their problems have been receding in the 1964 research on leisure, which deals with the urban population.

2) *Methods have evolved.* In the sciences as in the arts, form cannot be separated from content, and method from the problem investigated. This is not a mechanistic relationship. The same method (e.g. time-budgets study) may be applied to different problems (those of the Soviet Union by Strumilin and those of the United States by Komarowsky during the same period). The same problem (social inequalities as they affect leisure) may be approached by studying time-budgets (Prudenski, 1959) or interests (Grushin, 1967). Yet an evolution in the problems tackled is often accompanied by a change in method. If the latter is defined as the creation of a system of techniques and concepts required to treat a problem in a given situation in relation to a hypothesis, what becomes of it when the situation changes and the hypothesis is altered (even if the ideology remains constant)?

The 1924 survey reflected the situation and the dominant ideas of Soviet society at the time. The main objective was to stimulate the productive forces of the emerging socialist planning system. Economics, as a science of needs, resources and constraints, imposed its objective and qualitative method; time was treated as money. Social differences were given less consideration than common progress. Indicators were expressed as average times devoted, within a global population, to activities which were not finely analysed (e.g. men spend 453 hours a year reading both newspapers and books). The study of subjective differences between individuals and groups of individuals belonging to different social strata was neglected. There were few changes in these respects between 1924 and 1959.

After 1960, methods changed. Sociology was no longer reduced to social economics. It gained a place of its own alongside philosophy. Objective methods became more exacting. They were supplemented by *subjective* methods which investigate the content of activities, the interests and value systems of respondents. Social differences between socio-occupational categories, between the sexes, between age groups, educational levels and urban populations from cities of different sizes, etc. were no longer overlooked, simplified or covered up, but became the object of systematic observation, according to the rules of probabilistic sociology. Thus Grushin's survey in 1963—4 did not only provide the "concrete" results of a huge unrepresentative sample of 10,393 persons, but centered its scientific content on a stratified urban sample of 2,730. Thus generalisation becomes possible from a scientific viewpoint.

Conceptual and technological imagination is still less developed in Russian sociology than in other socialist societies (Szcepanski, 1969; Richta, 1969). Yet a change towards which the sociology of spare time has contributed (Dumazedier, 1967), has undeniably begun.

3) *Results:* Successive empirical studies have yielded a number of related facts of comparative interest. Whereas long-term research is lacking in the sociology of all countries, Strumilin and Prudenski have provided sets of comparable facts for two stages in the development of Soviet society, 1924 and 1959.[12] The results of Grushin's survey, though not comparable with the previous sets of facts because of differences in problems and methods, may still be considered in conjunction with them. All these studies deal with a national sample of urban factory workers. Of course the percentage of workers in the active population and the standards of living were unidentical in 1924, in 1959 and in 1963. However, it seems all the more interesting to study the change in the attitudes of the urban working population with the development of industrialisation, as well as its social and cultural implications. What does such a secondary analysis of the evolution of spare time problems between 1924 and 1959 or 1967 show?

Limitation of free time: According to Soviet researchers, free time is obviously limited by the duration of remunerated work, but also by the time devoted to other activities, which are unproductive though connected with production (hygiene after work, collecting or putting away tools etc.), the time spent on travel between the work-place and the home, and the time taken up by household and family obligations: housework, the upbringing of children (including playtime) and the activities necessary to survival: sleep, meals, personal hygiene.

As concerns the legal duration of work, the legal working day has been reduced several times since 1924, to reach 7 hours in 1960 (and 6 hours later). What is the situation in fact? The time devoted daily (except on Sundays) to work and to its corollaries seems to have increased over 40 years, at least for urban workers. In 1924, the average working day was 7.83 hours[13] with 1.17 hour for travel. In 1959 the corresponding averages were 7.17 hours and 2.30 hours. In 1963—4 the actual working day of the urban worker was 7.30 hours and travel times were as long as in 1959. Moreover Grushin endeavoured to measure, for the first time in the USSR, to the best of my knowledge, the percentage of workers who take on other jobs outside legal working hours. It has already been said that he rated it at 28.7%. According to him, the size of connurbations, the inadequacy of individually owned mechanical transport, and the wish to gain additional resources for consumption account for this state of affairs.

Obligations other than work: Household and family tasks impose another limitation on spare time. Has their duration decreased among workers? Despite the development of domestic amenities and of collective organisations for home maintenance, it has remained roughly the same: in 1924, 1.72 hours per day for a man, in 1959, 1.70 hours.

Consequently in 1924 the duration of free time amounted to 3.54 hours a day and twenty-five years later to 3.39 hours, i.e. approximately to the same. There are no comparable data for 1963—4, but Grushin considers that in future increases in free time should result from reductions in travelling times and in time devoted to housework, rather than from the legal limitations of the working day. At the 22nd Congress of the Communist Party in 1961 the development plan of the Soviet economy (for 1961—80) contained provisions for the extension of free time to 45 hours a week. These provisions concern both a reduction in work ti··· s, and savings of the time devoted to duties other than work, e.g. shorter travel due to the provision of electric power for transport, halving of the time spent on household chores, increased provision of consumer durables, etc.

"At present, the problem of increasing free time will not be solved by reducing work time, but by freeing non-work time which for the moment is largely absorbed by the daily tasks which do not serve the general development of man. The creation of crèches for children, the improvement of transportation etc. will free millions of hours for *leisure*." (Grushin, 1966).

Free time: This covers, on the one hand, spiritual and socio-political activities and, on the other, leisure. Soviet researchers, from Strumilin to Grushin, tend to define what free time is not rather than what it is. The relationships between the two dissimilar kinds of activities it covers have not yet been clearly analysed in the new Soviet society. However all spare time activities have been more or less accurately catalogued since 1924. How have they evolved over time? Religious practice will be mentioned briefly as there are no systematic observations on this subject in the urban workers sample. In a rural environment, 8.85 hours a month were devoted by peasants to religious practices in 1924. In 1934, the Kolkhoz members observed by Strumilin only spent 0.52 hours in this way. The information available does not show whether the samples and the conditions involved were strictly comparable nor whether this kind of results can be extrapolated to urban workers.

However, very interesting data has been provided on what Soviet researchers call "social activities". This category covers all forms of participation in spiritual, civic and political meetings, in collective celebrations and social events of any kind. In 1924 they accounted for about 109 hours a year of the factory worker's time, whereas in 1959, they had dwindled to 17 hours, i.e. six times less than before. In 1963–4, Grushin did not reckon the time involved, but worked out the number of workers who participated only "about once a month" in any social activity. He found that they represented 72.3% taking into account the fact that attendance at most union or political meetings is compulsory or strongly recommended as a result of organisational pressures. Since 1924 the evolution of Soviet society seems to have led to a decrease in the degree of compliance with socio-political obligations. Unfortunately, Grushin did not consider socio-political activities proper as a distinct category. He mentioned that political training, either compulsory or optional, is given about once a month to 44.6% of factory workers; this percentage decreases with the size of the community, from 45.8% in small towns to 29.3% only in Moscow.[14]

Leisure and studies: The information available does not discriminate between studies integrated with job, the union or the Party and those which constitute a form of leisure chosen as spontaneously as say fishing or a variety show. Among lecture and discussion group topics, it is impossible to distinguish between those which provide training for occupational promotion, family responsibilities, union or political posts, and those which concern less utilitarian or more disinterested topics and are merely intended to satisfy the body, the imagination or the mind. Adult education will therefore be considered as a whole, in an attempt to assess its evolution in relation to sport, shows and other "entertainments". The great efforts of the Soviet government to increase socio-educational facilities are well known; what has their impact on the life of the people been?

In 1924 manual workers devoted approximately 168 hours a year to study and twenty-five years later 175 hours, i.e. an increase of 4%.[15] However sport, in a wide sense, probably covering outdoor games, but not walks and tourism, increased from 18 to 74 hours per year, i.e. by approximately 400%. The highest growth rate applies to shows: 373 hours in 1959 as against 42 hours in 1924, hence an increase of 900%. During the same period other entertainments increased from 210 to 257 hours per year.

In 1963 TV had already entered one third of homes (Zvorikin, 1967); 37.5% of the people (36.1% of the men and 38.7% of the women) viewed for an hour a day, while 78.9% listened to the wireless. Their interest in various kinds of programmes is not analysed, but it is known that 73.3% (74.4% of the men and 73.3% of the women) went to the movies several times a month, 42.2% to the theatre, 36.6% to variety shows, 24% to museums and 17.8% to concerts, without indications as to frequency.[16] Hence in twenty-five years spectator sports, visits to shows and other entertainments increased among Soviet workers, while studying tended to remain stationary and the practice of "social activities" receded sharply.

Cultural inequalities according to social categories:[17] The social differences which endure despite the socialist state's intent to abolish them are obviously worthy of special notice. The study of this fifty-year-old experience is likely to prove more fruitful than dreams of a socialist ideal which indifference to reality and unwillingness to experiment within the limits of possibilities may render chimerical.

Unfortunately diachronic information is unavailable on this major problem of the sociology of leisure. Strumilin has not dealt with it and, to my knowledge, it had not been considered from this angle before 1960. It is the comparative analysis of spare time activities according to income conducted by Prudenski at Krasnojarsk which provided data on cultural disparities related to income (Prudenski, 1964). Grushin's study shows these disparities in relation to socio-occupational category and educational level (Grushin, 1966). Both sources have been used in turn to provide a maximum amount of information on each problem.

Which social categories worked most and presumably had least free time, in 1963–4 when the 6 or 7 hour day was made legal? It would have been interesting to know the differences between categories of workers (unskilled, semi-skilled and skilled), but Grushin did not discriminate between them. However, he provided additional data on employees, the technical intelligentsia and intellectuals, enabling their work times to be compared with those of manual workers. On average, employees and intelligentsia members work longer hours. This is particularly clear in the case of the technical intelligentsia with 43.2% working over 8 hours, as do 60.5% of intellectuals. Soviet society might be facing the problem of managers and intellectuals overworking, as are other types of industrial societies.

In addition to the comments already made on the evolution of "social activities" between 1924 and 1959, other equally interesting facts are revealed by Prudenski's survey at Krasnojarsk. Despite the great efforts made in Soviet society to give the masses an education in citizenship and in politics, an equal level of participation in civic and political life does not seem to have been reached by manual workers as by other social categories enjoying higher income or education. Thus at Krasnojarsk in 1960 those whose wages were lowest (less than 300 roubles a month) devoted only 6.2 hours a year to "social activities" as against 15.6 hours in the case of people earning between 501 and 1000 roubles. The latter category of wage-earners had a seven times higher level of participation in city management. Conversely, in 1963–4, Grushin noted that 38.2% of workers as against 70.4% of intelligentsia members attended political teaching courses.

As regards leisure, those who earned under 300 roubles a month spent about 36.4 hours a year taking walks as against 83.2 hours in the case of those earning over 1000 roubles. The former devoted 197.6 hours to reading either books or newspapers, the latter 332.8 hours. The former had four times less artistic activity than the latter. Lastly, the more affluent spent 395.2 hours on visits to museums or attendance at lectures, whereas the less well remunerated were content with 46.8 hours, i.e. *nine* times less.

In 1963–4, Grushin merely asked "who did what" in the various social milieux, without reference to frequency. He found that 21.9% of workers went to museums[18] as against 31.9% of intelligentsia members and 41% of students. There were more evening course students (during leisure time and under release from work arrangements) among workers (29.8%) than among employees (25.2%), but it was in the intelligentsia that adult education was most widespread (58.8%, as compared with 27.5% among workers). Attendance at concerts was reported by 13.2% of workers versus 30.2% among the technical intelligentsia.

Such are the achievements and the limitations of a forty-year policy aimed at raising the cultural level of the activities practised in their spare time by the population, and particularly by manual workers. Despite the incompleteness of the diachronic information available, despite rather crude analytical categories which make it difficult to isolate the relevant facts with any degree of accuracy, the general trend of the evolution seems clear. It shows an increase in free time and the collective determination of active social groups to secure further increases. Spare time appears to be turned mainly into leisure, rather than into the socio-political activities described as "social" and the more or less compulsory forms of adult education. Within the category of leisure, the highest growth rate pertains to entertainment of all kinds. Its predominance is most pronounced among factory workers.

The participation of the latter in artistic and intellectual activities at a high level is undeniably much greater than among their French or American counterparts. Will this still be the case when 90% rather than 30% of urban households have TV, when the standard of living rises, when weekends and holidays become as long as in the States or France? No critical discussion, no ideological tenets can replace systematic observations on current trends and probability forecasts for the near future. Despite the difficulties encountered in attempting to develop free empirical sociology, it is to be hoped that new information on a representative sample will be available soon.[19] Thus the problems of leisure, work and socio-political commitment in the future of advanced industrial societies under socialism will be explored further.

II.3. French Society. A Hypothesis Covering the Period 1955–1965.

The evolution of French society, particularly during the years 1966–67, gives rise to some objections against the theory of leisure. These objections were reinforced by the events of May–June 1968. The increasingly political character of some of the public and private interventions (public authorities or voluntary associations) stimulated by the new social and cultural problems of leisure blurred the *specific* characteristics of cultural policy, as it was beginning to be called. Such a policy is developed at the level of the country or of local authorities, of the State and of municipalities. Yet in my view the period 1955–65 was for French society one in which breaks tended to be more significant than continuity, especially with regard to leisure and to the corresponding cultural policy. Resistance to change remains strong, both structurally and psychologically. Our society is blocked, so is our school, our culture etc. But these blockages are more obvious in the context of the new situation than they were before. Changes affecting leisure time, services, organisations and values have been overshadowed by other problems which attract more attention. They have been underestimated in the studies of the relevant period. Yet they may contain the germ of a cultural renovation whose implications have not been assessed as yet.

The period 1955–65

This period initiated a change likely to prove very important not only for the economic, but for the social and cultural evolution of France. The system of production was virtually reconstructed due to the collective efforts of the post-war years, sustained by the Marshall plan. As a reaction against the Malthusian attitudes of the thirties, the modernising spirit gained ground, as the second national plan, "for modernization and facilities" proved in many respects. The Rome Treaty (1957) designed to set up a common market for large firms, began to be prepared in 1955. Perhaps more significantly, French industrial concerns, stimulated by the prospect of European trade, but faced with a tight labour market, and especially with a shortage of skilled manpower, stressed the need for rapid increases in output. It had taken seventy years (1880–1953) for the productivity index to double. Ten years sufficed (1954–1963) for it to double again (Fourastié, 1962). It may treble by 1985 according to some economists. The per capita consumption increased by 49% in 1950–59, despite an increased demographic growth; it may be multiplied by 2.5 between 1960 and 1985 (Commissariat au Plan, 1964). If these hypotheses were confirmed, despite the present slowing down, we would be on the brink of that mass consumption and leisure era which, according to Riesman, would be likely to determine the change of the "social character", whatever the regime (Riesman, 1950; Dumazedier, 1965; Touraine, 1969).

Prior to examining, in the light of my country's experiences, the great problems of change in post-industrial society which Riesman stated from the standpoint of his own country, a more modest task will be tackled. It will consist in observing some characteristic changes which occurred in France from 1953–55 in the demand for goods and services by individuals, and for goods and activities by commercial and non-commercial organisations.

Evolution in the demand for cultural goods and services by individuals

Obviously it is in the time freed from work and especially in leisure that adults may engage in the consumption of cultural goods and services. During the years 1953–65 the duration of the working week had slightly increased (except in agriculture), but the full weekend has become more widespread and the length of the annual holiday has been extended from eighteen to thirty days, despite the protests of employers and the unfavourable opinion of experts in the Planning Authority (Commissariat au Plan). Most of the time thus freed has benefitted the education of the young generation. The age at which productive life starts has been postponed as a result of longer school attendance (Cros, 1961; *Etudes Statistiques*, 1964). During the period considered, most young people continued their schooling beyond the age of fourteen (71.3% in 1964 as against 57.7% in 1954). In my view, the most durable features of the 1955–65 decade are double: a) a rapid increase in the value attached to leisure activities and expenditure in all urban and even in rural circles (Mendras, 1964);[20] and b) a widespread awareness of the specific problem of leisure in the equilibrium of the country's present and future social and cultural life.

The dimensions and patternings of these two recent phenomena are mainly as follows. The expenditure devoted to leisure does not amount to 8%, as stated in national accounts (1960), but to much more. Indeed the entry "Leisure and culture" extracted from the heading "miscellaneous" since 1953 does not exhaust all the expenditure actually made for leisure purposes. Owing to a study conducted by INSEE (National Institute for Statistics and Economic Studies) and CREDOC (1957–1961) we know that 51.7% of the mileage covered each year by motor-cars is connected with non-remunerated activities: pleasure drives, weekends, holidays etc. (Faure, 1963). This heading accounted for 8% in the budget of households during that year. Similarly expenses incurred in cafés, classified under the heading "Hotel-Restaurant-Café" (6.7%) corresponded for most people to leisure time social intercourse, rather than to the requirements of occupational or political life. Yet they were excluded from leisure expenditure

(CREDOC). Account should also be taken of housing expenses (holiday or weekend homes), of clothing (for winter sports or summer), of personal care and hygiene (from sun cream to sporting accidents), of food (additional expenditure incurred in connection with entertaining and outings). On this basis the present amount of household expenditures devoted to leisure is at least 16%. Even if it is difficult for the economist to collate it, its *common* meaning in relation to leisure is beyond doubt. During this period, expenditure on leisure has risen quicker than household expenses as a whole.

Yet the most significant aspect of this new way of life is the accompanying change in and sometimes even the transformation of cultural interests. For example, in 1950 about 10% of households had a motor-car, in 1965 almost half of the total population and 40% of skilled workers. There were eight million private cars in all. The 1985 group of the Planning Authority expects that there will be 19 million in 1985 (Commissariat au Plan, 1964). The possession of a car has changed the outlook of families belonging to all social classes. From 1950 to 1963 departures on holidays from towns of over 50,000 inhabitants increased from 49% to 63%. In 1964, 70% of French people aged over 14 travelled for their holidays, most of them by car (85%). Among them, 14% went abroad, i.e. 3,780,000 (Goguel, 1965). The contemporary Frenchman can no longer be described as a stay-at-home.

The city dwellers' exodus into the countryside is increasingly bound up with a search for closer contact with nature. After the Netherlands, France is the European country where camping is most widespread in all social classes, regardless of income (in 1964, about 21% of factory workers as against 11.3% of managerial workers). Casting, practised by 308,000 in 1950 and by 1,120,000 now, is the pastime of 41% of fishermen. This taste for nature is on the ascent, despite the overcrowding it generates (e.g. on beaches). It tends to predominate during the weekend. There are about 900,000 weekend homes (INSEE, Census for 1962); if makeshift huts, gardeners' dwellings, some unproductive farms, caravans parked on suburban sites etc. were to be taken into account, the figure would probably be doubled. Second dwellings are in fashion and the 1985 Group expect that there will be 1,250,000 new ones, bearing in mind the emerging development in the building of detached individual houses, which are the dream of a majority (68% in Paris in 1962). Frenchmen in old and in new towns may be discovering a new pattern of relations with nature.

Despite the growing attractions of outings in natural surroundings, the traditional interest in pottering in the house and gardening around it endures. Do-it-yourself does not seem as developed among the French as among their neighbours: only 21% say that they do odd jobs at least once a week, as against 29% of Italians, 37% of Dutch and 41% of British men (Piatier, 1963). But it is a strong interest: 60% of do-it-yourself addicts from Annecy say that it is exclusively practiced for pleasure (especially in the case of factory workers) (Dumazedier, Ripert 1966). The satisfaction thus experienced tends to be a compensation for depersonalised, fragmented industrial work. It is also a form of expression in which Levi Strauss detects a persistence of "pensée sauvage", of untamed thought in an age of scientific rationality (Levi Strauss, 1962). Though indicators to measure the extent and the meaning of this interest are lacking, I would assume it to be growing. It is likely to become less and less utilitarian and more and more psychological as rationalized production and the standardization of mass produced consumer goods increase. It may be argued that a handicraft culture already is and will no doubt increasingly become a major aspect of popular culture, as experienced by the majority of population. While crafts are receding in the productive sector, they prosper in leisure time, as does gardening.

The Sunday peasant is a product of industrial and post-industrial societies. Although since 1954 over three million dwellings have been built in small or large housing developments without gardens, the French remain very fond of gardening: 42% do some at least once a week as against 34% of the Dutch and 11% of the Italians (Piatier, 1963). This is motivated by a wish to save, but also to have "healthier" products than those sold on the market and by the pleasure experienced in working the soil and in coming in close contact with nature. This traditional relationship with the earth or with materials to be worked corresponds to a cultural need which neither a higher standard of living nor a higher educational level has reduced.

In the artistic and intellectual sphere, the major event of the time has been the advent of television. At first it spread slowly in households (53,000 sets in 1953), then rapidly (1 million per year since 1st January 1962). In September 1965 there were over 6 million sets. Thus over one household in two has TV (35% among managers, 21% among workers, in 1961). The average viewing time is 16 hours a week (Cazeneuve and Oulif, 1963). Listening to the radio is known to take up less time in households. Since 1957 cinema attendance has dwindled: only 27% of TV owners go at least once a month as against 42% of others (SEMA, 1965). During the same period (1956–1963) the sales of transistor radios passed from 150,000 to 2,000,610, those of long-playing records were multiplied by ten between 1954 and 1963, and a third of households have record players. Sales of magazines went on growing (11.7 mgs. per head in 1955 versus 15.4 in 1962). CREDOC expect this to continue in 1960–1970. The sales of books expanded too, with 10 million volumes sold in 1960 rising to 31 million in 1963 (Syndicat National du Livre, 1965).

The content of French TV programmes has not up to now been flooded by varieties and by commercial advertising, as in the United States where this covers 75% of camera time. The French programmes are better balanced, with 25% of varieties on a slightly higher level. The public's tastes are divided between easy games and high quality reporting, between serials (whose average level is higher than in the States) and plays such as "Macbeth" or "The Persians" which had a larger audience in one evening than in two thousand years of theatrical shows. The TV weekly whose standards are closest to those of the better educated viewers (Télé 7 Jours) has the highest readership (over a million copies). It has no counterpart in the United States. On the radio, songs are the most popular programmes, but "highbrow" singers meet with as much success as others and out of five hundred hours of transmitting, one hundred and fifty are devoted to classical modern music (1961). The French cinema is closer to the standard of quality literature than to Hollywood. In 1964 favourite films were "Les Misérables" (75%) and "The Guns of Navarone" (70%) but, "Quai des Brumes" is still selected by 43% and "Hiroshima Mon Amour" by 37% (Perspectives du Cinéma Français). Paperbacks have facilitated the expansion of popular crime novels, but also that of worthwhile literature. After the dictionary "Larousse" (1,300,000 copies sold), the most widely read books are *The Diary of Anne Frank* (750,000 copies), *The Plague* (650,000) and thirty books which sold more than 300,000 copies by 1964. Although paperbacks are not as common as in the United States, there is already the beginning of mass production and distribution of literary works (though not yet mass consumption).[21] In ten years the cultural situation has thus evolved towards growing complexity. In most social milieux of a town it is characterised by an intricate interpenetration of cultural styles and levels whose patterning is often original. Neither the refined concepts of academic culture and of avant-garde culture, nor the simplified concepts of mass culture such as the one which dominates in the United States, seem apt to describe the cultural content of the leisure enjoyed by the various social classes and categories in France, although some trends appear to be common to both.

Collective awareness

In this cultural context a general awareness of the specific problems raised by the cultural content of mass leisure has occurred in France. The value of leisure was certainly appreciated in that country much earlier. Foreigners have appreciated the quality of life ("douceur de vivre") in France. This is very unlike the "American way of life". Ever since the first manifesto for workers' leisure (1883) was written in France (Lafargue, 1965), leisure has been a frequent and important claim of the unions, especially in 1936. However, in the last ten years, it has become a general problem debated in an unprecedented number of congresses, round tables, seminars, and special issues of reviews, not only on the initiative of trade unions, but of employers' associations, advertising agencies, social workers' groups, educational associations, cultural organizations, religious bodies, State administrations etc. Leisure has become a truly national problem, on the agenda of various organizations. It is a widespread concern whose importance and whose meaning are wholly new.

Collective reflections on this theme, despite their diversity, offer some common aspects. Four problems have proved dominant:
a) How and to what end is the right of leisure to be asserted as a new aspect of happiness, despite the survival of earlier moral

imperatives concerning work, the family, politics or religion?

b) How and to what end are the constraints (working hours, type of work, or type of dwelling and travelling time, etc) which limit leisure possibilities for the under-privileged, to be reduced?

c) How and to what end are contradictions between leisure values and the authentic values of family, educational, occupational, unionist, political or spiritual commitment to be avoided?

d) How and to what end is an equilibrium between enjoyment and effort, escape and participation, entertainment and high culture in leisure to be favoured?

In reply to these questions, it should be noted that all the organizations of social life have been transformed or have undergone a faster process of change during that period. Firstly, marketing bodies have altered their advertising to make it more informative, more educational or more humorous. In 1964 the Paris Fair organized for the first time a "Leisure village" in which all trades of cultural goods and services were represented in an attempt both to educate the public and to promote sales (collaboration between researchers, writers and educationalists). National advertising groups met in 1963 to study ways of making the content and the form of advertising contribute to the development of balanced leisure in the life of the masses. The customary store which sells everything and knows about nothing is disappearing. In addition to the development of supermarkets, which often have special leisure departments, new specialised shops for cultural goods (sports shops, bookshops, music shops) are usually managed by competent salesmen who have received an appropriate training. These "salesmen organizers" are integrated in the life of the local society not as traditionalistic benefactors, but as technicians skilled in a leisure activity. Although this trend is still limited in its scope, it is a major aspect of the recent evolution in the trade of cultural goods.

A growing number of industrial concerns built in this period are unlike our old factories. They are still few in relation to industry as a whole, but they illustrate a new trend and offer a new frame of reference. New sources of energy and new working methods impose buildings which are more akin to administrative or school patterns than to the old factories and the wish to make life more pleasant leads the firms to add stadiums, playing fields, theatrical halls, meeting rooms, lecture rooms, and gardens to their workshops. Staff committees have increased their leisure activities and acquired greater expertise in this respect. In 1960 the main training officers of large firms met in order to study "general culture in industrial training."[22]

This new culture gives much scope to the new relationships between work and leisure values in the cultural equilibrium of managers. Most firms still offer anachronistic working conditions, but modern ones are less and less like the factories described by French literary works from Zola's to Aragon's.

During the same period, more than three million flats were built. Whole neighbourhoods and new towns were born. The protection and equipment of space for leisure is a major contemporary problem : parks, playgrounds, youth centres, social and cultural centres etc. A growing part of the activity displayed by social centres has been devoted to entertaining and informing the public. From 1956 onwards the role of the social worker began to evolve. She is becoming a "community leader" trained in the techniques of cultural action. The traditional "caretaker" tends in the new housing developments to be replaced by a complex system of guardians, delegates, assistants and leaders of diverse cultural centres for young, adult, and old tenants.

In a wholly different sphere, the traditional parish priest has undergone a comparable evolution. He has been the forerunner of leisure organizations. Yet the framework of "social work" within the Church has proved too narrow to meet new needs. Following a national congress on "pastoral action and leisure," in 1965 a general secularization of all these activities has been decided upon by the Church. The participation of the congregation in all new organizations for leisure has been steadily encouraged. Pastoral action is evolving towards forms better adapted to weekend leisure or end of year holidays and to the new outlook of the faithful. In addition to the traditional requirements of the priesthood, the role of guide within a team of cultural leaders is becoming increasingly common among the clergy.

The most dynamic municipal authorities have begun to approach the problem of leisure for the local population in new ways. Formerly committees for sport, art and associations followed fragmented policies without any overall perspective. For the last ten years, following the example of such pioneering cities as Rennes, Strasbourg, Metz, Rouen, Bourges, Avignon, Annecy or Grenoble, a more coherent policy of cultural development outside school, both in the short and the long term, has been gradually adopted by some municipalities, with the assistance of the State. The number of swimming pools, gymnasia and stadiums is increasing rapidly. Despite the delays accumulated over fifty years,[23] municipal libraries tend to become cultural centres. After similar delays, museum custodians are encouraged to become cultural leaders (Congress of the International Council of Museums Organization, Paris, 1964). Many theatrical centres set up under the Fourth Republic have been or are being turned into cultural centres (Maisons de Culture), six have been inaugurated under the Fourth Development Plan and nearly fifty are planned. Social centres, youth and cultural centres, and homes for young workers have more than doubled in ten years (there are now over 1200). The traditional municipal administration (mairie) is less and less adapted to solving all these new short and long term cultural problems.

Of course, all these innovations are still limited in scope. They meet with hostility among conservatives and with the inertia characteristic of all public and private administration. But there is no doubt that a cultural renewal movement began or gathered momentum during that period. It encouraged the realisation of many plans and has given an impetus to detailed projects which may very well gradually take shape over the next ten or twenty years, if the assumptions of economists are confirmed. These projects may be among the most concrete indicators of progress in "1985".

I have not exhaustively described the characteristics of the cultural evolution undergone by families and social organization during this period. Such was not my intention. I have selected some significant facts which show the appearance of new interests among the population and of new initiatives on the part of organizations in connection with the uneven but general premium on leisure expenditure and activities. Can one agree with Riesman that a "second revolution" is beginning to change the national character? It is too early to tell. My assumption is, however, that this cultural change is sufficiently wide and deep to durably affect the general outlook of the French, including unionist, sociopolitical or socio-spiritual attitudes. Despite the change in political climate since that time, despite the impact of the May—June 1968 events, these trends are proving lasting. No observation indicates the likelihood of change in this respect. On the contrary, all statistical data available since the period 1955—65 continue the trends of this decade with regard to leisure (Dumazedier 1972). Demands for a 40-hour week and for retirement at 60 may extend leisure problems to a wider public in the near future.[24]

A comparative analysis of leisure-time activities and of other activities in the daily life of advanced industrial societies leads to the conclusion that leisure tends to increase in the long run for the majority of workers. This trend is a general fact, but it does not apply to all and it is bound to come up against many obstacles in the present, as well as in the future. Considerable minorities do not benefit by this general evolution. The official ethics of work in an advanced industrial society where the means of production are under collective ownership, may give a different orientation to the content of leisure, but it does not alter the movement towards increased and more highly valued leisure for the majority of the active population. There is no difference with other types of advanced industrial societies in this respect. French society seems to have entered in the decade 1955—65 a phase of change in which leisure problems become more and more pressing in relation to all other sectors of social and cultural life. This is no longer a working class demand as in 1936; today leisure as a problem concerns society as a whole and its global culture.

I hope to have shown that the dynamics from which this phenomenon originates cannot be reduced to the economic factor. It is certainly the reduction in work times which provides for the increase in leisure-time; still the reduction in household and family duties, and the shorter travelling times between home and work have also contributed to the production of leisure. On the other hand, confusing free time and leisure may conceal the impact of two other important factors: a regression of the institutional controls of all basic social organisms and a high social valuation of personal fulfilment in all meanings of the word, at all levels, and despite all opposing economic, political and cultural forces.

Those socio-cultural dynamics transforming free time into

leisure are omitted from the studies which reduce the whole process to the impact of economic forces. One of the latest works based on this reduction is Lanfant's *Les Théories du Loisir* (The theories of leisure) (1972). The author's aprioristic position leads her to: 1) successively employ terms such as idleness, free time and leisure, without distinguishing between the socially different realities they cover; and 2) describe as "ideological" the social and cultural factors of the dynamics generating leisure, although they are indispensable to its understanding.

Joint work by historians and sociologists on this theme is still lacking. Thus it is not possible in each period, within different situations, to ascertain the existence of an explanatory *model* based on the three variables linked with the growth of productive forces, the regression in institutional controls and the social promotion of individual rights. However, studies based on these hypotheses about the dynamics of leisure in advanced industrial societies seem likely to prove successful.

Notes to Chapter II

[1] Since 1954 technological change and the dwindling of the primary sector have become faster in France. This sector employed only 17% of the active population in 1968 as against 34% in 1946. Though this rural exodus advantaged the secondary sector, which passed from 31% in 1946 to 35% in 1968, its main beneficiary has been the tertiary or post-industrial sector, whose increase was the most pronounced. It increased from 35% to 47% of the active population in 1968 and is now the leading sector. Although inadequately industrialised, French society has come in ten years to approximate a service economy which is the condition for the development of mass consumption and mass leisure. Of course the scope of what are known as "services" remains variable. In the U.S.A. the service sector already employs 63% of the active population.

[2] The opposite view is based on graduate women chosing the duties and leisure of home life in preference to employment (Friedan, 1964).

[3] For the population of the U.S., 48.5 years in 1900, 68.2 in 1950, 70.5 in 1967 (Historical statistics of the USA, Washington, U.S. Dept. of Commerce, Bureau of the Census, 157 p., p. 5).

[4] A different viewpoint is represented by Naville (1967).

[5] Some even refer to a new "cult of the sun" practised by tourists on the beaches. It is stretching the definition of religion rather.

[6] This information was obtained from the French Communist Party in 1971.

[7] This will be covered in my book on Leisure and the City, vol. 2: *Leisure and Society* (in preparation).

[8] See W. Kerr, *The Decline of Pleasure,* New York, 1965: "We are all of us compelled to read for profit, party for contracts, lunch for contracts, bowl for unity, drive for mileage, gamble for charity, go out for the evening for the greater glory of the municipality and stay home for the weekend to rebuild the house" (p.319).

[9] An economist, S.B. Linden, shows that consumer goods and corresponding activities are so many and so diverse that increasingly time for their consumption is lacking (Linden, 1970).

[10] See A. Grushin, 1969. This author, heir to a Russian tradition (Strumilin, Prudenski etc.) is well informed of the problems of empirical sociology. He belongs to the new generation of sociologists who were students in 1956–57 when Polish intellectuals began to apply the principles and the methods of empirical sociology to the study of socialist society. Despite many difficulties, that generation resisted for ten years the dogmatism and the academism of the Stalinist era, which threatened the utility of Marxist thought. After conducting opinion surveys under the aegis of a youth journal and later of an international review published in Prague, Boris Grushin is now in charge of the most thorough enquiry ever conducted in a Soviet town (Taganrog) about the sociology of culture. He has published a book on "public opinion". He has been a member of the Executive Committee of the Committee of

Leisure and Culture of the International Sociological Association since the World Congress of Sociology at Evian 1966.

[11] It is with this outlook that Soviet sociologists of the new wave participate in the comparative study of time-budgets initiated by Szalai. In his first comments, he stresses the limits which restrict real leisure in some countries and for some social categories. But the wealth of data gathered in twelve countries permits the treatment of other and wider problems, linked with the dialectical relationship between the constraints and the resources of the age.

[12] To my knowledge, this is the first sociological study on time-budgets conducted over a 25-year period.

[13] Minutes are expressed as hundredths of an hour.

[14] The author did not comment on these data; however, in the light of press information and of other research, it seems that two reasons may account for this: a) social (political) control is stronger in small than in large towns, as is citizens' participation in political life; b) as there are fewer alternatives in small towns, social meetings and ceremonies may be partly considered as substitutes for entertainment.

[15] Does such a statistical difference correspond to a genuine increase or to a random fluctuation? Probability calculations do not solve this issue, due to possible variations in reliability.

[16] The corresponding figures for theatre and concert attendance in France are much lower. It is a pity that Soviet surveys do not discriminate between the reading of books and of newspapers.

[17] Occupation, income, educational level. The present state of research makes it difficult to detect the relative influence of economic, socio-occupational and educational levels. Strumilin noted in 1959 that those who enjoyed a higher income had also reached a higher level of qualification implying more advanced education. Many Soviet sociologists consider that qualifications are now the main factor in the structuring of the social hierarchy in the USSR.

[18] In France the comparable percentage is 2% or 5% depending on the survey.

[19] Particularly the results of the first great modern survey of urban sociology conducted at Taganrog, a town of 200,000 inhabitants.

[20] See also the leisure survey of JAC (Rural Catholic Youth) which received 20,000 replies, 1961.

[21] Paperback versions of general literature are mainly bought by those who already read books, i.e. 42% of the French (according to the 1960 survey of the Publishers National Association).

[22] It is during this period that the social movement which was to extend and to result in collective bargaining and eventually in legislation on continuous training in industry (in 1970–71), originated and/or gained momentum.

[23] Thus in Paris, municipal libraries lend a quarter as many books as in New York and 10 times less than in London. (Hassenforder, 1965).

[24] See below *Leisure and the Third Age*, p. 92.

III The Quarrel over Definitions

After examining the difficulties raised by the diachronic analysis of leisure I now come to what might be called the quarrel over definitions. Here again the progress of scientific knowledge is hampered by epistemological and methodological difficulties constantly debated by sociologists. I shall attempt to outline the viewpoint which I have arrived at while undertaking research projects which are still far from completed. To my mind, a sociological definition should offer at least the four following properties: firstly, it should be logical and should enable its object to be located in the genus to which it belongs, while being distinguished from other objects within it by the least ambiguous specific difference. Secondly, it must be valid in relation to the major problems of society. Thirdly, it must attempt to be operational in relation to the corresponding social behaviours. Lastly, it must take account of the division of labour within sociology between various specialised branches (industrial, political etc.), and define its object as clearly as possible to demarcate it from that of other specialisms.

III.1. Definitions

In the light of these proposals, the four common definitions of leisure in contemporary sociology will now be examined. A basic distinction is made between activities: A) remunerated work, B) family obligations, C) socio-spiritual and socio-political obligations, D) activities external to these institutional obligations and mainly oriented towards self-fulfilment. Four types of definitions may be distinguished, depending whether they hold leisure to include one or all of these elements.

	A	B	C	D
	Remunerated work	Family obligations	Socio-spiritual obligations	Activities oriented towards self-fulfilment
Definition no. 1	X	X	X	X
Definition no. 2		X	X	X
Definition no. 3			X	X
Definition no. 4				X

Definition no. 1

Leisure is not a definite category of social behaviour. Any behaviour in each category may represent leisure, even work. Leisure is not a category, but a style of behaviour, which may occur in any activity: one can work while listening to music, study while playing, wash the dishes with the wireless on, hold a political meeting with a parade of majorettes, mingle the erotic and the sacred, etc. ... Any activity may become leisure. Riesman may have been the first to develop this theory in 1948; it is now widespread among sociologists; it has often been expounded by Kaplan (at least prior to 1973), and by Wilensky. Its advantage is to show that leisure patterns tend to infiltrate all other activities, that leisure may initiate a lifestyle and that its forms contribute to changing the quality of life. However, this is a psychological rather than sociological definition: it refers to the attitude of some rather than to the behaviour common to all. It confuses leisure and pleasure, leisure and play. It does not define a specific sphere among the various activities which perform different social functions. It does not illuminate the relationship, basic to the dynamics generating leisure, between the decrease in the time devoted to institutional obligations and the growth of the time freed for personal activity in the context of new social norms.

Definition no. 2

The second definition explicitly or implicitly situates leisure in relation to work only, and by contrast to it, as if nothing else existed, as if leisure could be equated with non-work. This definition is most common among economists, especially since Keynes saw leisure as the major problem of advanced economies. It is also found in most of Karl Marx's writings.[25] Industrial sociologists and sociologists of leisure (Meyerson, Parker) have often used it in comparing work and leisure. The advantage of this approach is that it locates leisure in relation to the main source of leisure-time and the main limitation upon it. However, it is too influenced by economic categories and by those of the sociology of work. It is less and less apt to deal with the specific problems of leisure in advanced industrial societies. An additional disadvantage is the juxtaposition of heterogeneous social realities under the label of leisure. For the clarity of this concept, it is regretted that the same term should cover activities occurring in a time freed from occupational commitments and those which take place in a time taken up by family obligations. The reduction of the latter gives scope for leisure pursuits, especially in the case of housewives and mothers, too often forgotten by the sociology of leisure. The non-work time devoted to parental, conjugal and family duties is not relevant to the sociology of leisure, but to the sociology of the family. However, in studying the relations between family and individual or collective leisure, the sociology of leisure could usefully cooperate with the sociology of the family.

Definition no. 3

This definition of leisure which excludes from it household and family obligations has the merit of showing the double dynamics of leisure creation and limitation for men and women, of emphasizing both the reduction of remunerated work and that of family tasks. However, such a definition has a disadvantage. The specific difference characterizing leisure is ambiguous. The term leisure covers socio-spiritual and socio-political obligations, whose decrease favours the development of activities pertaining to a new type, as well as these activities themselves. It has already been shown that the decrease in holidays and rites controlled by traditional socio-spiritual institutions has freed time, now taken up by purely hedonistic activities freely chosen by the individuals concerned rather than institutionally imposed.

Yet, even when the control of religious institutions on free time recedes, ambiguous activities, religious or pseudo-religious in character, often oriental in inspiration and containing elements of idealism and mysticism, of dream and metaphysics, of erotism and of the supernatural etc.... appear in some circles and especially among the young. These activities are performed in small groups or in large gatherings during weekends or holidays. Celebrating, feasting, collective leisure have a varying share in these occasions which are part-cult, part-leisure. It seems difficult to consider them as leisure phenomena which should be viewed as distinct and analysed sometimes by religious sociology, sometimes by the sociology of leisure. Such an analysis is of the utmost importance for the future of socio-spiritual activities in a society where the cultural patterns of leisure tend to be pervasive.

This definition embraces both the socio-political obligations required for the operation of a democracy and the activities sometimes described as escapist since they may detract from the performance of these obligations by the citizen. It strikes me as a mistake to use the same concept to describe realities which are heterogeneous from the viewpoint of relations between individual rights and institutional duties, and conflictual from the viewpoint of social dynamics.

In addition, such a definition of leisure covering socio-spiritual and socio-political obligations would merge political sociology and the sociology of religion with the sociology of leisure, letting the former two handle problems for which they are not competent. In order to describe the time freed from both occupational and family duties including socio-spiritual and socio-political obligations, I prefer to use the term *free time,* as Szalai and his team do. This expression should not have a normative meaning, in my view. It merely means the time freed from those double duties, whether they allow for self-fulfilment or not, whether this time is limited by social conditioning or not. Free time so defined does not allow, in my opinion, for the establishment of a special branch of sociology.[26]

A variation on the same definition excludes socio-spiritual activities from its scope. These phenomena are not mentioned in the definitions of free time given by such authors as Prudensky and Grushin. Sociologists of this school are content to use the same term for socio-political activities and for activities aimed at self-expression. I have already said why this confusion makes it difficult to deal with the major problem of future participation in socio-political activities in advanced industrial societies. To make this point clear: the institutional requirement for socio-political commitment is a democratic duty for the citizen, whether he likes it or not. The assumption of his socio-political responsibilities may give him a deep satisfaction, it may take place in a festive atmosphere, but it may also require discipline, even sacrifice. In either case, it is *above all* an institutional requirement of society, not an individual one. The participation in socio-political responsibilities, needed by society, cannot be treated as a leisure pursuit among others. If we wish to facilitate the scientific study of interconnections and dialectical relations between these two types of activities, socio-political activities and those which I shall term leisure should be covered by different labels. In time-budgets, the latter takes up fifty times more time than socio-political activities in the wide sense, whether in the Soviet Union or the United States, in Czechoslovakia or in France.

Definition no. 4

Both in terms of accuracy and of operationality, I prefer to reserve the word leisure for the time whose content is oriented towards self-fulfilment as an ultimate end. This time is granted to the individual by society, when he has complied with his occupational, family, socio-spiritual and socio-political obligations, in accordance with current social norms. It is a time made available by the shorter work-schedules, the reduced family duties, the lessened socio-spiritual and socio-political obligations. The individual frees himself from tiredness by resting, from boredom by entertainment, from functional specialization by developing the aptitudes of his body or his mind, as he pleases. This available time is not the result of an individual decision, but above all the product of economic and social evolution. As has already been said, it is a new social value of the person translated into a new social right to dispose of time for his own satisfaction. As shown by the international survey on time-budgets (Szalai, 1973), this time corresponds for each worker to four or five hours a day, Saturday and Sunday included.

Since time is defined mainly — though not exclusively — in relation to remunerated work, I have suggested a distinction between four periods of leisure, from 1960 onwards: leisure at the end of the day, at the weekend, at the end of the year (holidays) and at the end of life (retirement). These periods of spare time include many days of activity, but, according to time-budget studies, they are increasingly dominated by the dynamics of leisure. Their mutual relations have been uncovered recently and imperfectly as yet. During such times, leisure covers a number of more or less structured activities connected with the bodily and mental needs of individuals: physical, practical, artistic, intellectual and social-leisure pursuits, within the limits of economic, social, political and cultural conditioning in each society. These activities will be called LEISURE. They are determined by work and by other institutional obligations, but as the post-industrial stage approaches, they increasingly tend to affect the determining institutions.

Certain philosophers (Marcuse and his disciples) tend to deny the existence of the personal activities called "leisure". According to them, leisure is a form of alienation, the delusion of freely satisfying individual needs, since such needs are in fact created and manipulated by the economic forces of mass production and consumption, in the masters' interests. The point deserves consideration. Empirical sociology shows that for leisure goods and services (holidays), commercial agencies sell sunshine, adventure, exoticism in the most standardized forms in order to attract a maximum number of clients at lowest cost and for the highest profits. Leisure goods and services are therefore regulated by the same market laws as other goods and services. This is roughly the case of State or co-operative organizations in the emerging tourist industry of socialist societies, (Mamaia, Sotchi, Varna). Such commercial or political standardization sets or may set serious problems for the social and cultural development of society. Standardized social and cultural behaviour patterns limit creative and authentic communication between individuals and groups. However, standardization should not be equated with the abolition of possibilities of self-fulfilment. Socio-economic *conditioning* which limits possibilities of personal choice should not be confused with family, spiritual or political *constraints* which are normative and may repress the personal choice of leisure pursuits. The general concept of alienation propounded by Marcuse is one to which I am sympathetic. But why does it wholly disregard the subjectivity of individuals? It seems indefensible to speak of alienation *equally* about those who spend their holidays at Las Vegas or Cannes, as per touristic brochures, and about those (much more numerous) who have a family vacation in some "cheap spot" or who have a dream holiday with a boyfriend or a girlfriend on some lonely island.

The specific characteristics of leisure in today's society may now be outlined. Many surveys conducted over the last thirty years have shown the scope, the limits and the structure of this concept. I shall call leisure any activity which offers four properties: two "negative" ones, defined by reference to the obligations imposed by social institutions and two "positive" ones, defined by reference to personality needs. These four properties have appeared to be interconnected in almost all replies to a survey on leisure as represented in a sample of 819 urban factory workers and employees (Encyclopédie Française, vol. XIV, 1954). Leisure may, of course, have many other attributes and fulfill many other functions; it may be akin to consumer goods, to an educational service, to a propaganda theme etc. . . . It is undoubtedly a total social fact, linked with all others. However, these properties are not specific to leisure; they do not make up its social reality. On the other hand, the system of characteristics which will be discussed below is specific; it constitutes leisure, which would not exist without it. This is my basic tenet.

Liberating Character: Leisure results from a free choice. It would be inaccurate to identify freedom and leisure, to exclude any obligation from leisure. Leisure is freedom *from a certain number and from certain kinds of obligations.* Need I repeat that it is socially determined, as are all social facts? Similarly, it is dependent, as are all activities, on social relations, and consequently on inter-personal commitments (contracts, appointments). It is also regulated by the obligations emanating from the groups and bodies needed for its practice (discipline of a sports team, regulations of a film-society etc.). Yet it implies freedom from kinds of obligations which may be described as *institutional*, since they are imposed by the units which make up society: occupational institutions (or compulsory schooling for the young who have not yet entered active life), family, socio-spiritual and socio-political organizations. As compared with these primary institutional obligations, those which are imposed by leisure organizations, even when they are strict, appear secondary from the viewpoint of society. Leisure dialectically implies these basic obligations. It is opposed to them, yet it assumes their existence. They must end for it to begin. It is defined by reference to them. Thus leisure is, in the first place, freedom from work within the enterprise. For the child, it is freedom from schoolwork. Leisure *is* freedom from the basic primary obligations derived from the basic units of society: family, socio-political and socio-spiritual institutions. Conversely, when the leisure pursuit becomes remunerated occupation (as when the amateur sportsman turns professional), or a school (e.g. compulsory attendance at a film), or family duty (such as a walk made under pressure to go out), or a political or religious commitment (for instance a fete held for propaganda purposes), its sociological character changes, even if its technical content does not, even if the individual concerned derives the same pleasure from that activity.

Disinterested Character: This is a corollary of the previous attribute on the level of finality. Basically leisure serves no lucrative end, unlike work, no utilitarian end, unlike household duties, no ideological or proselytising end, unlike political or spiritual obligations. In leisure, the game, the physical, artistic, intellectual or social activity involved is not at the service of any material or social end, even when it is materially and socially determined, even when attempts to integrate it are made by professional, educational, family, socio-spiritual and socio-political institutions.

Consequently, if leisure is partly geared to profit-making, to a utilitarian end or to some form of commitment, it does not become a duty, but is no longer fully worthy of its name. It becomes part-leisure: I shall call it *semi-leisure*. It is as if the circle of primary obligations cut across that of leisure obligations and semi-leisure occurred when the two overlap. Semi-leisure is thus a mixed activity in which leisure mingles with an institutional obligation. This happens when a sportsman is remunerated for part of his activities: when the amateur fisherman sells a few fish; when the gardener who loves flowers grows some vegetables for his own table; when the do-it-yourself enthusiast does all repairs at home; when someone attends a civic celebration for the sake of entertainment rather than for the ceremony itself; or when an employee reads a novel to show his superior that he has read it. . . .

Hedonistic Character: First defined negatively in relation to institutional obligations and to the ends imposed by the basic limits of society, leisure is positively defined by reference to personality needs, even when the individual fulfills them within a group of his own choosing. In nearly all empirical surveys, leisure is characterized by a search for a *state of satisfaction,*[27] taken as an end itself.

This search is intrinsically hedonistic. Clearly happiness is not limited to leisure, it may coexist with the performance of basic social duties. Pleasure is not the automatic outcome of that social artefact which "should serve to promote pleasure:" the game (Cazeneuve, 1952).[28] However, the quest for happiness, pleasure or joy is a basic characteristic of leisure in modern society. Wolfenstein speaks in this connection of a "fun morality". When this state of satisfaction ends or deteriorates, the individual tends to discontinue the corresponding activity. No one is bound to a leisure pursuit by a material need or a moral or legal imperative of *society*; such is not the case with educational, occupational, socio-political, civic or socio-spiritual obligations. Though social pressures or the force of habit may hinder the decision to free oneself, such a decision is the individual's prerogative in relation to leisure, far more than to any other activity. The search for a state of satisfaction is the prime condition of leisure: "this interests me". Such a state may consist in the rejection of all tensions, of any attention or concentration. It may alternatively be a voluntary effort or a deferred gratification. In playing a game against elements, against another man or against oneself, an effort more intense than work, comparable with religious asceticism, may be required to achieve a level of performance or of wisdom. Rock climbing, to name but one sport, can entail a strict discipline. But such efforts, such commitments are freely chosen in the expectation of disinterested pleasure, not for utilitarian ends. This hedonistic character is so essential that when leisure fails to give the expected pleasure, when it is not enjoyed, it loses its intrinsic character: "it is not interesting," "it is not fun." Then leisure is no longer itself, it is impoverished.

Personal Character: All the manifest functions of leisure expressed by the individuals concerned refer to individual needs, as contrasted with the primary obligations imposed by society. Leisure is directly related with the possible degradation of the individual (e.g. alcoholism) or with the defense of his integrity against the onslaught of industrial and urban society, less and less natural, more and more run by the clock and stereotyped. It is connected with the realization, either encouraged or hampered, of man's full potential, conceived as an end in itself, whether it is related to social needs or in contradiction with them.

1) It offers man the possibility of freeing himself from the physical or nervous strains which counteract his biological rhythm. It enables him to recover or merely to be idle.

2) It provides an opportunity to free oneself from the daily boredom generated by repetitive and frequent tasks, in opening up the real or imaginary universe of entertainment, either socially allowed or prohibited.

3) It gives everyone a chance to escape the routine and the stereotypes imposed by the operation of basic institutions; it enables man to go beyond the confines of the self and frees his creative powers, whether to conform with the dominant values of civilization or to challenge them. These needs are more or less fully satisfied, depending on the kind and level of activities, as well as on the situations and the persons involved. In my view, the most *complete* leisure must satisfy these three individual needs and fulfill these three basic, distinct but interrelated functions. Any leisure which does not offer these three alternatives is incomplete in relation to the specific requirements of personality fulfillment, outside the network of institutional obligations proposed or imposed by modern society.

III.2. Classification Problems

Like the definition of leisure, the classification of leisure pursuits is controversial. Any classification is primarily an answer to a problem. It is constructed rather than given. In my view, any scientific classification should have at least three formal attributes:

(a) *It must be oriented.* It is made "from a given point of view" (Martinet, 1960). A criterion of selection discriminates between pertinent and irrelevant elements. Other criteria then split these two categories into sub-categories. The positivist delusion whereby classifications have an intrinsic worth, independent from the point of view adopted, has long since been forsaken.

(b) *It must be finite.* The criterion of selection separates all pertinent elements, without omission or repetition. It creates an exhaustive sub-set. Irrelevant elements are not forgotten, but rejected into an equally exhaustive second sub-set. They make up the remainder, in a mathematical sense. It is indispensible to be exhaustive so as to avoid relying only on favourable instances in accordance with the verification procedure. Probability calculations show whether the difference in the distribution of favourable and unfavourable cases, among all possible eventualities, is random or due to other factors.

(c) *It must be coherent.* Each class includes a smaller one and is subsumed under a larger one. The whole constitutes a coherent set.

The main classifications propounded by the sociology of leisure will now be examined, both from the viewpoint which inspired them and from that of the problems analysed here.

Starting from the standpoint of cultural development, a genetic classification springs to mind first. From the Middletown study (Lynd, 1925) in the United States to that conducted at Trovje in Yugoslavia (Ahtik, 1960), this mode of classification has often been adopted by sociologists. In the first study, Lynd distinguished between traditional leisure pursuits (lectures, reading, music, art), modern pursuits derived from discoveries (the motorcar, the wireless, the cinema . . .), and organized leisure (groups, clubs). This classification is oriented towards the problems of social control, compatible with social evolution. Thirty years later, Ahtik, guided by the progress of research on mass culture, adopted an equally historical approach. The effects of mass culture are already felt in Yugoslavia, a socialist country whose economic development is still weak. Ahtik classified the contents of leisure depending on their derivation either from traditional culture (family life, local outings, pubs), humanistic culture (lectures, popular education centres etc.) or "mass culture" (radio, cinema, magazines). These classifications are most interesting. It would be useful to continue such research in order to improve selection criteria and increase the coherence of the set and the sub-sets of various historical origins. However, diachronic classifications are less appropriate than synchronic ones to the solution of our basic problem, which is dominated by the gap existing *today* between the culture of learned origin and the culture experienced by the masses. Indeed synchronic classifications include categories whose components differ by their historic origins, but possess significant properties for this study. From my point of view, the origin of cultural contents matters less than their types (physical or mental, technical, aesthetic or scientific etc.) and their levels (elementary, medium or higher) by reference to various criteria of cultural development.

The example of linguistics is fruitful in this connection. Modern linguists firmly defended the synchronic approach against the general predominance of the diachronic. This is not tantamount to underestimating the importance of evolution; Jakobson and Lévi-Strauss have made it clear. However, as will be shown later, it is the only way of attempting to exhaustively describe the whole set of elements offering the same characteristics from the viewpoint of cultural development, without taking account of their historical origin.

From the synchronic viewpoint, which I am adopting, many attempts at classification have been made. Only the main ones will be examined.

In the study of leisure at Kansas City in 1955, Havighurst distinguished eleven categories (Havighurst, 1959):

1) participation in organized groups,
2) participation in unorganized groups,

3) pleasure trips,
4) participation in sport,
5) spectator sports (excluding TV),
6) television and wireless,
7) fishing and hunting,
8) gardening (flowers, vegetables and country walks),
9) crafts (sewing, carpentering, do-it-yourself),
10) imaginative activities (reading, music, art),
11) visits to relatives or friends.

This classification has the merit of grouping under the single concept of leisure activities which are often scattered under various isolated conceptual labels. Yet it resembles a nomenclature which covers several couples of opposite activities (e.g. participation in organized and in unorganized groups etc.). The author has obviously left to a later date the processing of these elements by reference to a criterion of selection on which a coherent ordering could rest. This is a temporary nomenclature rather than a classification proper. Furthermore, can it really be considered exhaustive?

Foote and Cottrell have worked along the same lines, but have made greater efforts to arrive at a coherent classification (Foote and Cottrell, 1955). They distinguish within leisure:

1) Physical play intended to explore and exercise the faculties and aptitudes of the body (formation, functioning, sensation).
2) Crafts. These come after physical play.
3) Dreaming.
4) Intellectual play, knowledge for the sake of research.
5) Artistic play.

This classification is at a more general level. Its unity derives from the concept of play and it appears to be more logical. However, the comparative analysis of dreaming and of artistic play ought perhaps to have been pursued further, before the two were dissociated. In addition, some gaps, especially about forms of sociability, ought perhaps to have been filled.

Lastly, Kaplan attempted, in a general study, to reduce leisure activities to six major types, connected with six foci of interest, grouped in couples by the author (Kaplan, 1960).

Types of Leisure	Foci of Interest
1. Sociability	Persons
2. Association	Interests
3. Play	Rules
4. Arts	Traditions
5. Exploration	Going out into the World
6. Immobility	Receiving the World

This classification is more systematic than previous ones. It deals with some problems which concern the educationalist. How can we complement spontaneous sociability based on inter-personal attraction with organized sociability (association) based on shared interests? How can physical activities be developed to encourage individuals to discover the world by taking walks, by exercising, by travelling, rather than to wait for the world to come to them (by wireless or TV)? Art which, according to ethnologists, is of the same nature as play, compels to make a creative effort based on tradition. To compare play and art in order to contrast them later is of obvious interest. However, though the underlying major criterion of this classification is effort (the search for a level of attainment), it has not in fact proved operational. Some of the included categories are not directly derived from this criterion. The internal coherence of the classification is weak, it is not exhaustive.

I shall now suggest some principles for the classification of leisure from the viewpoint of a sociology of cultural development. A synchronic approach will be retained and therefore my classification is not chronological. History will be used only to show the origin of the importance attributed today to the analytical categories suggested.

(a) The general problems raised by the modern history of culture in its relationship with leisure are constraints on a logical approach. A classification must possess some logical attributes (disjunction, coherence, etc.), but these are subordinated to their meaningfulness in relation to the historical problems studied. My classification will therefore be explicitly made "relative" to the unclear, but important problems arising from the connections between bodily and mental culture, and, within the latter, from those which are linked with practical, aesthetic or intellectual activities. Finally, I shall deal with the cultural issues raised by the content of organized or unorganized social relations, whatever the kind of physical or mental activity with which they may be connected.

(b) Within this framework of historical constraints, how can my classification have the logical attributes required from any classification? Firstly, a coherent analytical scheme is indispensible to identify the topics covered, to compare what is comparable etc. I suggest a reduction of all concrete elements to interests in the cultural content of leisure activities, or — to make the formula simpler — to "cultural interests". Therefore, whether they are actual behaviour patterns or opinions on such behaviour etc., explicit or implicit cultural interests will be considered as the common denominators of all these reactions. Thus the necessary homogeneity will be achieved by treating the sociology of leisure as part of the sociology of culture.

(c) In order to locate the various interests, associated with the content of many diverse leisure activities, in the categories corresponding to the problems I have already defined, I have to regroup them under five foci of interest: physical, manual, aesthetic, intellectual and social, which coincide with my categories of cultural problems. This is a logical necessity which entails operational difficulties. Indeed the interest generated by the content of leisure pursuits is *multidimensional.* Several contents may correspond to one interest. Thus an intellectual interested in the acquisition of knowledge may be satisfied by reading a novel, by watching a film or by perusing a dictionary.

Conversely, the same content may stimulate different interests, physical or mental, aesthetic or cognitive; for instance, a race of athletes or a walk in the woods. This is a classical taxinomic problem: how to order a collection of multidimensional elements into homogeneous classes? A solution may be found by drawing up a hierarchy of attributes and determining classes only by reference to dominant attributes. I shall call dominant attribute that which demarcates a class. By what method is such an attribute to be discovered? Several alternatives exist. The subjective assessment by individuals cannot serve to define basic categories. It is too unreliable about the intrinsic characteristics of each group of interests. I feel that an objective approach, external to individuals, is preferable. Thus even if, for a given individual, a walk is perceived as a poetical experience, we know that walking differs from reading a poem, because it *necessarily* entails *physical* movement, whether the individual cares about this or not. I shall call the dominant attribute of an activity *that whose presence is logically necessary to the existence of this activity*. It will be found among the attributes considered to define the scope of my problem, i.e. physical, manual, aesthetic, intellectual and social attributes of leisure activities.

I still have to define the various attributes corresponding to different groups of interest: physical versus mental interests. Among them, manual, aesthetic and intellectual interests must be defined *in relation to each other*. Finally, with regard to interpersonal relations, social interests associated with leisure must be distinguished from interests linked with the content of leisure pursuits. This systematic approach will facilitate the delineation of the attributes on which categories of leisure are based.

(a) For these categories of interests, thus relativised, reduced, disjointed and defined in relation to each other, to adequately deal with the general problems of the cultural contents of leisure, their patterning must *correspond* to the significant *patterns* of the general problems of cultural development. Hence the problem of the *formal structure* pertaining to these groups of interests, as a function of the major problems concerning the *cultural values* included in leisure. (These values are related to the free development of the individual's physical and mental personality through active participation in the cultural life of society.) It is important to attempt the application of an analytical scheme corresponding to the various contents of leisure pursuits. It can thus be ascertained to what extent common cultural problems may really be posited in different sectors of activity. Once again a logical approach adds precision to an empirical approach and makes its results more explicit, just as combined analysis complements empirical inference and sets out its limits. Categories, even empty or containing a single element, always generate a higher form of knowledge than an element considered in isolation. As the logician Peano stated, "a single match is not the same thing as a single match in a matchbox."

Firstly, cultural interests may give rise to different operations, either productive (achievement, invention, discovery, expression etc.) or unproductive (observation, contemplation, attendance). For instance, invention of a technical device or creation of a dramatic part, as against observation in the street, attendance at a show or visit to an exhibition.

The level of interest in productive or unproductive operations may vary with the adopted criteria; it may be low, medium or high, in relation to the values of academic culture, of the avant-garde or of other cultural referents. These levels are not to be confused with *kinds*. An interest in popular or classical music corresponds to two distinct kinds, each of which includes brilliant and mediocre specimens. Whether considered minor or major, these kinds of interest correspond to different kinds of knowledge, which by definition cannot be ranked (unlike cultural levels). Each kind corresponds to basic *sectors* of activity, in which physical, manual, aesthetic, intellectual and social interests are expressed. They may be compared with the sectors of interests external to leisure and associated with work, family commitments, socio-political obligations etc. The logical attributes of this structure enable one to detect whether the cultural contents of the various sectors are coherently patterned. A concern for structural coherence must never lead to an artificial description of reality, intended to bring out symmetry where none exists. On the contrary, it ought to allow for the identification and measurement of real differences (of kind and level) between sectors of leisure activity. Positing common categories makes it possible to solve some of the more general problems of cultural development, which must be tackled for *all* sectors, in order to ascertain whether *one* or *several* answers exist: e.g. the issue of an "active or passive attitude" towards leisure or that of the *quality* evidenced by the cultural content of leisure etc.

(b) Do these complex significant units exhaust the concrete units gathered by systematic observation? It is highly likely that the reply will be negative. There is a considerable danger of retaining those aspects of reality which suit the research design and of discarding "the rest". To surrender to this temptation results in the confusion between illustrating and demonstrating, between the verificatory and the experimental approach, which I have already denounced. In order to avoid this risk, the general classification of one's data must be analysed to test its *pertinence,* even if analytical rules cannot be applied to some sectors due to lack of information. It is only under this condition that the relative value of the cultural interest investigated here as against all the manifest interests shown in my data can be ascertained. I can even endeavour to treat this set or one of its sub-sets (e.g. interest in the plastic arts) as a lexicologist deals with the range of verbal signs corresponding to his chosen criterion (Dumazedier, 1964).

I shall thus arrive at a formal classification capable of dealing with real problems. Beyond its logical and epistemological interest, it can provide a frame of reference for two other kinds of classification: firstly, for a classification no longer based on logical attributes, but on connections experienced by my population between the various classes or sub-classes of cultural interests; secondly, for a classification founded on statistical correlations. Thus information may be ordered by reference to another classificatory principle: my a priori classes may be reduced to binary elements of varying dimensions (bodily/non-bodily interests; manual/non-manual interests; aesthetic/non-aesthetic interests) in order to reckon statistical correlations between sectors. Within classes of interests, categories may be dichotomised (interest in walks vs. other interests, interest in sport vs. other interests). *Statistical relationships* between the various sub-sectors, kinds or levels of interests can thus be made manifest. New cultural patternings, either similar to previous ones or contrasting with them, will be outlined. The a priori classification suggested in the light of existing problems may be compared with that which is founded on the statistical relationships between the interests of this population.

III.3. Implications

Such a definition and such a classification have implications for some research fields apparently external to leisure. The sociology of leisure enables one to conceptualize some kinds of activity, some phases of life which have until now fitted into other frameworks and other analytical categories. Yet I intend to show that the priorities and the relationships brought out by the sociology of leisure more accurately reflect the most specific characteristics and the dynamics of these phenomena. If my analysis is justified, their widespread representation is less and less accurate. My work contains many examples which have been analysed and which will be mentioned later. Two instances particularly meaningful in French social life will suffice for the time being: I refer to the use of cafés and to the stage of life increasingly called "the third age".

1) Cafés and leisure

It is a well-known fact that licensed premises make up one-third of commercial enterprises in France (Ledermann, 1965). The café — the equivalent of the pub — is a place where alcohol may be consumed under the provisions corresponding to the type of license held. There are four types of licenses, depending on the strength of the alcohol sold. The law on the siting of licensed premises tends to be restrictive (to protect some areas from such establishments). I would like to show that — though a minority may be drinking dens — cafés are in most cases *leisure institutions* with important social and cultural functions which call for legislation and a policy widely different from those of today (Dumazedier and Suffert, 1962).[29] This is the hypothesis I shall attempt to corroborate.

The main fact is the following: 17% of the male population never go to a café; the regulars (several times a week) are only 15%; over two-thirds of the population go less than twice a week (27%) or occasionally (41%). For most consumers going to a café is an activity which exhibits all the attributes of leisure or semi-leisure.

I have first attempted to find out on what occasions and with whom people go out. Nearly all individuals are not interested in drinking, but in contacts, in exchanges which enhance, complement, or compensate for, daily relationships at work and family or social commitments; above all, the café is a *framework for freely chosen social relationships.*

Some large firms have installed machines dispensing drinks in the work place. I have interviewed neighbouring licensees: it seems (but this should be checked after a longer period, the machines having now existed for three years only) that the rate of customers' attendance has not altered. On the one hand, factory workers enjoy the possibility of quenching their thirst in working hours and many make use of it. On the other, they still meet after work, at the café. Hence there are two distinct needs which are met under different circumstances: one at work, the other during leisure time.

Some cafés perform a special role in relation to working people, after they have left the factory, the workshop or the shop. This connection with work is mentioned in 35% of replies. The workplace often imposes relationships dominated by the requirement of production or distribution. The café allows far more selective, less rigid relationships better adapted to individual needs and desires. They may be derived from and determined by work, but endowed with a wider content. Alternatively they may be outside the scope of work proper and consist only in human, friendly exchanges. They continue working relationships, but with a new character of semi-constraint, semi-leisure. It is shopkeepers who most frequently mention work or business as grounds for frequenting a café (59% of replies). Tradesmen also refer to a connection with work (53% of replies).

The meaning of these replies is strengthened by a content analysis of conversations in cafés. Going there may be linked with working patterns, without work being necessarily mentioned in conversation. Yet work and business are still the most frequent topics: they are mentioned in 23% of replies. Factory workers talk least about their work (22% in the case of semi-skilled and the unskilled, 10% among foremen and skilled workers). However, industrialists and managerial workers discuss it more frequently (36%).

The age of respondents is significant. It is between 41 and 50 that going to the café for business and work reasons is most common (44% of replies). Between 21 and 30 years of age, only 22% of answers refer to work as a ground for attendance. These differences are also reflected in topics of conversation. "Business" is a more frequent subject between 30 and 50 than either before or after.

The café thus plays an important part in this sphere of semi-leisure, in between work and leisure; it links up two activities whose content and rhythm are so different that all categories of workers seek transitional situations, albeit to various extents.

A smaller part of the public (from 5 to 18% depending on the social category, 11.5% overall) go out *as families,* mainly on Sundays. It is an old custom. An "old boy" told me: "we used to take the child out for a grenadine, when he had had good marks at school." Some cafés, particularly in the main street and on the outskirts of the town are often much attended, as are those located near a lake or a river. It is among the middle ranks of managerial workers that the family plays the biggest part in such outings. Age is also significant and the age group between 21 and 30 enjoy this leisure or semi-leisure as often as other generations.

The main reasons for going to cafés concern extra-occupational and non-family relationships. Part of the public come in the first place to continue relations and exchanges started during a match, a film, a friendly, social, civic or political meeting etc. (from 2 to 21% depending on the social category, 9% overall). As could be expected, cafés located near picture houses, theatres, stadiums, headquarters of associations, labour exchanges and meeting halls have most of the customers prompted by such reasons.

Many individuals (27%) go to cafés in order to meet friends. This general answer probably overlaps in part with previous replies: friendship is no stranger to working relationships, to family outings, to the relations emerging from membership of the same groups. Yet it goes beyond these connections. Interviews have spontaneously and in numbers expressed this major attribute of all forms of social participation in cafés: the maintenance or the development of freely chosen personal relationships which express all degrees and all nuances of comradeship and of friendship.

Shopkeepers make fewest allusions to this phenomenon: only 5% of their replies mention friendly meetings. In all likelihood their occupation, though schedules are demanding, involves a sufficiently flexible activity to allow for encounters with friends in the work place. By contrast, members of the liberal professions and teachers refer most frequently to friendship (42% mention meeting friends as the main reason for going to a café). No doubt they find it more difficult to meet their friends at work.

Meetings with friends in cafés increase with age (23% of answers between 21 and 30, 26% between 30 and 40, and 29% between 40 and 50, 31% above 50). Differences between age groups are again minimal and, in each age group, a quarter or a third seek such meetings.

The café provides a focal point not only for spontaneous interpersonal relationships, but for organized ones, such as meetings and reunions of groups and societies. This is an old-established role. Before the First World War, the early trade-unionists met in cafés which were also the headquarters of political parties. "There were red pubs and white pubs, it created hatred and political dissensions; that is the party spirit" (a former industrialist). Such groups still meet in cafés, but debates are less heated and members fewer. However, an increasing number of leisure associations hold meetings there. Towards 1900 there were some thirty such associations in the town studied. Today the population has trebled and there are over 250 bowling, fishing, sporting, musical, reading and social work associations etc. Over 80 out of 244 cafés are headquarters or meeting places of such associations.

Some cafés are indifferent or hostile to this social role. But others are, so to speak, specialised in welcoming *associations*: 36 act as headquarters of 66 associations, among which leisure ones are dominant. Associations are subdivided as follows: 25 sporting, 18 bowling,[30] 10 of war veterans, the remaining 13 being centred either on games (billiards, chess etc.) or on social relationships (regional groups, professional societies etc.). The figures show that some establishments are the headquarters of several associations. In such cases, the atmosphere is determined to a large extent by these associations. Propaganda is made for their activities by posting pictures, circulars and documents. Help is given with lotteries and socials. Such cafés are mostly adjuncts to the life of associations. Is it fair that they are placed in the same category and submitted to the same financial regulations as others? For instance there are 30 bowling associations at Annecy, of which 18 have their headquarters in the same café. Except for seven of them they use a green attached to this establishment.

Thus cafés play a part in the development of participation in social life. They provide a framework for free, spontaneous relationships which continue, diversify, enhance, supplement or compensate for the relations imposed by occupational, family or civic responsibilities. All cafés cannot be viewed as interchangeable with regard to the social relations taking place there. Those which play a positive role in the struggle against social isolation, often experienced by the "lonely crowd" in towns and cities, and which contribute to the development of social relations and groups to make urban life more humane, should receive special consideration.

What is the *content* of the social relationships facilitated by cafés? It will be analysed through the kinds of activities and conversations which take place in these establishments. The subject is an important one. These *exchanges* within and outside the family group are among the main elements of the culture experienced by the masses of town-dwellers (Katz and Lazarsfeld, 1955). The mass media, as we know, fail to convey their message, whether serious or futile, to the public at large; they compete with various leisure pursuits (games, conversations, etc.). On the other hand, the content of broadcasts, films, newspapers or television programmes is mainly taken in by group leaders of various social backgrounds. Such messages are circulated by them to their relatives, friends or neighbours. From this angle, the content of activities and talks held in cafés may have a great positive, or negative, impact on urban popular culture.

As would be expected, pastimes in cafés are summed up or implied in their functions as leisure centres. Among the reasons for social relations or activities which prompt people to go out, many connect up with the general functions of leisure, already mentioned. It is striking that out of 148 explicit motives for going to a café, only 32 relate to the physiological needs for which it specifically caters (eating and drinking), while 116 conjure up the general functions of leisure: rest (24), entertainment (77) or disinterested information (15).

Among the favourite pastimes of customers, watching the street plays a great part. The preference for this sight is confirmed by the overwhelming majority who favour the cafés with pavement service ("terrasse") (85.5% as against 14.5%). Card games have survived; they have outlasted successive fashions for new games and remain the favourite game of one head of household in two.

Yet it would be wrong to assume that card games are associated with cafés. Games, including cards, take up an important part of modern leisure time. Only 1/5 (21%) of players choose cafés and this choice is highly differentiated according to socio-occupational categories: among card-players in cafés there are 49% of factory workers, 33% of craftsmen, 7% of medium level managers, and very few upper managers and teachers. People aged over fifty and the young play cards more often in cafés than other age groups.

New games have replaced skittles and have developed both in cafés and outside. They are mainly bowling games ("boules" and "pétanque") which are the favourites of 1/5 among Annecy heads of households. Over 2,500 players, participating in more or less sporting competitions, belong to 28 associations, whose headquarters — as has already been said — are held in 38 of the town's cafés (i.e. in 16%).

According to "old timers", the success of bowling games has significantly contributed to improving the atmosphere in cafés. According to the publicans, customers sit around less than they used to. They spend more time out of doors. They drink less alcohol. "I have stopped bowls and cards," said a publican more interested in profits than in the social function of his establishment, "people stayed for hours and drank nothing." There is more discipline. The game introduces a set of rules which provide standards for individuals and the concern for skill is an incentive to temperance. Not all players abstain from drink... far from it, especially when a victory is celebrated! However, according to elders, the general tone of many cafés has improved, largely under the influence of bowling games.

The young seem least attracted to open-air games. Among bowls players, only 21% are under 30, 30% are between 40 and 50, and 26% are over 50. The difference between these percentages is not very significant. All social categories play: factory workers more (29%) than employees and medium level managers (22.5%).

Somĕ cafés have a juke-box, a radio and/or television set. I have tried to ascertain individual preferences in this respect. In fact opinions are divided. The bigger variations are related to social category rather than to age, as might have been expected.

For juke-boxes, rejections range between 47 and 63%. The difference between the under-thirties (47%) and the over-fifties (62%) is significant, but less important than expected. Choices range from 53 to 38% depending on age. It is worth mentioning that among the young there are as many supporters of the juke-box as there are adversaries. These machines are concentrated in eight cafés whose public is mainly recruited among the very young. Differences between socio-occupational categories are bigger: rejections range from 41% among skilled workers to over 70% among artisans, managers and the liberal professions.

In most cafés the wireless is at the disposal of the public or of the staff. Who listens in? Who tries not to hear? Again views are divided. There is a slight predominance of rejections. Negative opinions increase steadily with age: from 51% under 30, to 64% over 50, with 54% and 57% for the intermediary age groups. In cafés it is mainly music which is heard: do the older customers find it too loud?

The problem I am most interested in concerns the quality of the programmes (songs, concerts or reporting) chosen by or for the public and that of the advice or comments uttered by the regulars or the management. If those who run a café are passive or ignorant, they may encourage the worst habits among an unrefined public, but if they have some standards or some knowledge, they may influence the cultural level of their customers. Most publicans belong to the former type, but there are some innovators. For instance, a café near a youth centre, whose owner gets on very well with the youth leaders, has attracted a young public by the quality of the modern music he has introduced or developed in the town. It has become a focal point for genuine jazz music.

This analysis of the content of social relationships in cafés highlights the attractiveness of some activities and some topics for all age groups and occupational categories. This content is wide, it is varied, it reflects the various functions of leisure and the related interests in entertainment or information. From this angle, great differences exist between the social and cultural atmosphere of various cafés. The law and the inland revenue take no account of these differences. No policy has been applied to help the cafés which cooperate with associations in developing sport, out-of-door activities, musical tastes or citizenship among the urban masses. Selection and assessment criteria in a new legislation centred on the needs for social and cultural development could replace regulations wholly based on the alcoholic strength of the beverages sold.

III.4. Leisure and the Third Age

The analysis which I have just made of a kind of activity can be repeated in connection with a period. As has already been seen, retirement corresponds for the adult to one of the four periods, linked with the shortened duration of working life. This abridgement has often been sacrificed to favour the young who are receiving a longer education. The topic will be resumed later. Bertrand de Jouvenel points out that while the amount of spare time is growing, it is mainly for the young because they do not work yet and for the elderly because they work no longer. Though this statement is oversimplified, it expresses a thought I must agree with, once it has been qualified. The same author expresses some surprise that the two periods are not equally "visible": "it is a psychological fact worth mentioning that the first of these two masses attracts attention and that there are leisure policies for it, while such is not the case of the second; the contrast must be due to a difference in visibility" (de Jouvenel, 1972).

There are approximately seven million retired people in France. All demographic estimates announce a rapid increase of this category during the next twenty years. I shall endeavour to demonstrate that the active participation of the retired in various basic institutions (occupational, family, socio-cultural, socio-political) refers only to minorities. For the majority it is leisure which represents the most extensive and the most significant set of activities at that age, even when disease or poverty interfere.[31] It is through such activities and through the corresponding values that chances of self-fulfilment during the third age are greatest.

Yet studies of social gerontology have omitted these activities until now. It is one of the least well observed and interpreted sectors. Some analyses conceal leisure under "activities" in general or "family activities". Others hide it under the alleged pervading nostalgia for work among the retired, though no representative survey ever managed to prove its existence. Yet others split up the phenomenon of leisure into many atomistic activities (rest, vacations, walks, television, etc.), treated as residual in relation to "noble" pursuits such as work or family duties. When leisure activities are interpreted, they are often negatively associated with boredom, emptiness, and expectation of something to "compensate" for disengagement from the occupational and social duties of the "second-age" (the age of work). They are not interpreted in the light of the possible creation of new values specific to the third age and of the conditions required to sponsor them.

This undervaluation of leisure, which is not geared to the way of life experienced by the majority of the retired population, dominates the outlook of gerontologists and is accompanied by an *overassessment* of work and of family duties. Both these assessments express ideological interpretations handed down by a society which is now disappearing. A close cooperation between social gerontology and the sociology of leisure would result in a more scientific observation and interpretation of leisure in various milieux of the retired and would highlight its connections with work, family duties, and participation in socio-spiritual and sociopolitical activities, as they are experienced. This is the basic hypothesis I shall attempt to substantiate.

The retired at work

The age of retirement does not always entail giving up work altogether. However, the more advanced a society with regard to industrialization and urbanization, the fewer of those over 65 who go on working. In France, the highest rates of work among the over 65's are found among managers: 33% (Caisse Interprofessionelle de Prévoyance pour les Cadres, 1965).

The meaning of continued work after retirement is, according to survey data, not only financial, but ethical for the minorities involved. To go on working may be a deliberate choice, rather than the result of financial constraints, in the case of a small minority whose occupational life is dominated by a high level of responsibility or of creativity. Apart from this minority limited to between 10 and 20% of all workers, a number of occasional or part-time occupations of various kinds are developing, which may be interpreted either as semi-leisure (the main objective being other than financial) or as semi-work (the main objective being financial). Still it is important to stress that, to our knowledge, all empirical research shows (Shanas et al, 1968) retirement to be desired by a vast majority. Contrary to widespread ideas, it is not forced upon most people and merely tolerated by them. In the

U.S. two-thirds of those who retire do so through choice. The desire to return to work after retiring is experienced only by a minority: in France, the highest rate of return to work is found among managerial workers. Moreover strong pressure is being brought to bear by wage-earners for a reduction of the age of retirement from 65 to 60: this item heads the list of current union claims. A major aspect of the dynamics of retirement consists in the will of most workers to enjoy it.

Retirement and leisure

How do elderly people employ the time freed from work? Some data on time budgets in the United States are available.

The amount of time devoted to leisure activities increases: 80% of those aged 65 and over have at least 5 hours of leisure per day and 5 to 6 hours during weekends and vacations. Among American time budget surveys, I shall examine one based on a sample of 5,000 Social Security beneficiaries aged 65 and over, from which people in gainful employment were excluded (Dumazedier et al, 1950). As against 6.7 hours of time taken up by domestic and family duties (meals, housework, personal care, shopping, caring for others), there are 8.3 hours of free time a day, out of which only 0.2 hours on average was taken up by non-leisure (religious and socio-political activities in a wide sense).

No time budget studies are available in France. However, the survey conducted by the French Institute of Public Opinions (I.F.O.P.) gives some information on the schedules of the retired, without providing any indication about the average duration of various pastimes. During weekdays, apart from household and family duties, leisure activities take up almost all their time; religious activities are almost non-existent among men, a little more common among women. As for "various meetings" which might cover socio-political activities, they are not mentioned by women and concern only 4% of men.

The limited scope of this survey results in general comments only, but suffices to show that only an infinitesimal part of spare time is devoted to pursuits *other* than leisure. Time budget surveys in general have demonstrated that leisure takes up most of the spare time enjoyed by the elderly and even *more time* than the unavoidable activities of personal and family care. It has been shown that work goes on only for a minority of the old; other ways of filling spare time must now be examined.

Socio-spiritual obligations and leisure

What happens to socio-spiritual commitment after the age of 65? Is there an intensification of spiritual activities, and particularly is greater importance attached to religious practices, towards the end of life? In France, the survey conducted by the National Institute for Demographic Studies (I.N.E.D.) (Paillat, Wibaux, 1969) points to the small importance of religious activities among those of elderly persons. In reply to the question: "Among the following activities, is there one to which you devote an important part of your time?", it is seldom mentioned by men (2 to 5%), a little more frequently by women (10%). This difference between the sexes is also found in a survey of Building and Public Workers: the rate of total withdrawal from religious practice is 18% among women, but 31.5% among men (Pergeaud, 1968).

More advanced research in the United States shows that retirement does not basically influence the rate of participation in socio-spiritual activities: the majority trend is towards continuity. While, by comparing the various generations of adults, no notable differences in roles of attendance at religious services are detected, surveys (Shanas et al., 1963) among people aged 60 and over show a trend towards a reduction in religious practice in relation to the individual's past. This regression is probably the effect of the general lessening of religious influence in advanced industrial societies.

In fact, there are two patterns: a sizeable minority of the old practice less, whereas a smaller minority practice more (McKain, 1947). It is among the latter that religious organizations or organizations connected with the church achieve the highest rate of participation. The intensity of this participation ranks just after fraternities, secret societies and mutual help societies (Riley, Foner, 1968). Lower rates of church attendance after a certain age may be imputed to ill health. A study of old people in good health shows greater attendance by the over-75's than in the 65 to 75 age group. (Riley and Foner, 1968). Moreover, listening to religious broadcasts, which requires no outing, hence no effort, increases with age.

Socio-political obligations and leisure
Do socio-political activities change with age?

1) Participation in associations. Participation in political associations, trade-unions, friendly societies, charitable organizations, etc., may be considered as indicative in this respect. Membership remains high. In France, 38% of men and 18% of women aged 65 and over belong to associations (Paillat and Wibaux, 1969). However, membership does not necessarily imply any activity: some members never attend meetings (a little less than half of women and about a third of men). Among Building and Public Works workers, results are slightly different (Pergeaud, 1968): 9% of women and 26% of men belong to an association, but active participation is greater among women (41% as against 32% among men). Participation in voluntary associations is in general mainly linked with socio-economic status.

After 55, the rate of participation decreases, education and income being held constant (Foskett, 1955). The average rate observed in the United States is 51% for men and 61% for women (taking account of trade-unions and of the wide range of different organizations and societies). Groups reserved for the elderly (Golden Age Club and Senior Citizen Centre) have a low participation rate: 1% of the elderly in New York, 5% in Syracuse, N.Y. High rates are definitely local phenomena. This is also the case in Britain, where one working class district in London boasts a 12% rate (Riley and Foner, 1968). Such groups are mostly centred on leisure rather than on citizenship or religion. The associations which attract most of the elderly are mainly concerned with sponsoring social relations rather than social action (Youmans, 1961). In a survey in the United States, half the respondents referred to a decrease in their social activities, generally after the age of 50, whereas only 3% noted an increase (Taietz et al, 1956).

However, political participation proper can and should be studied by using other indicators: the vote and identification with a political party. How does this form of participation change with age?

2) Participation in elections. Its highest rate is reached between approximately 45 and 60; it then goes down, with a big drop after 70, especially among the less educated. The same applies to women, whose rate of voting is lower than men's, except among the highly educated for whom it is almost the same. As concerns identification with a party, results are different: it increases with age among all those who are interested in politics, in the case of conservative parties, e.g. Republicans in the U.S., Conservatives in the U.K.

Overall, political interests do *not* seem to decline with age, but political activities proper reach a peak between 45 and 65, and then decrease. It is worth noting that in political life, the threshold of decline occurs at a later age than for all other basic social obligations, at least among those who have an interest in politics. One cannot in this respect talk about a disengagement of the old. This observation coincides with the conclusion, reached by Leo Simmons about the status of the elderly in pre-industrial societies, where the quest for *influence* is a constant, as well as the pursuit of security (Riley and Foner, 1968).

The analysis of this data, mainly from France and the United States, shows that active minorities, committed to work, to socio-religious and to socio-political life, exist among the elderly, but that for a *majority* these activities decline or become of little importance. The general trend is towards a form of continuity in relation to the former type of participation, except of course as regards work.

Family obligations and leisure

Time-budgets show that the family retains a great importance. However, the confusion which surrounds what is known as family life, makes it difficult to interpret these results. The various components of family life should be more thoroughly analysed to clarify their meaning both for the individual and for contemporary society. I must begin by repudiating a syncretic approach whose totalitarianism is more akin to ideological interpretation than to reality. Family activities ought to be sub-divided into obligations and leisure (Dumazedier, 1972, Chapter Two), and an intermediary category of semi-obligations or semi-leisure.

Relations between parents and children are not always characterized by mutual duties. In the United States, about half of the elderly state that they give no assistance to their relations (White House Conference on Aging, 1931). In France a recent survey has shown that 82% of grandparents report giving no active help to their children in housework or with family commitments (Pastaud and Laballe, 1969).

Both parents and children increasingly prefer to be further apart, as society evolves towards the post-industrial stage. This trend is linked with the financial independence of the elderly from their family: in the United States only 1% of the resources possessed by the over-65's come from aid given by relatives.

Contacts between the elderly and their children are frequent. They are a basic aspect of intergenerational relations in advanced industrial societies, but they pertain to leisure spent within the family rather than to family obligations. The thesis whereby the family is reduced to the nuclear unit in advanced industrial societies does not fit in with the facts shown by many surveys. Cain sums up the main results achieved in this field (White House Conference on Aging, 1971): there are two major categories of *family structure:*

(a) the family as a residential unit; couples and people living alone are most frequent; couples with children range from 7 to 14% depending on the country (U.K. – U.S.A. – Denmark) and adults alone with children from 9 to 20% (Shanas et al, 1963).

(b) the extended family, which is that of the majority and which covers three or four generations (Denmark 75%, Britain 68%, U.S. 76%) (Shanas et al, 1963).

Contrary to ready-made ideas, the children's departure from home is not a traumatic shock. It is often experienced as a liberation from domestic and financial commitments, as a new opportunity to rest, to travel and to be oneself for the first time after they have gone (Riley and Foner, 1968). Children can play a negative part in relation to their retired parents self-expression. Thus Cain reports that a survey of one hundred marriages during retirement showed the children's negative attitude to be a serious obstacle to their parent's remarriage, since their expectations may be perceived as a normative constraint. All these indices reveal that for a growing number of retired people complete compliance with family obligations is no longer a strict imperative. They gladly provide a service, but neither a permanent nor an unconditional one. They increasingly aspire to a personal life related to their own personality needs. *Family obligations* tend to *decline.* Family relationships are increasingly characterized by distance, as well as intimacy and by mutual independence. Again there are two patterns: for a minority, family obligations are likely to be the main ones, but for the majority their strength is dwindling.

Types of leisure activity

The most common pattern points to continuity between the kind of leisure activities undertaken as an adult and in old age. The socio-occupational category is often a better discriminator than age. In a survey conducted by the Danish Gallup Institute in Denmark in 1951, the elderly respondents stated that they had engaged for years in most of the leisure activities characteristic of their old age (reported by Havighurst, 1960). However, the survey conducted in Minnesota by Taves and Hansen in 1961, showed than nine-tenths of the respondents aged 62 and over mention an activity to which they devote more time than before. In addition, there are some significant changes in the way of life: a development of activities centering on the home and a regression of those practised outside. (Bulletin Statistique du Commissariat Général au Tourisme, 1970). The spatial tightening of social life is thus reflected in leisure. With aging, time devoted to relaxation also increases.

Besides the most common pattern, characterized by continuity of kinds of leisure before and after retirement, there are discontinuous behaviour patterns originating mainly from the leisure structures devised for the elderly; outside intervention thus stimulates the learning of new activities (development of vacations[32] (Donfut, 1972), attendance of clubs).

To enlist the leisure activities of the elderly is to discover that they overlap with the cultural classification of leisure into five big categories based on the criterion of the needs for physical and mental fulfilment experienced by individuals.[33]

a) Physical Leisure. Predictably the practice of sport is less frequent among the elderly. According to a survey conducted by SOFRES (Piatier, 1963), it is almost exclusively limited to men, mainly active ones belonging to medium or high managerial levels. Among the 2% of people aged 65 to 75 who have during the last ten years practised one or several sports, the most common is fishing, with bowling coming far behind. According to the INSEE survey of 1967 on leisure in France, 0.9% of those over 65 regularly practise a sport all year, 1.4% do so periodically and 22.8% have done so in the past, but have given up.

Thus two related phenomena are reported: one relates to age, the other is generational. The latter seems more important: 75% of people aged over 65 have never practised any sport in their life. In the United States a marked decline in the rate of sporting activity with age has also been noted.

However, walks and rambles are common among the elderly (18%). They are mentioned among the two main activities in the SOFRES survey. Their rate declines slightly with age (from 19 to 15%): it is roughly the same for both sexes. In the United States, walking seems less common, but drives in cars are more frequent, though less than among the young.

Besides walking, a growing amount of time is given to relaxation. In the SOFRES survey, rest and relaxation are considered as one of the two main leisure pursuits (by 16% of respondents). The rate increases with age to 18% for the 70 to 75 age groups. In the United States surveys show a marked increase of napping and idleness or sitting and thinking, with, on the other hand, age and, on the other, the dwindling of income: 56% of the elderly spend on average two hours a day relaxing. The "average time-budget" based on all social security beneficiaries includes 1.4 hours of napping: in this case, research is needed to demarcate leisure from biological requirements (Riley and Foner, 1968).

Among leisure pursuits requiring physical efforts, travel and vacations play an important part. In France the rate of holiday travel for vacation for the elderly may be lower than the average rate for the whole population, (Le Roux, 1968), but the deviation may be largely imputed to lower incomes or poor health. If income levels are equalised, differences in departure rate between age groups fade and are only characteristic of very old age, when health is a more significant variable (Paillat and Wibaux, 1969).

Vacations are keenly desired by the elderly (Le Roux, 1970): the INED survey shows that *half* of elderly town-dwellers would like to travel and organized trips are mentioned in the greatest number of replies as initiatives which they would like to see developed. The same trend prevails in the United States (INSEE 1967 survey).

b) Artistic Leisure. Vacations and travel may be viewed as kinds of shows: landscapes of various regions, museums, monuments. This is often how holiday-makers perceive them, especially the elderly, for whom shows generally play a growing part in leisure-time. This is confirmed by the rate of TV viewing, which, together with the wireless, takes up on average 2.8 hours of the day in the life of retired Americans (Riley and Foner, 1968). In France, there is a reduction of viewing rates with age, due to the inadequate supply of sets to the elderly. 83% of the French watch television (of whom 51% do so every day and 17% every week), but only 64% of the over-65's (of whom 43% view every day and 9% every week (Le Roux, 1970).)

The low rate of attendance at shows outside the house is mainly socio-cultural in origin, but is also due to age: 5% of the 65-plus age group have never been to the cinema, 41% to the theatre, 43% to any variety show, 66% to a concert, and 63% to a sporting event. Of those who have been at least once, 77.5% never or hardly ever visit a cinema, 51% a theatre, 52% a variety show, 30% a concert and 31% sporting events (Le Roux, 1970).

Thus it can be argued that the elderly are less used to shows than the young and also that this pastime decreases with age (Le Roux, 1970). According to the INED survey, other artistic activities are only practiced by 5% of men and 3.8% of women.

c) Practical leisure. I have already mentioned in connection with shows how important it is for daily leisure activities to be practiced at home. It is therefore hardly surprising that manual tasks (pottering, gardening, needlework) which are generally performed in the home should be very common as leisure pursuits among the elderly. The rate of gardening steadily rises with age; a survey conducted in the United States has shown this evolution over the generations: 24% of individuals do some gardening between 20 and 29, 33% between 30 and 39, 38% between 40 and 59 and 42% from 60 onwards (Opinion Research Corporation, 1957).

In France, among town-dwellers (whose opportunities for gardening are limited) *one-third* of men and 1/10 of women engage in gardening. This activity declines only after the age of 80 for men and 75 for women (Paillat and Wibaux, 1969).

Manual activities are most often quoted by the elderly in France as being among their main activities (by 46% of the 55 to 75 age group and this rate increases with age until 70, to decline thereafter) (Bulletin Statistique du Commissariat Général au Tourisme, 1970). They are more widespread among country dwellers and in the lower income brackets. These activities are either utilitarian and linked with family duties and semi-duties, or entertaining and subsumed under leisure or semi-leisure. In all likelihood the latter characteristic is the dominant one, *above a certain level of poverty*, but surveys on this problem are lacking.

d) Intellectual leisure. Intellectual activities mainly consist in reading (Le Roux, 1970). The INSEE survey has shown that the elderly spend more time reading newspapers than the rest of the population: the average time spent reading papers is about half an hour a day for the population as a whole, as against three quarters of an hour for the 65 plus age group. It is mainly the reading of dailies rather than that of weeklies or monthlies which increases with age.

By contrast, listening to the wireless slightly decreases with age, though it remains an important pastime for the majority: 67% of the French listen in every day and this rate declines to 57% for the over 65's. Conversely the 11% who never listen in become 22% in the over 65 age group.

In the United States, time devoted to reading (of all kinds) varies from 0.8 hour between 20 and 49 to 1.3 hour at 50 plus, among men; for women, the corresponding times are 0.7 and 1.4 hour.[34]

Reading is therefore a leisure activity which develops with age. The attention paid to daily papers and to the radio is linked with the interest in current affairs displayed by the elderly and evidenced by their greater receptiveness to the mass media. The reading of books and magazines tends to decrease with age, between 15 and 59, but rises from 60 onwards.

e) Social leisure. Social leisure, in the guise of entertaining, paying and returning visits, plays an important part in the life of the elderly.

In the "time budget" of retired Americans, it takes up on average 1.6 hour a day. This form of leisure decreases between the ages of 20 and 60, but slightly rises thereafter. In the SOFRES survey (Bulletin Statistique du Commissariat Général au Tourisme, 1970), 10% of respondents aged from 55 to 75 mentioned gatherings with friends among their two main leisure activities. In France, 76% of elderly town-dwellers entertain at home and 44% pay visits, either on a regular or on an occasional basis (Paillat and Wibaux, 1969).

However, not all the old engage in social leisure. The results of surveys in France and in other countries on social relationships always point to a considerable minority of isolated individuals (20 to 30%). Special problems of social therapy are raised by this category of retired people, described by researchers as anomic, partially isolated or withdrawn. At this level, leisure activities and relationships may have an important socializing function to perform. It is within this perspective that medical centres for the elderly increasingly include leisure organizations.

In conclusion, a considerable healthy minority are oriented towards the continuation of full-time or part-time paid employment. Some American writers, such as Stephen Miller, Eric Pfeiffer and Glen Davis[35] have been able to conclude that the ethic of productive work needs to be reintroduced in the third age. Yet surveys of representative samples have shown that among the healthy retired, not only is employment limited to a minority, but the majority do not regret work and do not wish to resume it. Hence hasty generalizations ought to be distrusted. As has already been said, there is a danger of relying on the views of people who belong to the second age and of projecting their values into the third. Since 1961, a reaction has started against this unjustified projection of life styles pertaining to the working phase onto the third age. It has resulted in what is known as the disengagement theory. This is based on an undeniable observation: among the retired, a majority withdrew not only from work, but from other family and social obligations.

This theory derives from observing a functional ethic for the third age. People of that age "adapt to aging and prepare for death." In my view, this negative approach is insufficient and overlooks behaviour patterns and aspirations increasingly common in the 1960s, especially in the warm regions of the United States (Florida, California etc). The same features are beginning to appear in French society, as has been shown above. I refer to a growing lust for active leisure in the third age, an appetite for new experiences, a wish to satisfy curiosities which remained unsatiated during the period of work and responsibilities in middle age. Sometimes even poverty and ill health cannot frustrate these new aspirations of the "undignified elderly." Social gerontology and the sociology of leisure have recently begun to co-operate in order to initiate new studies and to prompt a change in established outlooks, as well as a reform of old-fashioned institutions for the elderly.

Notes to Chapter III

[25] With the aid of a Marxian expert, M. Rubel, I have found five definitions of leisure, but all of them are with reference to work.

[26] I approve of Bush's analysis in this respect. Is this to say that she is right in asserting that leisure cannot be dealt with by a special branch of sociology? A confusion between free time and leisure underpins this assertion, but weakens the conceptional analysis, in my view.

[27] I prefer this item to happiness, or pleasure or joy, as it is less emotionally loaded. However, these alternative words have occasionally been used, as clearly as possible.

[28] Cazeneuve's book is important for the cooperation of the sociology and the psychology of joy, though the concept of leisure is not used.

[29] The results quoted below are borrowed from a survey conducted in 1957 at Annecy and covering 244 cafes out of 650.

[30] The French game of bowls and its Southern variation (pétanque) are slightly different from the English game.

[31] There are no accurate statistics to show how incomes are shared among the elderly French population. According to data supplied by the fund for social assistance, out of about 7 million retired, 2,300,000 old workers receive assistance. Those who have unsolved or badly solved financial worries, whether they are granted assistance or not, may be assessed at 1/3. A national survey (by Paillat) has shown that 7% of the retired population are in bad health. Even for these categories, financial or health aid are no longer enough. Despite the primacy of material needs, their needs for entertainment, conversation, reading, walks, shows, travel, etc. become wider and more pressing. In homes, clubs and hostels, it is becoming increasingly clear that the majority of the retired population, whether fit or not, whether well-off or poor, are in a state of leisure; new activities are developing or should be developed for them, despite insufficient interest in, and biased views of, this problem.

[32] A national enquiry among those working in the building industry and public works in France revealed that 17% of retired people went on holiday for the first time ever after their retirement, which was mainly due to the campaign for holidays for the aged (CNRO, 1973).

[33] The objection often raised against this view is that my analysis does not apply to the poor and the sick.

[34] Unpublished data collected by J.A. Ward in "A Nationwide Study of Living Habits," New York, 1964, and quoted by S. de Grazia in R. W. Kleemeier, ed. *Aging and Leisure: A research perspective into the meaningful use of time.* New York, OUP, 1961, p. 125, note c.

[35] Report to the Round-Table on "Leisure and the Third Age", Tampa, November 1971 organized by the Gerontology Department of Rhode Island and the Leisure Institute of Florida University.

IV Work-Leisure-Time-Space

The relationship between leisure and work is the most emotionally loaded issue in the history of industrial sociology and of the sociology of leisure, from their very beginnings. From the outset of industrial society, socialist theoreticians have been divided on this point. For some, labour is the ultimate aim of human activity, for others, it is a "disastrous dogma", unless it is reduced to a mere instrument.

In the eyes of some, time is a "means of recovering the strength to work", while to others it is a framework for human fulfilment. Karl Marx founded on "work the prime need of man" a theory which has made countless disciples and still does. Yet the finest praise of "idleness mother of the arts and of noble virtues" was made by his son-in-law, Paul Lafargue, in *The Right to Idleness* (1883), (see above, p. 10). The two approaches still clash in socialist thought (Richta, 1969).[36] As I have already mentioned, at least five or six interpretations of leisure, or rather of time freed from work, may be found in Marx. Today, research into the specific characters of leisure or into its relative autonomy from determination by work and by related social relationships seems to some sociologists an infringement on a dogma or a taboo.

Other thinkers adopt the opposite attitude, as if leisure escaped economic determinism and evolved in an ideal era of freedom. This springs from a confusion between rules for action and explanatory theory, between the desirable and the real or the probable. Despite my doctrinal preferences based on Marxian ideals, I have endeavoured to empirically investigate: 1) The probable relationship between the various social components of work and those of leisure in the various social categories (classes, generations...) and 2) the evolution of this relationship in connection with change affecting work and non-work time within advanced industrial societies. I have stressed a reduction, at the end of the XIXth century, of the cultural gaps between socio-occupational categories, and also the persistance of social stratification in some leisure activities, mainly artistic and cultural (Dumazedier and Ripert, 1966). I have then dealt with the problem of relations between work and leisure.

IV.1. Relations between Work and Leisure

In a first stage, I have observed the distribution of interest *in work* in the active population of a town (37.7% of factory workers, 11.3% of employees, 21.8% of supervisory workers, 26% of heads of industrial, commercial and artistic firms). Despite appearances, this is a difficult question to ask. Indeed, to the question "do you find your work interesting?" sociologists everywhere get a majority of affirmative answers. My survey is no exception, 79% of respondents other than factory workers and 80% of factory workers find, to a varying extent, that their work is interesting and not boring. However, if work is linked with their other daily activities and if the respondent is asked to identify his *main* interest among them, replies change. In the town surveyed, 77% of workers are interested by an activity other than their job, only 23% of the active population see their work as their main interest. The percentage is higher (31%) among heads of firms, supervisory and clerical workers, as might have been expected. Moreover the aspects of work which stimulate interest should be analysed: some are specifically technical or organizational, others derive from human elements common to all group activities (relations with comrades or with leaders).

I have therefore found it necessary to analyse work by using objective (situational) and subjective (reactional) indicators, and to split up leisure into several kinds and levels of cultural interests in the spheres of artistic, intellectual and social activities. Having worked out the correlations between work variables and leisure variables, I have equalised age (−35, +35) and socio-occupational categories (factory workers, others) by using a kind of multivariate analysis which gave a better grasp of interactions and of their true complexity. It goes without saying that the correlation is not an explanation. It may be a co-variation, mainly due to variables I have not checked. Still this means facilitates the discovery of compatibility in situations or reactions which are generally perceived in terms of incompatibility or at least of antagonism. Apart from negating such stereotypes, this treatment also highlights inaccurate relationships of causality, shown up by negative correlations. The introduction of age groups and of socio-occupational categories as variables will bring out interactions which are closer to reality as a whole. As is well known to control the socio-occupational category is also to control income, social status and educational level, which in most cases operate to reinforce each other.

IV.1.1.

The dimensions and the indicators of work and leisure which were selected and the reasons for these choices will first be outlined.

A. Work

The concept of work covers a number of very diverse components and the individual may be more or less committed to one or another of them. Therefore this option cannot be considered globally. Possible links between each component and leisure behaviour patterns will have to be checked. This is why I have differentiated between components which are almost wholly independent from the individual's will and those which are dependent both on an imposed situation and on the individual's reactions to it. The former may be analysed by situational indicators, the latter by reactive ones.

A1. Duration of work: in order to ascertain whether the duration of work is an important factor in the choice of leisure activities and in their cultural levels, I have distinguished between respondents who work under 48 hours a week and those who work over 48 hours (1955—56), so as to distinguish work with long hours.

A.2. Type of tiredness: in order to ascertain the burden of tiredness on the choice and level of leisure activities, I have distinguished between: a) respondents who state they are *very tired* and others, and b) respondents who state that they experience *nervous stress* and others.

A.3. Type of work: in order to ascertain the effect of various types of work on the choice and level of leisure activities, I have singled out firstly the industrial and building workers, who belong to two major sectors of industrial society, and secondly those employed in the retail trade and the civil service, two rapidly growing sectors in the post-industrial stage, which France is approaching in some respects.

These different variables define a situation whose effects on factory workers and on the other occupational categories in my sample will be comparatively studied.

A.4. The reactional indicator is interest in work: To ascertain the incidence of this factor on the choice and the cultural level of leisure activities, I have first distinguished between those workers who are interested in their job and those who are not.

A.5. Satisfaction at work: among the former, I have then singled out those for whom work is the "maximum satisfaction," to the exclusion of any other activity. I have then sought to detect which aspect of work gave this maximum satisfaction to each of the respondents and to this end I have distinguished between:

A.6. Satisfaction with work well done due to the old concept of a "job well done" handed down by the craftsmen of traditional society.

A.7. Satisfaction with the organization of work: since this is a developing feature of the modern firm and since it has been posited that in the post-industrial phase of technical civilization organizational systems embracing workers and their leaders will increasingly grow (Touraine, 1969).

TABLE I

Breakdown of situations and attitudes towards work depending on membership or non-membership of the working class

I Situational Indicators	Total population N – 415	Factory workers N – 139	Others N – 276
1. DURATION OF WORK			
−48 hours	38%	46%	34%
+48 hours	45%	10.5%	5%
Others	17%	43.5%	21%
2. TYPE OF TIREDNESS			
Low nervous stress	25%	22%	29%
High nervous stress	7%	5%	8%
High nervous and physical stress	3%	3%	3%
3. TYPE OF WORK			
Building and industry	38%	74%	20.5%
Commerce	23%	7%	32%
Civil Service	14.5%	8%	17.5%
Others	23.5%	11%	30%
II Reactional Indicators			
Maximum satisfaction in			
4. INTEREST IN WORK	81%	80%	79%
Work well done	23%	31%	19%
Technique	34%	37%	33%
Organization	18%	11%	21.5%
Relations with comrades	34%	47%	27%
Relations with superiors	11%	37%	5%
5. Overriding concern for job	23%	7%	31%
6. Wish for occupational promotion	48%	44%	62%
7. Dreaming of another occupation	38%	28%	43%
8. Participation in union	32%	21%	36%

A.8. Satisfaction with relations with comrades: for some workers, work is predominantly a human environment, a network of social relationships, particularly with comrades, colleagues or mates.

A.9. Satisfaction with relations with superiors: I wanted to know whether this satisfaction matters or not, and how it varies with levels in the occupational hierarchy.

Finally, it seemed important to find out how interest in leisure varies depending on the worker's plans for occupational promotion, or his dreams of another occupation or his involvement in union activities.

A.10. Plans for occupational promotion either with a view to occupational mobility or to status betterment. Sociological work on social mobility has shown the importance of this attitude and its repercussions on the worker's life style.

A.11. Dreaming of another occupation: this attitude has seemed all the more interesting since in post-industrial society occupational turnover is likely to be more frequent than before (Husén, 1968). This variable may therefore have more impact on the dynamics of leisure, provided of course, that a connection may be demonstrated between them.

A.12. Participation in union: on the one hand, discontent with social and economic conditions at work may be expressed through participation in unions; on the other, with new forms of claim and control, unions retain much impact on economic and social dynamics.

I shall attempt to discover how behaviour patterns and attitudes relating to work and shown by these indicators are linked with leisure behaviour and attitudes.

B. Leisure

The concept of leisure also corresponds to various components which it is important to single out, since the individual may be tied to one only (or only to some of them). If a linkage exists between leisure activities and work, it may depend on the choice made between the various components of leisure.

The distinction previously drawn between physical, practical, intellectual, artistic and social leisure interests provides a basis for this analysis.

I have pointed out that the two first categories: physical interests (walks, sport) and practical ones (do-it-yourself, gardening, breeding a few animals) vary much less with social class and generation than the three last sets of interests; artistic, intellectual and social. It is especially interesting to see how the latter three sectors of leisure link up with various aspects of the working life.

I am thinking in terms of the post-industrial society, which will probably be characterized by a steady growth in the importance of innovatory knowledge, whether in the technical, the scientific, the aesthetic or the ethical field. (Bell, 1960, Richta, 1969, Touraine, 1969).

If it is wished to reduce cultural lags or inequalities between the leisure patterns of different social milieux, one ought to know whether a given life style corresponds to a high level of culture. Would a change in type of work be conducive or not to a rise of cultural interests? Hence a distinction between the various cultural levels of leisure must be drawn.

For all these reasons, I have selected indicators in the three sectors of leisure activities which most closely correspond to three types of knowledge (aesthetic, intellectual and social). Whenever possible, I have distinguished at least two levels, either on the basis of a quantitative (frequency of activity) or of a qualitative criterion (low or high cultural level at which an activity is practiced, by reference to explicit standards of invention, creation and participation) (Dumazedier and Ripert, 1966).

In each of these sectors, I have selected the following indicators:

In the artistic sector: indicators of artistic taste in daily life: visits to theatres, to concerts, to exhibitions, to the cinema, listening to a certain type of songs (so-called literary or highbrow songs).

In the intellectual sector: purchases and borrowing of books, desire to have a cultural holiday and choice of a theme for this holiday, reading of literary, religious and political journals, reading of scientists' or politicians' biographies.

In the social sector: taste for family gatherings and parties, and active interest in the various types of voluntary associations which can take up leisure time. Indeed, the political evolution of modern societies is characterized by an increased opening of the family group onto the environing milieu, and by the participation of its members in voluntary groups and associations, whose number and whose variety are growing, while their meaning is ambiguous for social evolution: do they complement, compensate for, or replace political bodies? (Riesman and Glazer, 1950).

Hence the following table of leisure indicators:

Artistic sector	*Intellectual sector*	*Social sector*
Visits to theatres	Purchase and borrowing of books	Participation in family gatherings
Visits to concerts		
Visits to exhibitions	Approval for idea of cultural holiday	Participation in life of associations
Visits to cinema	Choice of a type of theme for holiday	
Listening to a type of music	Reading journals (literary, political, religious)	
Listening to a type of songs		
	Reading scientists' and politicians' biographies.	

IV.1.2. Results

How can the behaviour patterns of factory workers and of other categories of the active population, as well as those of the young (under 35) and of the "elder" age groups be broken down by reference to the various components on which this analysis is based?

A first comment must be made: differences between factory workers and others with regard to various interests never exceed 20%. Many of these workers therefore have the same reactions as other social categories and a slightly smaller number exhibit different ones. In 1954 could there already have been two "working classes" distinguishable by their actual attitudes? Factory workers are characterized by a greater interest for technical matters (37 vs. 33%) and for work well done (31 vs. 19%), by less frequent dreaming of another occupation (28 vs. 43%) and by the satisfaction they experience at work through relations with comrades (47 vs. 27%). The latter point has already been noted: do factory workers have a stronger sense of comradeship? or should it only be construed as a sign that their social life is more limited to the work place?

The other social categories are distinguished in my sample by a greater interest in work organization (21.5 vs. 11%) and mainly by a higher rate of participation in unions (36 vs. 21%). Is this the rise of white-collar unionism among those who have both cultural and political aspirations?

Do linkages between leisure interests and duties at work appear to be different in the case of factory workers? For both categories (factory workers and others) I have made a qualitative analysis of linkages between work situations and attitudes, on the one hand, and different leisure interests on the other.

A. *Situational indicators*

A.1. *Duration of work*: This is linked with interest in leisure, which in turn, varies with age and socio-occupational category. Thus for participation in cultural holidays, the positive factors of short work times, of age and of socio-occupational category interact: young factory workers accept such holidays more willingly than older ones and other occupational categories than factory workers, especially over the age of 35.

A correlation has been noted between the duration of work and the reading of articles on literary life, artistic taste for reproductions, and level of union participation; subsequent analysis shows that these choices are in fact determined by membership of a socio-occupational category much more than by the duration of the working week.[37]

On the other hand, while a correlation had been noted between the short duration of work and visits to the cinema, it is in fact membership of an age group which is the main determinant of this choice.

However, among *categories other than factory workers after 35 years of age* the short duration of work is always linked with a *high cultural level* in leisure. This group has a cultural level which is not only higher than that of non-factory workers under 35 whose work times are long, but also than the remainder of the population, e.g. with respect to the reading of literary columns.

On the other hand, a correlation has been observed between long working hours and a high level cultural interest in concerts, among the young (factory workers and other categories). I had already mentioned that lack of time is often given as an excuse and is in fact an alibi for a lack of interest in culture.

A.2. Type of work: Cultural interests during leisure time do not appear to be dependent among manual workers on the type of work, i.e. according to the analytical categories of this survey, on their membership either of industry or of the building trade.

By contrast, membership of the civil service or employment in commerce affects workers of the corresponding category. Thus civil servants of 35 plus pay frequent visits to the cinema (interaction between type of work, socio-occupational category and age), shopkeepers of the same age pay less regular ones.

A.3. Type of tiredness: It does not differentially affect the members of various socio-occupational categories, but does affect the various age groups. For all workers aged over 35 (but not for younger ones), nervous stress is correlated with a high level of cultural activity.

B. Reactional indicators

According to my multivariate analysis, relations between these variables and leisure variables appear to result even more than relations between situational indicators and leisure variables, from the network of relationships between three types of variables: controls (age and socio-occupational category), independent variables (attitudes to work), and dependent ones (leisure activities).

In addition, my analysis shows in some cases which variable has the greatest impact in this interaction. The results are as follows:

B.1. Interest in work: Holding age and socio-occupational category constant, the initial negative correlation between interest in work and high cultural level in leisure time endures only among non-factory workers, although the distribution is roughly the same for both categories. When these workers find their work interesting, they exhibit a lower cultural level in some artistic spheres (e.g. exhibitions, artistic tastes).[38]

A similar kind of correlation is found among young factory workers: those who are interested in their work listen e.g. to fewer highbrow songs than their comrades.

The positive correlation detected between interest in work and family parties is confirmed by multivariate analysis for all age groups and occupational categories.

B.2. Satisfaction with work well done: The initial negative correlation between satisfaction with work well done and interest in various leisure activities depends on an interaction between controls (age, socio-occupational category) and an independent variable (satisfaction with work well done); it is stronger among non-factory workers under 35. Indeed, when they state work well done as a source of satisfaction, the latter are characterised by a low level of interest in sport, in buying books, in cultural holidays, in the choice of a possible theme for such holidays, and in reading articles.[39]

Among those aged over 35 (in both occupational categories) a connection which was not initially obvious appears between satisfaction *with work* well done and the reading of articles.

It is only in the case of the correlation between satisfaction with work well done and the buying of books that a determinant influence of the socio-occupational category may be discovered through multivariate analysis. The initial negative correlation between satisfaction with work well done and the fact of *not* buying books is cancelled out among non-factory workers of under 35, who experience this satisfaction and yet purchase books.

B.3. Satisfaction with the organization of work: Holding age and socio-occupational category constant, this satisfaction is positively correlated with the level of the following cultural interests: visits to highbrow exhibitions, purchasing of books and wishing for cultural holidays.

However, multivariate analysis shows that it is membership of an occupational category which is the main determinant variable of the choice of exhibitions visited and of the period in life during which cultural holidays would be wished to take place. It is also the main determinant of book buying: indeed, the correlation between satisfaction with work well done and book purchases is stronger among factory workers, but reduced in the other category.

On the other hand, multivariate analysis shows that age is the dominant variable of the wish for cultural holidays: indeed, the correlation between satisfaction with work organization and this wish is stronger among the over 35s and weaker in the younger age group.

Finally, multivariate analysis shows the connections between visits to theatres and concerts to be the product of an interaction between control variables (socio-occupational category and age group) and independent variables (satisfaction with organization). In these correlations, which are more pronounced in the 35 plus age group, it is membership of a socio-occupational category which is comparatively most important. It will surprise nobody that membership of the working class should be an obstacle to visiting the theatre.

B.4. Satisfaction with technique: This type of work satisfaction diversifies the behaviour patterns of non-factory workers[40] towards some sort of artistic and intellectual leisure visits to theatres, choice of cultural holidays and the reading of articles. In this occupational category, a connection between a high cultural level of artistic and intellectual leisure, and satisfaction with technique is observed. This correlation is stronger among the under 35s.

Once more, these correlations are due to interaction between controls (socio-occupational category and age group) and an independent variable (satisfaction with technique). The main variable determining interest in the reading of articles, the theatre, and classical music is again membership of a socio-occupational category: that of non-factory workers.

B.5. Dreaming of another occupation: Multivariate analysis shows that positive correlations between dreaming of another occupation and (respectively) visits to the theatre, to the cinema, listening to highbrow songs, buying books and the choice of exhibitions visited, result from an interaction between control variables (socio-occupational category and age group) and an independent variable (dreaming of another occupation). It is age (under 35) which seems the main variable determining visits to the cinema, but for the theatre, highbrow songs and kinds of exhibitions, it is membership of the non-factory workers category which is decisive.

B.6. Union participation: It is the socio-occupational category which has most impact, interacting with age and with union participation, to "account for" differential rates of interest in the theatre, in concerts, in visits to artistic exhibitions, and in reading about religious and political life.

Union participation only differentially affects leisure behaviour among those who are not factory workers: Unionists in their midst have a higher rate of participation and of activity in associations and visit concerts and theatres more often. Under the age of 35, they go to more artistic exhibitions and read more political and religious journals.

Union participation tends to diversify the behaviour patterns of factory workers in the following respects: the under 35s visit more exhibitions and the over 35s read more biographies of scientists.

What conclusions may be drawn from this analysis of the relationships between work and leisure?

Firstly, for the indicators selected, the relationship between interests connected with work and with leisure seems to be differentiated *according to socio-occupational categories* derived from the division of labour rather than to age groups. I have already noted that the dominant leisure pattern is that of the under 35s (Dumazedier and Ripert, 1966), but the differentiation into kinds and cultural levels of leisure is much more dependent on membership of a socio-occupational category than of an age group.

This differentiation is *quantitative*: Such a relationship is nearly *five* times less frequent among factory workers than among others. Only four correlations concern the former, whereas thirty-five involve the latter only.

The impact of situational indicators is less strong on factory workers than on others. There are more correlations between the duration of work and the choice of leisure interests among the latter (8 as against 4 for factory workers) and it is only in their case that the type of work is correlated with some leisure behaviour patterns.

The impact of reactive indicators is concurrent: it is very strong on this category, whereas among factory workers it is almost possible to speak of a dissociation between these indicators (attitude to work) and leisure behaviour patterns. If one takes two indicators particularly significant of commitment to the sphere of work (high degree of work satisfaction and union participation), there are 6 correlations with leisure behaviour patterns among factory workers as against 15 in the other category for the first indicator, and for the second, respectively 4 and 11.

What conclusion may be drawn? I have started from the well-known tenet whereby work determines leisure. I have asked myself *to what extent* this coincides with the facts in today's advanced industrial societies. Taking French society as an example, I have questioned the population of an economically advanced town at the beginning of a period of prosperity for the country as a whole. I have split leisure and work into various dimensions and introduced age and socio-occupational differences. The conclusions yielded by my multivariate analysis are complex.

It would be interesting to interpret these results and thus to explore from an unusual angle (that of leisure) the new structure of working class culture in relation to the culture of other social categories. This analysis would go beyond the framework of the present chapter and I have undertaken it elsewhere. In order to answer the initial question, I can conclude in three points:

It is clear that the breakdown into classes and socio-occupational categories based on work affects leisure as all other spheres of activity. I have observed that, with the indicators selected, differences in leisure behaviour are mainly due to socio-occupational differences. The differences reported are statistically significant at 0.10. Undeniably, despite all statements on the standardization and the growing homogeneity of modern culture (school, mass media...), the cultural isolation of the working class remains a fact not only in relation to education, but also to leisure.

However, this insulation is not absolute and does not contrast with general participation in culture by all other classes. In fact, such a participation is a myth (Havighurst, 1959). The cultural insulation of the working class is relative and is merely expressed by a variation in percentages of cultural participation. I have never come across drastic differences of the kind in which 80 to 100% on one side is matched by 0 to 20% on the other. The division of labour is not reflected by leisure differentials as sharp as the contrast between the job of a semi-skilled worker and that of a manager. Any attempt to dichotomise the cultural content of leisure strikes me as an over-simplification and a deformation of reality.

Moreover, despite real differences between the dominant cultural contents of factory workers' leisure and the other workers' leisure, I have not found a single instance in which the correlations were reversed. The same relationship between work variables and leisure variables obtained in both categories. These significant correlations varied in number from 0 to 3 for each type of leisure among factory workers and from 0 to 6 for other workers. Social differences were never expressed by contradictory trends and correlations specific to factory workers alone were almost nil. Obviously, the selection of other leisure pursuits and of other indicators might have led to different results, but I doubt whether there are many leisure activities which are in so sharp a contrast that nearly all factory workers practise one and nearly all non-factory workers practise another. This would probably be untrue even of golf and whist. Other variables, such as age, positively or negatively interact with the determining influence of socio-occupational ranking.

The influence of work as a technical and organizational system and as a network of relationships is a common topic of debate. It can be inferred from the significant differences I have observed in the correlations between various aspects of work and some forms of leisure (age and socio-occupational categories being held constant). Yet these various aspects of work do not always act concurrently. Their influence varies and most often appears to be non-existent. Out of some two hundred theoretically possible correlations, twenty are significant (χ^2 at 0.10).

There has been little empirical research on the relationships between work and leisure. Nevertheless, I am not aware that any multivariate analysis at least in part comparable with mine, contradicts its results (Parker, 1971, Wilensky, 1961, Morse).

IV.2. Relationships between Work and Leisure

How is this question approached today? From Elton Mayo to Georges Friedmann, the interest of industrial sociologists in leisure arose from a concern for the improvement of working conditions and for the elimination or offsetting of imperfections in the work situation. In the years 1950 to 1960, Friedmann emphasised the importance of a distinction between the entertainment function implicit in doing an interesting job and the compensatory function which is (or ought to be) attached to a job carrying no important responsibility, involving no real creativeness and hence incapable of fulfilling the individual (Friedmann, 1946, 1950, 1956). Nearly at the same time, in the sixties, leisure activities were considered by many writers as a future alternative to work (Wilensky, 1961, de Grazia, 1962). This trend is still represented by some sociologists of industrial societies, either capitalist or socialist (Filipcova, 1963, Grushin, 1969). It is changing, however, as a result of more refined analyses conducted into the complex relations of work and leisure. It has adopted the form of an opposition between what Parker calls "segmentalists" and "holists" (Parker, 1971). The former emphasise the relative independence of leisure in relation to work (Bell, 1960) and the latter its relative dependence. Following

Wilensky, Parker outlines the possible political repercussions of each theory (Wilensky, 1960). The one might lead to the development of creative leisure patterns to compensate for degrading labour, among those who feel most alienated in their work situation. The other might stimulate a revision of work situations, progress in the technical and social meaningfulness of jobs and consequently, the promotion of higher quality leisure (Parker, 1971). Is such polarization of thought into two theories equally unable to account for the dialectical complexity of life, conducive to research progress? There seems to be a sufficient number of available surveys whose results converge despite referring to different societies, to avoid a limitation of the debate to dichotomous over-simplifying theories (Dumazedier, 1972).

A radical change not only in work and leisure situations, but in outlooks and values may be detected towards the mid-sixties. The dispute between those who foresee a growing separation between leisure and work (nomadic weekends, holidays etc.) and those who conceive of them as increasingly intermingled with work (coffee break, table tennis matches between assembly lines etc.), seems already dated.

1. Although it is conditioned, leisure creates new values by dissociating itself more and more from the patterns of mere compensation for work.

2. These values tend to change or to infiltrate not only work, but also all the obligations which I have called institutional. In my view, this is the focus of the main problems which empirical sociology has not yet been able to tackle broadly and rigorously enough.

A growing distaste for some forms of secondary (industrial) or tertiary (administrative) work is observed, especially among the young. It is hard to assess how many after completing their studies, live in a state of unemployment or of semi-unemployment, semi-idleness, and reject a life style different from leisure. A recent survey of INED in 1972 has shown that this phenomenon, observed in the United States, is also reaching France: official statistics record some 400,000 young people out of work between the end of compulsory schooling and the age of 25, but this research points to over a million (INED, 1973). Those who cannot *and* do not want to accept work as it is, lead an unstable life, taking on small temporary jobs dependent on market fluctuations. Since 1968, more frequent strikes have taken place not only to secure rises in living standards or reductions in working hours, but for improvements in life at work. Simultaneously, surveys such as Michel's in the United States (Barrett, 1961) or Goldthorpe's in England (Goldthorpe et al, 1959) show a general decline in work centered values not only among factory workers, but among a growing number of supervisors and managers, who value spare time and self-fulfilment more than the previous generation, that of Burnham, did. Work values are increasingly instrumental; part-time work expends to benefit some of those who have ended their period of compulsory work (the retired) and those who wish to do housework in addition to a job. Flexible work schedules are being devised; a new formula limiting work to four 10-hour days is being tried out by 2,000 American firms (Barrett, 1961). At the same time, breaks for P.T., for indoor and outdoor games, and study groups bring leisure patterns to bear on work. From 45 or 50 onwards, some activities preparing for retirement are part of the working schedule (Barrett, 1961). An important OECD conference on the organization of work time has dealt with new relations, desirable for the economy, society and individuals, between work on the job, in the household, at school, and leisure at the end of the day, the week, the year and the working life. Henceforth the positive or negative influence of work on leisure is no more a source of problems than that of other factors which also condition leisure; family life, education, socio-spiritual and socio-political commitments.

Furthermore, as the impact of leisure patterns on modern work, family and town life styles is observed, these problems tend to be included in research projects on desirable or possible policies. This is a major aspect of recent social conflicts. As the economist Glukman said (at the OECD conference in September, 1972), we seem to be on the eve of undertaking a large scale social experiment with new ways of organizing work and leisure. The investigation of these prospects shows that there are still large gaps in the information required. Our studies clearly need to be carried further. It is obvious that economic research, even quantitatively increased and qualitatively improved, cannot replace sociological research: work on *liberating* time, after reaching a threshold in the development of the productive forces, can no longer be dissociated from the problems of its *utilisation,* both for economic and for socio-cultural reasons. To free time in order to have what as a result and mainly to be what? To free time in order to free whom and how? How can the sociology of leisure contribute the necessary data to improve not only the standard of living, but the life style of a society?

In connection with what general problems of liberating time and of utilising this free time can one conceptualize the relationship of work and leisure? These problems should be tackled from the angle of the probable evolution of whole societies, bearing in mind the differences due to the degree of pre-industrial, industrial or post-industrial development of the forces of production reached by each society.

IV.3. Can the Duration of Work be reduced?

IV.3.1. Increase in production and reduction in the duration of work?

Free time is primarily generated by the development of forces of production. For any society, the basic choice, whether conscious or not, is between increasing either production or free time. The most rational condition for generating free time is achieved when progress in outputs enables increased production to co-exist with reduced work times for producers. Still a society aware of its motivations might, in so far as the economy allows, refuse to free time from work in order to produce even more. Some will argue that this is an economic, not a sociological problem. This is not my view. It is the economy which delineates the productive potential, but the purposes to which additional production may be put have social and cultural implications; they pertain to a sociological study guided by the possible alternatives for short or long-term development.

Thus additional productive labour may be used to eradicate some inequalities in consumption between classes or social categories (policy of redistribution). It may be used to bridge the gap between existing collective facilities (roads, hospitals, schools, stadiums, swimming pools, libraries, theatres etc.) and expressed or forecast needs. Alternatively it may be invested to benefit countries whose productive force is under-developed. Giving up free time might then result in long or short term loans or in gifts of staple goods to societies unable to produce them. It is of course by a political decision that such a choice can be made, but it is the sociologists who, in co-operation with economists, must study the likely or certain implications of possible alternatives for society or for culture. It is mainly economists who have started such studies until now, partly because sociologists have not yet taken enough interest in them, despite the topicality of development problems in all societies.

The meaning of free time is not the same in a society whose prosperous economy is characterised by the full employment of the whole population and in one where the work-force is under-employed. In an advanced industrialised society, free time itself is a product. It corresponds to the working time the economy does not need or no longer needs to develop at the foreseen or pre-ordained pace. In societies whose economy is retarded, the problem is, by contrast, to turn into work time the idle time wasting an often considerable work-force. This conversion into work time is as necessary as capital or talent, to exploit the country's resources. It is not industrial labour which yields this idle time, it is the use of such time which is needed in order to generate industrial labour. Idle time is not free time, it is a type of unemployment or under-employment; it might be called *dead time* from the viewpoint of society, and compared with that which *work studies* endeavour to eradicate in order to make the modern plant more productive.

In pre-industrial societies, another specific problem is raised by the co-existence of two kinds of non-working time: traditional idle time and modern free time: The patterns which ensure individual fulfilment in the latter may be pernicious in the former, by hampering the social patterns required for the conversion of idle into productive time. The danger of alienation for the traditional, idle and poor population, confronted with the ideal type of leisure from rich and industrious societies is considerable. The individual may thus be trapped in an artificial world, damaging to the development of awareness and to the effort needed to transform his environment by adopting modern working methods.

The search for leisure activities adapted to the transformation of the traditional attitude towards idle time into a modern attitude of national organization towards time, productive activity and corresponding social relationships, is essential. The development of sport is particularly meaningful in this context. Experience has shown that it fosters a rational attitude towards training, teamwork, etc., which can facilitate the assimilation of modern methods in work.

Hence the practice of sport in free or idle time may fairly be construed not only as a consumption of leisure, but as a cultural investment, useful to change traditional outlooks into the modern ones required for development.

IV.3.2. Increase in consuming power or decrease in the duration of work?

It is equally useful to consider free time from the vantage point of consumption as of production. Indeed, while industrial civilisation increases the need for leisure, it also increases the need for consumption. The pressure of mass consumption patterns in post-industrial societies, centring on goods for comfort and leisure, often creates such needs that the more one earns, the more one needs to earn. Thus in 1963, 85% of factory workers in French-speaking Canada bought on the instalment plan, as against 10% ten years before (Fortin et al, 1964). A survey in a town near Montreal has shown that the leisure civilisation is very far from a general philosophy of maximum profits (Laplante, 1969). Some leisure needs in turn prompt the need for expensive items: TV sets, sailing boats or motor-cars for holidays or weekends. The desire to purchase these goods is an incentive to work overtime, and thus limits spare time in both capitalist and socialist industrial societies. In Prague, registrations for the purchase of a car are made three years before delivery and its price may exceed an engineer's yearly salary: how can it be paid for unless by working as hard as possible? In 1963, the French Institute of Public Opinion (IFOP) asked a national sample the following question: "Would you prefer to have an increase of 6% of your income or a reduction of your working hours by 2¾ hours a week, i.e. 16 days a year, without any change in income?" 30% preferred to work less, 65%

to earn more (Dumazedier et al., 1966). The choice made is strictly dependent on the amount earned, and varies with it. Even in the United States, where mass consumption is more widespread than in any other society, the need for spare time long remained weaker than the need for money. It is only quite recently (1964) that a new trend seems to be emerging among the working class towards more spare time in accordance with union policy.[41] The results of the survey in the Renault factories, which I have already quoted, show a comparable trend among French factory workers since 1968.

It is easily understood that in societies whose economy lags behind, needs for food, clothing and accommodation are such that workers who have already internalised the values of modern civilisation will probably want to earn more rather than to gain spare time.

IV.3.3. Improvement in working conditions or reduction in the duration of work?

We know that the continuing scientific organization of labour has increasingly divided and rationalised the various tasks — slack periods have been cut out, rhythms speeded up, and assembly lines developed, despite job enlargement. This evolution has always met with the workers' spontaneous resistance. The prospects of automation seem no less antagonistic to the deeply felt needs of working men. In post-industrial societies where the highest outputs have already been reached, and even in industrial societies, the time freed by greater productivity might perhaps serve, in so far as the economy allows, to relax the pace of work, to introduce a greater alternation of work time and breaks, to expand the concept of work so as to cover not only productive tasks, but information, training and participation in management devised by the firm, the union or mixed management/labour committees. Such a trend would reflect Fourier's dream of more pleasant work schedules which would "gradually make (work) a need and a pleasure for all."

As has already been said, pre-industrial societies must first slowly insulate the rationality required for modern work into their population. Another hypothesis is that the new masses of African or Asian workers will approach the rational working processes devised in Europe with a fresh outlook. Will they be better able to solve the problems of reconciling man's traditional approach to time with the modern needs of industrial plants?

It is the daring plan of some and the dream of many. From their point of view, the main problem of free time is the organisation of work time in order to alter the very style of work. This is a very topical problem.

IV.3.4. If a decrease in the duration of work is possible: increase in free time for some social categories?

If consideration of the three issues outlined above leads to the conclusion that the duration of work may be decreased, will the workers' free time increase as a result? Outside, work-time activities which cannot be described as free time, and which in fact limit its scope, take place. For some, work-time is prolonged by other constraints connected with it or by *other forms of work.* Hours freed by high outputs might first benefit the poorest strata of the active population, who are compelled to work overtime (openly or in secret) to give their family a decent livelihood. It is a fact that the wealthiest post-industrial societies cannot extend prosperity to the whole population and that a sizeable percentage (20 to 25%) in the U.S. (Harrington, 1967) are still underprivileged.

The case of those compelled by the very structure of large cities to make long daily journeys to work should be given consideration. In Paris, the average return journey is about 1¼ hours, but for a minority it may exceed 3 hours a day (Villeneuve, 1970). According to international time-budget surveys, the duration of travel to work does not tend to decrease with advances in industrialization and urbanization;[42] it is at a comparable level everywhere, in Eastern Europe, in the West, and in the United States, regardless of the stage of economic development and of the social structure of investigated cities.

Could time freed from work first benefit the city population whose free time is curtailed by exceptionally long travel which might then be viewed as a kind of overtime? It is a hypothesis worth investigating.

Another category of extra-occupational constraints deserves

special attention due to the magnitude of the problems they generate in industrial societies. I refer to the double work performed by women, which has already been discussed (see page 00 and following).

In post-industrial societies (U.S., Canada) and in some industrial ones (France) where households are particularly well equipped with labour saving devices these constraints are less binding.

However, part-time work, especially for women, is rapidly increasing. This way of performing their double role is not without danger for women who may be given the duller jobs, be badly paid and exploited. In France one observes a spontaneous trend towards more part-time employment and shorter work-times in plants where female labour is dominant. More widely, throughout the world, occupations which entail longer weekly or yearly holidays are taken over by women, e.g. teaching. All this is evidence that the problem is being tackled, but in unplanned ways, without any conscious social policy of differentially allocating time freed from work. This problem is even more serious in countries where labour-saving devices are still scarce. In Europe, it is probably one of the reasons why women have even less free time in Eastern than in Western countries; the percentage of women working in industry is higher and the level of household equipment lower in the East, according to the international survey of time-budgets.

In pre-industrial societies, where the status of women remains still very close to the traditional rural pattern, the very concept of free time is often alien to them, except on feast days. Even in industrialised countries, it is only recently that society gave to housework the noble status of work. Consequently many countries have adopted a new legislation. Today, sociologically speaking, free time is a time freed not only from work on a job, as a main or as a secondary occupation (plus the travel entailed), but also from housework. At all stages of economic evolution and regardless of their social structure, industrial societies need to reassess the impact of women's double task on the free time of the active female population, and to adopt plans or policies in this respect, before they envisage equal increases of free time for workers of both sexes. Some equalities in relation to work perpetuate inequalities of free time. Modern societies have already introduced maternity leaves in order to offset the effects of natural inequality between the sexes. They might perhaps resort to shorter working hours in order to reduce the social inequality which results everywhere from the conjunction of paid work and housework. In order to show the scope of this problem, Daric in 1946 estimated the number of hours spent on household and family tasks at 45 billion versus 43 billion hours work in employment (Dumazedier, 1966). It is unsurprising that policies should be envisaged whereby time freed from work would as a priority be turned into free time for female workers, who do a double job outside and in the home, rather than equally distributed between all workers.

IV.3.5. If a decrease in the duration of work is possible: lengthening of compulsory schooling?

There is another important relationship worth examining: that between the workers' free time and their childrens' schooling. Although this connection is not obvious it is a direct one in the social dynamics of this age. It has some practical effects: the release of free time is, in fact, limited by the lengthening of school attendance. In the more advanced societies, which are already instituting mass secondary education, it is often forgotten that school attendance has been gained at the expense of the young people's work in employment. Many children give up studying because their families need their earnings. It is in the poor countries, where illiteracy still endures, that this general connection is more apparent. It is clear there that, from the earliest age, school attendance makes inroads in work time; one of the greatest obstacles to attendance, even when literacy is gaining ground, is the need for the child to earn a living. Thus the relationship is a general one: the increase in time devoted to schooling is always at the cost of reducing the labour force. Grown-ups must work more for the young to be able to study instead of working. As educational expansion at all levels, primary, secondary and higher, has been exceptionally fast throughout the world in 1955–56, the amount of time freed from work for the active population has certainly been limited in consequence. Orders of magnitude of the time devoted to learning are often impressive. Thus, in France, for about 14.5 million wage-earners in 1965, there were over 10 million youngsters in full-time education. This ratio is by no means exceptional, but illustrates the situation in industrial societies. Although the trend towards the extension of compulsory education and the resulting delay in taking on productive work is increasingly challenged in its basic tenets (Illich, 1971), it is still gaining momentum and affecting all societies. Nearly everywhere an "education explosion" and a simultaneous educational crisis are taking place.

The institution of universal primary education is aimed at by all societies whose economy is underdeveloped and efforts which are often exceptionally great, but which vary from country to country, are made to this end. In industrial societies, it is usually secondary educational expansion to the majority of the population which is occurring or is about to take place. In France, a majority of the age group remain at school till fifteen and in the Soviet Union, beyond sixteen. In post-industrial societies, almost everyone remains in a secondary establishment till seventeen or eighteen (U.S., Canada). Despite the educational crisis of the seventies, secondary and even higher education are still growing, except perhaps in the United States in the very recent past. During the OECD Conference of 1972 on the organization of work-time, it was viewed as necessary to continue compulsory schooling till eighteen, in order to fit the individual for active participation in increasingly complex economic, social and cultural patterns.

If this were to become a fact, workers would have to give up a very high number of free hours in order to make up for the growing lateness with which the young would undertake productive work. This is easy to reckon approximately and the approach is the same for each country. An extra year of education for the present generation of 800,000 French children would abolish two free hours a week which wage-earners could in theory be granted, if that generation went into active life. Of course, this "loss of earning" is theoretical, but it illustrates a very important connection.

Thus, in most societies, during the last twenty years, the economic possibility of freeing time from work has in fact benefited the education of the young rather than the leisure of adults. It might be more accurate to speak of an educational than of a leisure civilisation.

*IV.3.6. If a decrease in the duration of work is possible:
development of continuing education?*

A sociological study of free time should, however, challenge this evolution. Indeed, the problem arises whether these quasi-mechanical patterns of educational development are adapted or not to the needs for cultural development in today's and tomorrow's technical societies, at various stages of evolution and with various types of social organisation. What is the present correlation between the time devoted to the education of children and the amount of time spent on voluntary study by adults in their spare time, in the context of the needs and resources characterising industrial societies? What could an optimum correlation be in the future?

Firstly, if changes in ways of feeling, of thinking and of acting are often faster than generational change, will not society, by constantly lengthening the period of compulsory education, pay a high price in money and time for the inculcation to masses of youngsters of knowledge they will have to revise in under twenty years? In a fast-evolving society, would not education spread throughout life be more adequate, given a minimum level of basic instruction, than the extension of compulsory schooling to ever-longer periods? Some American sociologists have already asked this question, both for the reasons mentioned here and for many others connected with the dependence and irresponsibility in which many young adults without special aptitude for learning are artificially maintained by long schooling. The growing complexity of society requires a long apprenticeship for many, but the pace of change makes it even more imperative to alter the outdated patterns of learning (Dumazedier, 1969). Today, the "lessons" of experience alone do not suffice to supplement schooling. Continuous change compels society to devise a continuing education of a new kind for all the ages of life. This problem is indirectly linked with the use of the time or of some of the time freed from work. It must be tackled by the sociology of leisure, in collaboration with the sociology of education. Of course, it can be partly approached during work time. All modern firms need to inform, to train and to retrain their staff in order to keep up with frequent technical and social change. This post-educational work is an aspect of what I have described as a broad concept of modern work. In France, recent legislation (1966–67) on continuous training in the enterprise is indicative of this new outlook. There are many examples to borrow from other societies (Dumazedier, 1955). However, a large part of adult education, probably the main one, is certainly taking place in the workers' leisure time. This connection between leisure and adult education was the main theme of a European international conference held in Prague in 1965 under the auspices of UNESCO. In Europe, this voluntary education is particularly widespread among the Yugoslav and the Danish working class (Dumazedier, 1963), but it is expanding in all countries. In a post-industrial society like the United States, voluntary adult education has trebled between 1948 and 1964. A national survey in 1961 showed that about 25% of Americans were receiving systematic instruction, two-thirds of them with the wish to study subjects unrelated to their occupation, despite the constant and ever-present pressure of commercial entertainment, particularly on TV (Johnston and Rivera, 1965). *Two thirds of the voluntary education mentioned takes place in leisure time.*

In African, Asian or American pre-industrial societies, rapid development, in so far as the infrastructure permits it, can only result from an extensive educational campaign relying on voluntary study. Thus, when, in 1961 Cuba nearly eradicated illiteracy, which receded from 25% to some 1%, a policy of voluntary education was launched four years later, to include a number of adults equal to one-third of the compulsory primary schools' intake (primary attendance being 85%). Industrialising societies, instead of following the usually anachronistic educational system of more "advanced" countries, might be better inspired to set up from the start a continuing education network for children and for adults, with a mixture of compulsory, optional and free activities backed by the mass media and by voluntary associations. It can be assumed that such centres for cultural action would be better adapted to the apprenticeship of a new society and a new culture. Research on such solutions has started in Brazil and in Niger, and deserves to be expanded and deepened. Thus, in a "leisure civilization" the individual would have more opportunities for satisfying his lasting and spontaneous curiosity, indispensible for active participation in societies where there is a constant need to innovate. Special efforts to provide social and cultural facilities and leadership, especially for the least educated groups, which are also most hostile to full-time schooling for the group, would further our knowledge of the conditions needed to make attempts at educational democracy more effective.

It can be assumed that, since the mid-sixties, all societies have been evolving towards a second kind of vacation, study leaves, added to holidays proper. Part of the time which need not be devoted to work is thus invested. The Soviet Union was among the first countries to attempt this on a large scale. If continuing education is taken seriously, other societies may be expected to follow its example. Research on leisure voluntarily spent studying will be required as a result of such an expansion.

IV.3.7. If a decrease in the duration of work is possible: earlier age for retirement?

As has been shown, adults give up time which could be freed from work, for the sake of their children's education. Alternatively they can give up part of it for the older generation's sake. Indeed, there is a direct connection between increasing the workers' free time and changing the age of retirement. If this age is to be advanced, part of the labour force must be replaced as a result. It is difficult both to reduce the number of working hours and to institute earlier retirement.

In most European societies, the majority of workers retire at 60 or 65. However, new problems arise in industrial and post-industrial societies, as the physical and nervous strains caused by the tension of modern living increase, as life expectations improve and, consequently, as a longer "third age" must be contemplated and made more fruitful for the individual, as well as for society.

In this double context, the age of retirement should be made less rigid in two ways: some people should be allowed to work longer in specially devised jobs with a lesser output, while others ought to be enabled to stop working at an earlier age, without any decrease in pension rates.

Sociological observation shows that some individuals adapt with difficulty to not working any longer. A transition should therefore be made by gradually reducing from the age of 45 the time devoted to production. This form of gradual preparation has been tried out in Canada. For working life to end not with decline into old age, but with fulfilment throughout the third age, training must be provided for a new life dominated by leisure activities and values.

This training problem arises in industrial societies at all stages of their evolution, but it is most acute in the most advanced one: on the one hand, average life expectancy is longer, on the other, the stresses of urban living are greater. Hence there are more people to whom the problems of the third age apply and training them for this new way of life is more difficult. New claims have been made in this respect in the United States (Conference on the Third Age and Retirement, Washington, 1972, and International Courses in Social Gerontology, 1972).

In the more advanced economies, after life expectations have reached a certain level, training for the third age and the organization of appropriate activities for that age group may appear more imperative than increasing the working population's leisure time. Research on this topic is only starting.

IV.3.8. If a decrease in the duration of work is possible: increase of free time for the whole population?

After examining those various alternatives, there remains the hypothesis of free time being made available to the whole population. It has been shown (in Chapter Two) that time freed from work is not synonymous with leisure. It has been pointed out that socio-political activities seem to be receding, yet democratic societies, confronted with the growing pressure of consumption and leisure patterns, need a high level of voluntary citizen participation in all the forms of public life. Research and forecasting seem required to outline the conditions for promoting voluntary civic work on a lasting basis. Even those societies which attempt to limit the diffusion of information are penetrated by different patterns of consumption and leisure. According to recent surveys in political sociology, neither education, nor ideological pressures, nor the censorship of some leisure patterns, have been successful in maintaining a lasting equilibrium between the values of leisure and those of socio-political participation in mass culture. This is one of the two major problems of socio-cultural development in a society dominated by leisure values. It may be assumed that a long-term policy of priorities in allocating free time, linked with new forms of continuous education, would prove more effective. Voluntary leaders for all kinds of civic activity whether at the level of the State, of government, of Parliament, of the town council, of political parties or of civic groups, could thus be helped and encouraged in their promotion, their initial or in-service training and their work, by a policy of civic leaves whose duration and frequency would vary (from a day to one or several years). This category of active citizens would also get an additional amount of free time. In France a project along these lines is being studied by Parliament: special leave might be granted to town councillors, to receive information on and training in increasingly complex matters. Some societies, particularly socialist ones, are already applying such a policy of civic leaves on a large scale. All democratic societies will probably have to give consideration to this problem, unless they want to become democracies without supporters.

The basic issue is to what extent democratic societies want to balance leisure and socio-political participation, and what price they are prepared to pay for an equilibrium between these two sets of patterns. The policy of granting free time, which I have outlined, would be a kind of social investment required for the purpose of democratic development. A *voluntary social labour force* would be created and developed for social developments as a counterpart of the occupational labour force for economic development. It would provide a nucleus of democratic spirit, without which the future of citizen participation in the management of civic affairs might well become problematic.

In conclusion, the questions raised (in Chapter Three) about the likely future of leisure can be considered again. Under present conditions and without any drastic, innovatory policy, which formula of time allocation is most likely to prevail in the next ten or twenty years? As has been shown, there are factors which favour an increase in free time and factors unfavourable to it. On the one hand, growing outputs, pressures from the unions, the fear of unemployment, the need to sell, the decrease in institutional controls, the new aspirations of individuals ... tend to make shorter work time likely. On the other, production mechanisms, growing consumption needs, the rising costs of collective facilities, etc.... tend to slow down this reduction. Yet, although we are still far from the forecast made by Morris, who in 1955 envisaged a thirty hour week for the United States in 1976 (Morris, 1955), a general and moderate trend towards a decrease is probable in the future, and would be a continuation of the past. In which periods would it take place? According to public opinion surveys made after May–June 1968, it is not the shorter working day or working year which appear to be requested at the moment, but an extension of leisure at the weekend and through earlier retirement, although the desire for longer holidays is still overwhelmingly strong.[43]

In my view, problems of production and of leisure time in different societies are now inextricably connected with all these issues. It is no longer enough to consider the functions of leisure in relation to work alone.

Many other factors must be taken into account, including some spatial ones, such as the distance between house and work, town or country dwelling, housing standards, town and country planning, all of which have an impact on the leisure patterns of the various social categories.[44]

IV.4. Leisure and Space: The Need for a Policy of Cultural Development as Part of Town and Country Planning

In 1966, the United States has divided its territory into leisure areas (Outdoor Recreation Resources Reviews Commission, 1966). In France no overall study of this kind has been made: the dynamics of leisure areas in the country, in the mountains, on the seaside, in relation to the space devoted to production, transport, housing etc. should be investigated. The concept of "forsaken areas" is no longer operative. Ground forsaken by agriculture may serve as a leisure area, whose integration with surrounding rural territories creates new problems and often conflicts. (This was the central theme of the 1973 Congress of the National Federation of Agricultural Labourers.) The creation of regional and national parks is an important, but limited aspect of a wider problem, whose urgency is even greater in towns. The town, in the sense of a settlement with a regional calling has often been studied as an economic, an administrative or a military centre. Its role as a cultural centre, although it is well known, has not been investigated to the same extent. When it is analysed by economists, geographers and sociologists, it is from the angle of cultural creation (poets, writers, musicians). The town is seldom shown as a cultural centre covering, apart from these creative activities, all forms of relaxation, entertainment, disinterested information and voluntary participation in cultural life of all kinds and at all levels, for all social groups. Town planners are only beginning to realize this general leisure problem in today's civilization. In 1972 it was for the first time a major theme at the World Congress of the International Union of Architects.

Urban populations have now become aware of the role played by education in the cultural development of towns. The "educational explosion" of the last decade has already been mentioned. However formal education is only a part, and an increasingly challenged one, of urban cultural development. The cultural function of a town is also expressed by a wide range of (physical, practical, intellectual, artistic and social) leisure activities which are independent from schooling. This concept of cultural *function* has become so important that it contributes to the attractiveness of some provincial towns for the managerial workers invited to settle there (as is shown in the documentation provided by the French Town and Country Planning Agency, DATAR). If they want to become centres of development, they must and will increasingly have to turn themselves into centres for relaxing, entertaining, instructive leisure, to meet the needs of all socio-occupational categories and all age groups for outdoor recreation grounds, stadiums, cinemas, theatres, museums, concert halls, meeting rooms, cafés, societies etc.

These are some of the reasons which enable one to forecast that leisure will become increasingly important in modern urban and regional planning. Hence the problem of leisure must be included in a general policy of cultural development expanded beyond the sector of formal education. Thus schooling and cultural activities outside the school, each with its own characteristics, would be both more clearly distinguished and better coordinated. Physical training learnt at school could be continued for adults by a style of leisure which the town-planner would sponsor by designing streets free from traffic for walks, open spaces, a green belt, parks and gardens, playgrounds and sports grounds in the centre, the outskirts and the neighbourhood of the town. Similarly manual pastimes are so important for the leisure or the semi-leisure of all social categories that new problems arise. Organization, equipment and leadership are required to develop leisure time handicrafts. To provide a basis for a truly popular culture, semi-utilitarian and semi-disinterested handicrafts must be encouraged, stimulated and guided by specialised advisers and group-leaders, whose part cannot be performed by a salesgirl in a supermarket or a street corner shop, no matter how well-meaning she might be. Artistic and literary initiation patiently undertaken by masters, needs to be fostered by a whole network of film, theatrical, artistic and literary activities which cannot be sponsored only by papers and magazines. There ought to be an increase in the number of publications, institutions and groups which encourage an enlightened choice and which disseminate worthwhile and attractive works in all circles. What purpose would be served by teaching techniques, science and philosophy to millions of young people, regardless of difficulties, if no institution or association attempted to refresh their memory, to increase their initial knowledge, and to help them apply in everyday life these complex and abstract ideas? Why teach the history and the philosophy of democracy, if nothing or hardly anything, after school, counteracts the conformity, the apathy and the passivity of well-entertained, fairly uninformed and badly taught citizens?

Hence, to avoid incoherence or inefficiency, a policy of cultural development is needed, so as to achieve a balance between relaxation, entertainment and the continuing development of aptitudes and knowledge in the leisure of the urban masses, as well as between leisure values and work values or family, social, civic and political commitments. The town increasingly becomes a centre for the dissemination of culture in all its forms, physical, technical, intellectual, artistic, individual and social, not only through an improved telecommunications network, but through the availability of equipment for leisure organization and of a growing number of committed and skilled organizers for each type of leisure activity. The problem of free access to the highest level of physical and mental culture for the greatest number should be brought to the attention of the community. It should be debated by all interested agencies and optimum results should be sought by a *local or regional committee for cultural development*. The building of a few additional stadiums, the modernisation of some public libraries, the creation of a few centres of culture or of a second thousand Youth Centres, are not enough. All such provisions are, of course, useful, but what is now needed is global research, comparable to the work done on economic development, in order to devise the best solutions for the complete and coherent development of urban communities. Criteria for this development need to be defined and its public and private, commercial and voluntary agents to be classified. A bold policy is required to reform the legislation, the infrastructure and the men concerned. The quest for an equilibrium between physical and intellectual activities in mass culture may lead to far-reaching institutional reforms, or even challenge the structure of urban settlements. For this new type of development to prove productive, the facilities required for entertainment and culture will have to be improved and also perhaps more importantly the structure of urban socio-cultural leadership will have to be transformed (associations and group leaders). Unless this condition is met, the undeniable but limited growth in equipment for sport, tourism, artistic and intellectual activities might be unproductive or have a social output far too low in relation to mass requirements and to the potential of the present system, imperfect though it may be. The town-planner should attempt to provide for a solution to these problems by the ways in which he devises, equips and integrates an appropriate space: the *leisure space*.

The work I have conducted in cooperation with architects and town planners, particularly with J. Duminy, shows that leisure space must have functional unity. It is too often arbitrarily scattered: green belts, water space, playgrounds, noiseless zones, walking grounds, picturesque sites, halls in which artistic or sporting events may take place, meeting rooms, etc. In this sense, leisure space is atomised, since it has not been globally planned. Consequently coordination becomes difficult and a policy of harmonious growth, based on criteria of cultural and social development impossible. If functional divisions replace administrative categories, i.e. if this space is divided into coherent zones for predominantly physical, craft, artistic, intellectual and social activities, it becomes possible to coordinate efforts, compare costs and relate the output of each sector to the needs of the population. This regrouping of leisure space and its subdivision into *zones* provides the means of stimulating a balanced growth of culture for the body and the mind, of handicrafts, and of an artistic or intellectual culture, depending on the social groups which utilise it. Such a structure of leisure space, which is functional for the overall needs of individuals in leisure situations, makes alternative uses of the same area or a balance between scattered specialised zones equally possible.

Leisure space must be integrated with the whole urban area, since it provides space for culture: the functional structure which has just been described, makes this integration feasible, even when there is overlap with other kinds of space, as is often the case. Thus, it occupies enclaves within space devoted to productive work-zones reserved for cultural activities in factories, e.g. yards, gardens, stadiums, halls for entertainment, managed by the social services or the union management committee, and often by inhabitants of the neighbourhood. Similarly, within schools there are playgrounds, gymnasiums, sports grounds, and libraries (it should be mentioned in passing that they are, as a rule, out of proportion with the pupils' cultural needs). Leisure space can also be found in churches and chapels, some of which are not only designed for religious services, but for meetings, games and concerts. . . . It is also infiltrating the family space where, with the rise in the standard of living, the garage is being turned into a workshop for do-it-yourself, the living room into an entertainment centre (shows on TV, film projections, small bar etc.) and even the bedroom into a study or a bedsitter for entertaining friends. From the viewpoint of a leisure space to be created on the scale of current needs, the formula of early 20th century town-planning: "to work, to dwell, to travel and to cultivate oneself" is clearly deceptive. It is too simple, it lumps study and leisure under one label ("to cultivate oneself"), and it does not reflect the interpenetration between leisure activities, which are constantly increasing, and all other activities. It stems from inadequate sociological thinking about "human needs" and about their implications for urban development.

Leisure space, like space devoted to culture, is a social space in which specific relationships between people, between groups, between milieux and classes, are formed. It is determined by the characteristics of the user population, by the life styles of the various social milieux from among which its users are recruited. Their cultural diversity must be respected and sponsored to avoid uniformity, standardization and social boredom. Yet cultural deviations, disparities and imbalances which deprive some social strata of what urban culture could give to them, must be reduced.

Leisure space must also be, so to speak, time-bound: its limits, its equipment, its uses must be capable of varying with time. As has been shown, leisure activities have a rhythm dictated by the specific characteristics of periods in time: thus the pattern of seasons associated with that of work results in migrations at the end of the day, of the week, of the year (holidays) and of life (retirement). These patterns create periodic problems of shortage or glut which affect the design of leisure space. Wogensky described the modern town-planning of a highly mobile society as "relative, dynamic and dependent on time;" the same expression could apply to this design (Wogensky, 1964).

Both private and public facilities are included in leisure space. All too often, civil servants only take account of the latter, disregarding private (commercial or non-profit-making) services. Yet it is obvious that what matters to the people interested in various activities (from weekend trips to musical concerts) is the balance between supply and demand (both manifest and latent), rather than the ownership of the relevant facilities. Music rooms, whether publicly or privately owned, youth centres, cafés, record shops, fishing areas, whether public or private etc. are part of a space which constitutes a whole for the sociologist, even when administrative distinctions disregard this fact. Public and private space cannot be considered separately, if a harmonious and effective development of leisure activities is sought.

Leisure space must be geographically located in the spot best suited to each particular case. How can this be found? Since it may be located at various levels of the urban area, there are alternative choices, affected by and evolving with the degree of motor-car ownership and the density of the population etc. The present trend is to extend the urban leisure space further and further from city centres and to locate a growing part of this space in the neighbouring or even the remote countryside, where people go for the weekends or for short vacations, where they have a second residence, even, in some cases, their home. However, in making this geographical choice, the town-planner ought not to consider only this temporary (weekend, holidays) or final (living in the country) migration whereby a growing mass of town-dwellers go to suburbs, near or far. He ought not to forget another trend, also very important, which still attracts growing numbers from the country to the town (rural exodus) or which transforms village life. The joint effects of both trends will have to be taken into account in organising the work space of former villagers and the leisure space of "the new villagers" (Gans, 1962).

Lastly, leisure space must be open to the future, for, in the sphere for which it caters, needs vary and may do so not only following technical discoveries, but the evolution of social relations and of cultural patterns. No matter how techniques and ideas may change, one comment strikes me as essential for the future of town-planning. Within the next fifty years, leisure space may be expected to become increasingly necessary for human equilibrium in ever-bigger cities, whose population will be ever wealthier and more educated and will work less and less. As a rule, the town-planner designs for a period of over fifty years (Fourastié, 1966). Whether evolution is slow or fast, global or fragmentary, convergent or divergent for the various social classes, its general trend towards the end of the XXth century will be in this main direction. Leisure even if its duration is not extended as much as some foresee, will be more widespread, more sought after, more highly valued. It reflects an old human dream, expressed in myths and utopias. Moreover, it is in accordance with the logic of a tertiary economy to promote jobs for the production of leisure goods and services in order to make up for the decrease in employment for the manufacturing of primary and secondary goods. An increased consumption of leisure is required for the operation of an economy which will be more and more centred on the tertiary sector. Unlike needs for food and health requisites, leisure requirements are virtually limitless. It may be asked whether their growth on such a scale is desirable in a world where inequalities endure and where one third of mankind has too little to eat. Yet, as societies become wealthier, change in consumption patterns is always accompanied by an accelerated growth of the relative share of leisure. It is as if, in tertiary or post-industrial society, urban culture put a premium on what has been called *homo ludens* (Huizinga 1970).

How can tomorrow's town planning take account of this trend? In industrial societies, town builders had a primarily utilitarian outlook; nature was changed at the cost of its enjoyment, social relationships were subordinated to productive work. New times are coming, in which leisure will stimulate the need for new relations between man and nature, and between man and society. Emerging from centuries of workers' poverty, followed by rebellion, *we are still unprepared for life in the new society.* The old framework of our lives does not fit this new life style. Most towns are still shaped by their founders' utilitarian ideology, by the social segregation and struggles which accompanied the tragic advent of the industrial age. These struggles and tensions are enduring, but their content will in all likelihood change more and more, as a function of new relations between work problems and those which arise outside work, between production and consumption problems, between social commitment and individual happiness. Towns and cities will become increasingly unfit to live in, unless they are wholly transformed under the pressure of new needs. As society becomes more productive, wealthier, better educated, the mass requirement for leisure residences and migrations turns into the *biggest source of demand for space.* Despite all financial and ideological obstacles, the bold, progress-oriented, planned creation of a leisure space commensurate with the new needs of *homo ludens,* may be most important; it may be indispensible to the construction of cities in which the men of 1985, our children, will be able to live.

IV.5. Some Conclusions

Thus, by observing the integration of leisure time and space in the general dynamics of time and space, the sociologist can make a concrete analysis of the role played by leisure in social and cultural change. In turn determined and determining, in a dialectical relationship which evolves with change in society and culture, leisure tends to gradually transform our ways of feeling, of thinking and of acting (Dumazedier, 1960). This is not only due as McLuhan says, to the impact of the mass media. They are only one aspect of leisure. As I have shown, it is in all the sectors of leisure life that new values appear in man's attitudes to nature, to other men, to himself, to his own body, his heart and his mind. These limited changes, shaped by situations at work, in family life, at school, in socio-political and socio-spiritual life, tend to affect such situations in turn. It is as if leisure were the privileged sphere of a *genuine ethical and aesthetic revolution,* at once the product and the negation of the scientific and technical revolution which has prevailed in respect of work and organization.

It does not suffice to assert that leisure permits expressive activities in which the individual is an end, in contrast to instrumental activities in which he is a means. In the new society characterised by the scientific and technical revolution, leisure becomes the privileged setting for the second cultural revolution which is both aesthetic and ethical. To a world geared to the rational production of goods and the rational management of organizations, corresponds another world, centred on the free expression of human beings and their affective relations with others, considered as an ultimate end, despite social conditioning to the contrary. In the new generation, the strongest innovating attitudes find in leisure an expression which challenges the primacy given to a utilitarian transformation of nature and rehabilitates disinterested contemplation. The objective is no longer only to fulfill man by transforming the natural world and his own nature, it is to preserve the world and to live in a symbiosis with it. It is no longer to discipline, to needlessly repress his own nature, but to allow self-fulfilment with a minimum of constraint for a maximum of individual or collective contentment. Leisure is a rebellion against repressive culture. In the new society, it is less and less in relation to the virtues of work that leisure is lived. It has been said that "the vacancy of values makes for the value of vacations" (Morin, 1970). This is yet again a negative definition of the phenomenon leisure by reference to values which are alien to it, and a consequent unawareness of the new values emerging from it. Leisure assumes its new dimension by asserting the right to fulfill the deepest aspirations of the individual, repressed in the practice of his institutional duties. The value of play, which used to cease at the age of work, to disappear with childhood, is thus restored. Childhood and youth, permanent sources of inspiration for the poet, tend to become a universal art of living. *Humo ludens* is promoted, alongside *homo faber* or *homo sapiens*, as part of humanism. In relations with others, affective exchanges are no longer confined to institutionalised forms. In the quest for an ethical system based on individual or collective enchantment, music, dance, dreaming recover the major part they used to have in ancient societies. McLuhan has called the new generations neo-tribal. Moreno has contrasted relationships or groups based on spontaneous affinity (psycho-groups) and those which are institutionalised (sociogroups). This change is occurring in various categories of activity which together form a new cultural system whose prestige reflects on all sectors of human action. It is likely that this system will change in the future, to assume a direction and in forms difficult to foresee, but which may well be very different from the models anticipated a century or two ago, by Adam Smith and by Marx, by the French revolutionary assemblies or by Napoleon's Civil Code.

In post-industrial society, the various types of activity which correspond to needs of the body or the mind, of imagination or reason, are mainly practiced in the company of other individuals, in groups. What is the distinguishing characteristic of these leisure groups? They make up the majority of what Riesman called peer-groups, as distinguished from family, educational, occupational or political groups. Their development has been very fast indeed. Within them affinities are stronger than the statutory ties of blood relationship or of a common trade, but, like all groups, they are conditioned by social class. Hence they are undeniably very different from the tribal groups or archaic societies, which were mainly based on kinship systems. Communities which are to some extent marginal or in revolt against institutions are emerging; they are founded on the affective and emotional bonds born of love, music or drugs.

From an existential point of view (temporarily discarding all their own ideological interpretations of themselves as well as those which are made of them, largely from the standpoint of industrial society), these societies are primarily oriented towards leisure. Their setting up would be inconceivable if the duration of work were such as to leave little time over for education or leisure. Such marginal societies all locate themselves in a time which is neither taken up by work, nor by family, civic or spiritual duties, nor even by study. As a rule it is precisely to escape work as it is, family life and political life as they are, that some youngsters, in growing numbers, start a marginal society whose initial characteristics are all those of a leisure society, geared to satisfying not only the individual, but his inner dreams, and to seeking love relations perceived as universal models for social exchanges and organisation. At all times, such wishes have generated utopias, sometimes implemented in part, but for more or less short periods and without leaving any trace; they have been part of a protest movement against the standards of work, of politics, of the family and the churches. Some aspects of this negation are found in Plato's Republic, in Rabelais' Abbey of Thélème and in Fourier's Phalanstère. What is new about the post-industrial age is that leisure society introduces patterns which challenge the norms and values, both collective and individual, of the previous society. In the new utopias in which leisure patterns are lived, the work sought is less distant from leisure and feasting: working the land, or handicrafts, or travelling musicianship. The family becomes more open, more flexible, more compatible with the libertarian aspirations of individuals. Religiousness is more closely linked with hedonism and eroticism. Politics blend with an aspiration for peace and love. These patterns are related to an increasingly radical protest against repression, against the standards of production and the consumer society. Their influence is felt by all social strata and amounts to a fascination among the better educated strata, whose importance is, as Karl Mannheim foresaw, a new fact in social dynamics. The criticism of daily life which is thus made may generate a change more drastic than that of social structures; it may be a personality revolution. This trend witnesses to the topicality of Rimbaud or Freud, at least as much as to Marx's. The most far-reaching consequence yielded by the historical production of a leisure civilisation might be a drastic reassessment of all the patterns which have regulated the relationships between society and individuals from the traditional to the industrial age.

Fourastié writes: "to choose one's leisure will be to choose one's life." How is this daring thought to be understood? How can an effective resistance be made to everything that limits, distorts or alienates free choice? For society, the choice of leisure will always rank second to that of family, occupational or socio-political obligations. However, these institutional alternatives will probably be increasingly influenced by the choice of a type of leisure, and, in addition, determined by new cultural values.

Two Important Issues

There was a time when the progress of culture was more or less assimilated to that of universal rationality. The first duty was "to make reason popular." The expansion of schooling derives from this tenet. Later, in the course of the XIXth century, a reaction set in, which favoured a less disembodied culture, closer to technology and to manual work. Thinkers and poets protested against a rational, scientific or technical, civilisation, whose somewhat oversimplifying optimism might overlook the values of the body, of passion, of myths and of spirituality. They contrasted culture and civilisation. They strongly stressed that each culture was relevant to a prehistorical or historical period, to an ancient or a modern society. Culture has been opposed to nature, in order to be more closely associated with society. The concept of universality dwindled. In our industrial society, universal culture was denounced as a class culture which dared not admit its name. Today all these problems still exist, but many of the disputes they caused appear superseded. Nearly all these streams of thought are still represented. They have been progressively embodied or they will gradually be incarnated in the cultural practices of various social groups. The definitions of "mass culture" which take no account of them remain superficial. In my view, the new problem of cultural development in a society which has reached the stage of mass production, consumption and leisure, is double.

Firstly, will this society introduce a balance in the daily life of the people, between the values of occupational, social, spiritual or political commitment, and the values of comfort or leisure, so that the masses may be increasingly associated in shaping their own destiny? Or will the masses give up to an oligarchy of technocrats and politicians a prestigious, but onerous power, to merely enjoy more leisure and the increasingly plentiful goods provided for more and more people by higher work outputs? This danger is, of course, far from threatening the whole population. There are still serious social and regional injustices to fight as a priority. However, what will happen in the next two decades, *must* be foreseen. The warnings of American sociologists about mass culture are worth remembering.

Secondly, what are leisure values today, what will they be tomorrow? To launch the absurd idea that the corruption of Sodom and Gomorrah in 1985 will deserve the punishment of fate would be ridiculous. The second problem of cultural development for the urban masses of capitalist society may be more plainly formulated. Will the growing supply of obsessive, cheap or nasty entertainment, influenced by the unregulated system of commercial distribution, inhibit in the long run the nobler aspirations which could be associated with the free activities of the masses? Will these aspirations to make unfettered efforts of scientific research, artistic creation and voluntary social participation be in effect reserved for the leisure of a limited elite, while the well-entertained masses will only be capable of enjoyment in a land of plenty? Which part of the population will spontaneously participate in the more exacting forms of scientific exploration and of non-conformist or challenging culture, if the abundance of relaxing entertainment substitutes for culture? If the meaning of tragedy is to express a higher form of vitality rather than morbid enjoyment or outdated asceticism, if for the truly great creator the noblest game is a constant drama toying with the contradictions and uncertainties of human destiny how many will enjoy the efforts involved in a dialogue with such a creative artist? If we want to achieve a genuine cultural democracy at all levels, what is the necessary cost of a cultural action to reduce lags and inequalities, on a mass scale, in other words within and between all social classes? Disinterested effort is probably the prerogative of an aristocracy to which only minorities can aspire in all classes. However, should not cultural development sponsor conditions conducive to extending this circle of the elect, so that the leisure civilisation far from accentuating the natural inequalities between men and groups, reduces them? Thus it might become, at least from time to time, a passionate dialogue between creators and a mass of active participants in the austere games in which man challenges his own self!

Notes to Chapter IV

[36] In contemporary American society, contrasting attitudes towards the ethics of work, as formulated by Max Weber in his analysis of capitalism, can be observed.

[37] Except for non-factory workers aged over 35 so far as the reading of literary columns is concerned; this cultural activity is correlated with short work times.

[38] However, after the age of 35, the less interest they have in their work, the less they participate in associations.

[39] By contrast, young factory workers aged under 35 who do not refer to satisfaction with work well done as a source of gratification have the highest level of interest in all my population for these same kinds of leisure activities.

[40] Yet, as has been seen, satisfaction with technique is similarly distributed among factory workers and others.

[41] In the United States in 1953, 21% of wage-earners supported the 35 hour week, in 1963 29% did (40% among unionists). These are the results of two comparable nationwide surveys published in the Report "How do people feel about free time?", of the Eighth Yearly AFL-CIO National Conference on Community Services, New York, 1964. Union activity to this end goes on.

[42] See the results of the International Survey on Time-Budgets at the Evian Congress, in *Proceedings of the Sixth World Congress of Sociology*, 1970, Vol. III.

[43] Survey conducted by I.F.O.P. at the request of the Planning Authority (Commissariat Général au Plan) and of the Town and Country Planning Agency (Délégation à l'Aménagement du Territoire) *Revue 2000* 6, 1967.

Evolution of attitudes held by the active population about time freed from work between 1963 and 1969

If the duration of work were to decrease, would prefer	1963	1969
a) shorter working week	20%	35% + 15%
b) longer paid holidays	64%	53% − 11%
c) don't know	10%	12%

1968: Attitudes of the active population to various ways of granting free time:

If the duration of work were to decrease, would prefer:

½ hour less per day:	6%
½ day of free time added each week:	21%
2 weeks of extra leave a year:	26%
to retire two years earlier:	38%
don't know	9%

[44] Breakdown of the French active population according to the duration of their daily journeys between home and work (INSEE, 1960).

−10'	10–20'	20–30'	30–40'	40–60'	+60'
21%	41%	13%	11%	7%	7%

V Frames of Reference and Methods

V.I. Cultural Development: Concepts and Dimensions

What framework can sociology use to deal with the issues which I have raised in previous chapters? On what sociological conceptualisation can one rely to define and order the research area for scientific observation, to process the most pertinent data on all aspects of reality amenable to scientific knowledge and to systematic intervention?

To analyse the content of leisure in the fifties, the sociologist could be interested by the concept of mass culture. Indeed, the mass media *play an increasingly central part* in a mass society characterized by the gradual integration of the majority in the participation in comfort and leisure goods. They introduce this majority to new forms of culture, distinct both from inherited culture, from the verbal culture traditional in origin, and from the humanistic culture conveyed by schools and/or universities. It is the content of the mass media which is called mass culture (Wilensky provides an empirical, as well as a theoretical elaboration of this concept).

It is all the more necessary to investigate mass culture in order to analyse the cultural content of mass leisure, as time-budget surveys show that most individuals in all social classes spend on average half their leisure time watching television, listening to the wireless, reading newspapers and periodicals, and going to the movies. The decline in visits to the cinema, which is uneven anyway, is made up for by the increase in time spent televiewing (Steiner, 1963). The split between areas which seems implicit in the almost simultaneous publication of two anthologies entitled *Mass Culture* and *Mass Leisure*, in 1957 and 1958 respectively, is artificial. I am not alone in having wondered at it at the time. [45] Yet the concept of mass culture only offers limited and deceptive advantages to deal with my two basic questions about cultural change in post-industrial societies. This is why I have rejected it from the start, despite its obvious contribution to the progress of scientific knowledge in the fifties. To clarify the point: this concept is useful in grouping *under one* name distinct cultural contents disseminated by the mass media. It has shown that the media are not a mere support for the message. Their influence on the public's sensitivity and imagination is relatively independent from the message. Later, MacLuhan, summarizing and simplifying sociological observations, went so far as to write that the medium is the message (MacLuhan, 1964, Cazeneuve, 1970). Moreover, mass culture, in its most common forms, is not regulated by the same laws as artistic or scientific creation in high culture. Its production follows laws which are comparatively independent from creative requirements, and remains subordinated to the market, defined by mass consumption needs. These characteristics and these laws must obviously be known to study the problems I have raised.

However, another conceptualization is required to integrate them with a wider set of data. In addition, the implications and connotations of the concept of mass culture are not without offering serious disadvantages.

Firstly, the content of leisure cannot be reduced to that of the mass media. Conversation of the traditional kind, whether in the family or in other primary and secondary groups, retains an importance which may be independent from mass culture, but may also deeply alter its content. Empirical research has gradually highlighted the enduring centrality of "personal influence" (Katz and Lazarsfeld, 1955). Walking, sport, gardening, do-it-yourself etc. are activities which constitute a physical and craft culture, influenced by the content of the media, but influencing it in turn and regulated by other laws. What is the impact of my two major questions on this area comprised by the cultural content of leisure?

Is the cultural content of the mass media characterised by the unity postulated in essays on the "massification" or the "standardization" of culture? Empirical research convinced me of the reverse. Part of this content clearly supports the massification and standardization theses (some general information, some songs etc.). Nevertheless, a content analysis shows that all kinds and all levels of knowledge are aimed at, even in those societies where advertising has most control over the media (Steiner, 1963). In France, the wireless is the greatest provider of quality concerts: over 150 hours of highbrow music a week. Listening in is very *selective* and related to the system of social stratification (living standards, life style, educational levels etc.). Not only is the message irreducible to the medium, but its content is of paramount importance for the choice of programmes, depending on social background: political speeches or songs, religious services or travelogues, information on strikes or news from seaside resorts. The public is not the same in each case and all networks are not equally easy to tune in to. In songs, travelogues and serials, different levels of artistic, technical, scientific or philosophical knowledge are involved and they are not equally accessible to all. These differences within mass culture are more important for analytical purposes than its apparent unity.

Another problem is essential in my view: how does the cultural content of the leisure enjoyed by the majority of workers break away from or continue the movements of cultural emancipation which accompanied the social movements of the 19th century? To what extent is what has been called popular culture facilitated by some components of this cultural content of leisure, and hampered or negated by others?

Furthermore, we need to know the new criteria of a culture favouring personal fulfilment and social participation for the greatest number and the conditions and processes required for the development of such a culture by the mass media, as well as by new forms of information and education throughout the life cycle. No conceptualization of mass culture helps solve these problems. Some attempts were made in this direction, but the necessary epistemological and methodological considerations were not produced (Friedmann, 1965). We need a *sociology of cultural development,* dealing both with school and with later life, thus challenging the present borderlines between educational and leisure sociology. Many obstacles hinder its growth and it is still in infancy. Indeed such a sociology challenges habits of thought, by requiring us to go back on the split made in the XIXth century between humanistic and anthropological culture. Thus the one could advocate or promote values and criteria corresponding more closely to the observed culture which the various social categories and classes experience; the other could carry out the selective observation required for a better solution to the problems (raised by the former) of widening categories or raising the cultural level of the various social groups.

The sociology of culture must be able to distinguish several sectors within the area of culture. If culture is the whole set of symbolic relationships between the individual, on the one hand, the world, society and himself, on the other, cultural change is the modification of some relationships over time. Change occurs as a result of innovations, time-lags, inequalities, and conflicts between the old and the new, depending on the group, class or milieu considered. Cultural development is not just any change, but a symbolic one, assessed as positive by the criteria of any social subject (who may be an expert, a group, an organization, a State, a class, or a society through its deputies or delegates); it may be considered positive for economic, socio-political, or individual development, or for all three. Hence, convergence, divergence and conflict can arise. Cultural development is thus *both* relative and positive; it enables us to raise pertinent problems and to formulate useful hypotheses for action as well as for knowledge.

Cultural development may be grasped through observable indicators. Its results may conform or clash with the values which underpin it. If offers a concept for the formulation of problems, the selection of pertinent information, and its scientific treatment and corroboration.

This development may or may not be induced. It may result from the interplay of forces in a "laissez-faire" situation or from an action, i.e. the interaction between a system of intervention by a social subject and the favourable or unfavourable factors of a situation. Such action may be the outcome of short or long term planning.

Karl Mannheim was the first sociologist to raise the problems involved in the sociology of planning culture development in connection with leisure (Mannheim, 1950). Since his death in 1947, this sociology has made little progress, far less than the sociology of knowledge or of information. However, recent discoveries by the social sciences of action and critical thought on the first experiments in liberal planning showed me in what direction to seek the framework and the method required to create a sociology of cultural development planning. In my view, Karl Mannheim grasped the importance of this problem, both in active research and in relational action, when he wrote of planning for freedom. I shall not dwell on his contribution to the sociology of knowledge, which Georges Gurvitch outlined and critically assessed. Nor shall I allude to his epistemological study of utopia and ideology, the best known aspect of his thought among French philosophers and sociologists (Mannheim, 1929). *Ideology and Utopia* is the only one of his eight books to have been translated into French. I shall refer only to his last book, posthumously published in 1950: *Freedom, Power and Democratic Planning*.

This analysis of "planning for freedom" covers all aspects of the daily life of the various social classes and categories, but stresses the new relationships between work and leisure (especially in part III, chapter XII "Work and Leisure") in what Mannheim called "the new society". He denounced as anachronistic the high valuation of work, which increasingly corresponds to few responsible and creative functions in industrial society. Most jobs are characterized by the work carrying no responsibility, involving no creativeness, which Friedmann was soon to searchingly analyse in "The human problems of the industrial age" (Friedmann, 1946). Mannheim boldly asserted that "for a majority" leisure instead of work has become the path to civilisation. At the same time, he pointed to a double failure:

a) that of *laissez faire* which abandons the content of leisure in mass society to the degrading organization for whom cultured goods and services are merely a source of maximum profits;

b) that of regimentation which reduces leisure to a means of controlling the people for ends alien to personality fulfilment.

Starting from this double analysis, he outlined a sociology of planning whose problems and methods would enable it to process the data required for understanding the operation of a planned society based on free consultation and for guiding its planners. He thought that sociologists should produce "intelligence tests," interviews and a skilful observation of "physical and mental development and aptitudes," so that a sociology of planning would exist on the cultural, and not only on the economic, level.

However, these epistemological and methodological considerations remained very general. Mannheim spoke of "planned and predictable developments," but did not show how the sociology of cultural planning can make forecasts, or how the sociology of cultural development which studies an induced change can be objective. While conceptual and methodological tools which were lacking in the thirties are now available, the manifold epistemological obstacles which delayed the development of Mannheim's thought, are far from having disappeared.

I shall analyse the situation in France, where "indicative planning" is prepared on the basis of sociological research and mainly of ideological confrontations within cultural committees. I shall endeavour to show how epistemological obstacles endure and how experience has made it possible to develop the premises contained in Mannheim's work.

The notion of cultural planning is suspect on the grounds of the origin imputed to it. As it appears in official texts, some have generously attributed its paternity to the government: this is a mistake. It originated in fact in the thoughts of some independent high-ranking civil servants, some researchers interested in the problems of cultural development, some unionists keenly concerned with popular education and some associations for popular culture — in the French rather than the American sense (Charpentreau, 1967; Girard, 1964; Lestavel, 1964). The first coherent draft of a cultural development plan dates back to 1960. It went beyond the usual confines of the public sector and covered both the non-profit-making and the commercial private sectors. It suggested also by-passing the administrative barriers which prevent a global approach to the problem of cultural creation, dissemination and participation. It was presented to, and adopted by the General Assembly of a national voluntary association which has for twenty years perpetuated a tradition initiated by the Resistance Movement (Peuple et Culture, 1960). This idea emanated from a collective wish, stimulated by the ideals of 1936 and 1945, applied to the new social and cultural problems of the sixties; the wish to promote a voluntary policy for raising the cultural level of the population in all social classes and categories.

In 1961, the Commissariat au Plan, anxious for better information prior to decision-making in the cultural sphere, proposed to set up a Committee for cultural facilities and the artistic heritage (Commission de l'Equipement Culturel et du Patrimoine Artistique). Seventy members were appointed and the main leaders of cultural life, representing all trends, were heard. In 1963, these problems were on the curriculum of an International Summer School, led by Georges Jean and attended by one hundred and fifty cultural workers. In July 1964, Jean Vilar and Michel Debeauvais organized, on the fringe of the Eighteenth Avignon Festival, a meeting on the problems of cultural development. Representatives of the theatre, scientific research, public administration and private associations, the unions and political life, were invited to attend. Politicians interested in these issues were selected from opposition parties and from the majority party. The debate continued on the fringe of each Avignon festival, in 1965, 1966 and 1967, with an ever-improving background of documentation. However, the most important meeting on this theme is still the Bourges Round-Table, triggered off by "a meeting between the leaders of the association Peuple et Culture and some research-workers of the Ministry of Cultural Affairs and the Study Group for the Expansion of Scientific Research" (Crémieux-Blanc, 1965). It was held at the Cultural Centre at Bourges in November 1964 and attended by about a hundred civil servants, organizers and research-workers, under the leadership of A. Piatier. Its main theme was the development of the social science research required to provide a rational basis for planning.

There are still more questions than answers, despite a first batch of research projects (in 1963—66), variously adapted to the specific issues of cultural planning. The origins of this new attitude towards cultural planning show that it does not emanate from the government, or from the opposition, or from any right- or left-wing party, but from a group of *cultural activists* (Touraine, 1965), aware that they were innovating and determinate to fight both their political partners and their opponents for innovation to prevail.

One of the greatest experts on liberal planning, J. Friedmann, wrote recently: "We no longer ask whether planning is possible or compatible with a democratic ideology, but how to improve the present practice. The problem of planning has become a methodological one" (Friedmann, 1959). Methodology should be understood in the widest sense, to cover methods of thinking. It is a new way of conceiving the cultural development of society which a group of cultural activists endeavoured to introduce in French planning in the sixties. This new way of thought went almost unnoticed by politicians, both in government and in opposition, as was shown by the low level of the parliamentary debate on this aspect of the Fifth Development Plan, regardless of political party.

On the other hand, many experts on cultural creation or dissemination reacted strongly; some located any attempt to measure current cultural phenomena (area of dissemination, content, costs etc.), "half way between a joke and sacrilege" (Girard, 1964). Others interpreted it as the invasion by "arrogant Boetians" of art's marvellous realm. Certain critics alleged that they were "terrorised" by sociologists who opposed the results of systematic surveys to their subjective representation of the public. Some writers asserted their own humanism against the new "cultural technocracy". Left-wing intellectuals traced in cultural planning a renewal of ideological action, no less than a rebirth of fascism. They waved the flag of freedom and, in a sensational interview, J. L. Godard said that it was a sacred duty to obstruct any planning. All these are real and sometimes serious problems: the cultural activists who are fighting to promote cultural planning are well aware of them.

How can these differences be explained?

I shall endeavour to analyse the type of cultural planning which, more or less consciously, prompts the new "crusaders of culture" in their campaign. Of course, it is only an ideal type in Weberian terms and I am outlining it in its rational form. I feel that *the emergence of this attitude indicates a new expansion of the scientific spirit in a new sphere* (Aron, 1962), *that of cultural development policy.*

To dispel a misunderstanding: those who support cultural planning do not intend to turn rationality in general, and science in particular, into a preferred content for cultural development. Their aim is not to impose by scientific methods an official culture defined by those in power. It is merely to apply more rationality to cultural development as a function of each individual's, each group's, each class's and each society's needs. Cultural planning allows for a better detection of constraints as well as a more coherent and effective use of resources. It enables meeting, to the greatest possible extent, the cultural needs of a population, taking account of preference criteria selected by itself, by organizers or creators of cultural values. The ultimate choice of criteria pertains to those who hold political responsibilities.

Local authorities are increasingly asked to formulate a planning policy for *cultural development* in and out of school. Each body responsible for cultural planning must begin by thinking out the criteria of this development and their objective implications. It goes without saying that the public and private agencies of a town are not undertaking to promote culture, or cultural change in general, but only the cultural development of the various social strata and the urban population, for a period usually limited to one term of office. Cultural development is only one part of culture and of cultural change. It is limited to a change in the cultural systems of a population, assessed as positive by reference to the needs of the economy, society and personality, defined by a competent body according to explicit criteria for betterment. Indeed under defined conditions, gaps or discrepancies become needs, i.e. imbalances to be rectified or differences to be retained, only if assessed against development criteria.

I have not decided to explain "why" such an attitude emerged. The fact remains that when the French economy entered a phase of rapid prosperity (approximately in 1953–55), it became clear that a wealthier, more mobile, more complex society can bring about new lags and inequalities. Socio-cultural imbalances may increase despite the "education explosion" (Cros; Bourdieu and Passeron, 1964). The potential for research, invention and creation, increasingly needed to preserve a humanist attitude of protest seems more and more threatened by passivity, conformism, and academism. Communication between the intelligentsia and the rest of the population is more and more necessary to cultural democracy, but seems more and more difficult to achieve.

Despite the growing cultural unification or standardization due to the educational expansion and the growth of the mass media, imbalances between the urban and the rural culture, between the culture of the ruling classes and of the ruled, between that of the educated and of the others, between that of the leaders and of the groups, do not vanish; they merely change. They are no longer polar opposites, as in the last century, but more numerous, more relative, more subtle differences, located on another level (Dumazedier and Ripert, 1966). The problem of preserving social or regional diversity adds to the difficulty of reducing disparities. The problem of reducing cultural alienation is made more complex by the crisis of social participation in a more effective system of mass consumption, by the crisis of social solidarity in relation to mass leisure values, and by the crisis of cultural values related to the growth of a certain mass culture.

To deal with these constantly growing problems, the means available are becoming less and less adequate. To neglect exchanges in cultural goods may increasingly be considered as absurdly wasteful. Yet the responses of the public authorities in and out of school may appear more and more outdated, conformist and ineffectual, despite all reforms or promises of reform. How can these contradictions be overcome?

1) Cultural action must first be designed to match existing and *future* needs. Hence these must be studied, instead of implementing the whims of a cabinet minister, the habits of an administrative agency or the dreams of intellectuals. In her book *The Republic and the Arts,* Jeanne Laurent shows how decisions without follow-up and episodic achievements rest only on the good will of politicians in power. This attitude should be different, it should even be reversed: there ought to be a will to base cultural action on an objective study of cultural needs for entertainment, information, training or in-service training, depending on social background, urban or rural, manual or supervisory etc. There ought to be a will to study cultural needs as a whole; culture for the body and for the mind, craft, artistic or intellectual culture, individual or collective culture. These needs should be studied in their concrete entirety, without being divorced from the conditions in which they are expressed. The demand expresses both

the individual and the conditions in which he lives. If conditions are changed, will not the demand change too?[46] And to what extent? Needs are not reduced to the expressed demand, but the demand may be part of the needs (Cazeneuve and Oulif, 1963). There ought to be studies, by listening not only to the population, but to artists, group leaders and educationalists who influence them, as well as experts on cultural development, who can foresee the impact to be made on them by probable change in the conditions generating them.

In an increasingly mobile society, to observe needs is no longer enough, they must be foreseen and short- or long-term future hypotheses formulated. Just as no agents of economic development make rational decisions anymore without making a forecast of the market, so those responsible for cultural development can no longer do without forecasts of cultural needs. What will be the effect of the likely rise in living standards, urbanization rate, car-ownership rate, TV ownership rate, educational level etc.? The operation of some cultural administrations, both public and private, now seems out of date and even unworthy. To decide on a cultural policy without scientific hypotheses about the future, is not to decide "freely", but blindly. To formulate hypotheses on the various likely changes in society and in mass culture over five, ten or a hundred years, is to limit not the freedom to intervene, but the chances of failure. To limit uncertainty about the future by hypothesizing likely changes, is to increase the power of intervening and to reduce the scope for abstract statements about what "the people will like" or what "the masses need."

2) The study of needs is inseparable from the choice of *development criteria*. How can desirable criteria be formulated, when we are faced with the likelihood of change which relieves us from both sterile fear and naive hope? It is a delusion, in a way, to believe that needs are observed. They are constructed on the basis of observation and of a reference framework which is both ideal and possible: a cultural gap becomes an inequality only by reference to a desirable frame of equality and a *possible* frame of equalisation. This *double* reference framework must therefore be made explicit.

The illusory belief that they may replace preference criteria, often makes the most fecund ideologies sterile. It accounts for the powerlessness of great declarations about progress in the face of actual passivity. This delusion weakens the united front of innovatory forces and strengthens the forces of conservation. When ideologists are in power, they imagine that from ideologies a cultural policy can be directly derived. The progress made by the social sciences of action (Bross, 1961; Rosensthiel and Mothes, 1965) has shown, however, that development criteria result both from the choice of an overall ideology and from an analysis of desirable and likely outcomes, taking account of possible interventions in probable cases. Thus development criteria are a partial system of values selected and ordered by reference to a probabilistic assessment of a given period and sphere. The sociologist of planning must of course begin by unearthing the ideological choices concealed under coherence or efficiency calculations (Cuisenier, 1964). Two meanings of the term ideology must be distinguished to facilitate understanding: 1) permanent and global value system: 2) temporary and partial value system, determined up to a point by the general global ideology, capable of implementation as a probable outcome of a possible intervention. Only the second meaning is operational for decision-making. It is on this level that preference criteria are worked out.

Among the impersonal calculations and the coherence or efficiency tests applied to planning, it is the researcher's duty to uncover the hidden political criteria disguised as technical choices. The man of action, on the other hand, must not forget that planning is, in a sense, only a technique of thought, intended to clarify the big alternatives for political decision, taking account of probable change. The last word belongs to the politician, even if the first does not. However, planning thought, based on probabilistic thought, modifies political decisions. Global ideologies are less likely to change what is ideologically desirable into what is historically probable than successive systems of development criteria, appropriate for likely situations, in a given society and at a given time. Hence to draw up criteria for political preference implies several operations.

a. to define a period and a setting;
b. to formulate hypotheses about probable change without any new intervention by the social subject studied;

c. to formulate hypotheses about the probable results related to possible interventions;
d. to select the criteria for choice desirable in the general system;
e. to rank order them under various possible alternatives;
f. in the end, preference criteria pertinent for a given time and society will be available for policy making.

3) When preference criteria have been chosen after a study of needs, it becomes possible to select *objectives*. The social sciences of action have also adopted new attitudes in this respect. An objective is now no more than a hypothesis about the probability of a result. From among all conceivable projects, the only one which can be retained is that which stands the greatest chance of truly meeting needs after desirable criteria, the probable situation and possible means have been taken into account. However, this new rational approach to action does not exclude either improvisation or originality. It attempts to reduce the uncertainty about the outcome of any given intervention. It compels the mind to hypothetically control the result before acting. The choice of targets for action can thus be scientifically made, in a sphere in which the project becomes a hypothesis and implementation, its corroboration. Action is no longer the reaction of a subject to a situation he experiences, but a reasoned conjecture about a future situation, modified in so far as possible by the intervention of an active subject. In this process the force of routine and the weight of social determination, which limit the freedom of the innovating and creative subject, are most likely to be reduced to a minimum. Thinking about objectives merely continues thinking about needs: the one attempts to reduce uncertainty about the future, if no intervention by the social subject creates new events; the other adopts the same approach to the opposite case in which such an intervention is to occur. This is a complete break with the pre-scientific approach to decision making, which contrasted the analysis of the situation and the decision. The former belonged to knowledge, the latter to action. Both are today the object of probabilistic knowledge.

Moreover, planning thought no longer approaches an objective in isolation. Despite administrative and other demarcations, the objective is integrated with a whole which tends to constitute itself into a *coherent system*. A systematic effort is made to fill gaps, eliminate overlaps, and harmonise the operations of conservation, creation, dissemination and stimulation in a given sector of cultural activity, for a given kind and at a given level. Thus a network of unilateral, bilateral or multilateral relationships which form a structure may be discovered. This very structure enables the establishment of priorities and the detection of coherences to implement if one criterion is preferred to another. As André Piatier writes, "economic analysis may be very useful here by following chains of 'manufacturing and using' goods; there is a symmetry between the chain iron ore, cast iron, steel, agricultural machinery, wheat, flour, bread, and cultural chains: if full awareness prevailed, there would be no archaeological collections unexhibited for lack of room, no rooms closed for lack of staff, no museums empty for lack of visitors, due to lack of information" (Piatier, 1964).

4) Lastly, the relationship between thinking about objectives and thinking about means is renewed. It has always existed in common sense decision-making, but it has now become more rigorous. To the same objective correspond several possible choices of means and of combinations of means. Which are most likely to be effective in promoting the most desirable objective at the lowest cost? Studies are required to formulate all *possible alternative interventions* in a given field and a given period, and to foresee the likeliest result of each given occurrence. Such an approach to the problem makes it necessary to fully review the relationships "between end and means." The problem of mystique degraded into opportunist politics or of policy degenerating into mystical words, that of pure minds and dirty hands, does not vanish. It arises in a new perspective which makes the relations between the ideal and its implementation, probabilistic. Firstly, the science which draws up a probabilistic inventory of means, leads to their integration in the set, exhaustive if possible, of available *resources* in a given time and place, to solve the problem at stake. To the planning mind money is a resource, but so are time, space, and even men and institutions. All these resources are always more or less limited, "scarce," within a system of possible interventions to meet cultural needs, as well as all others, in a

given period. Resources are interdependent. It is therefore necessary to study, for short or long term action, *the whole* of the monetary, spatial, temporal, human or institutional resources as a system to be used (or to be created), in order to achieve the best result. Should priority be given to equipment or to the men who operate it? Should there be more public or more private institutions? and what should the ratio be? etc.... However, the support given by resources is always ambivalent. All these resources may be small and instead *constraints* may limit development. These constraints are part of social determination mechanisms and hence are a favourite subject of sociological analysis. Still, in a developmental policy, resources matter more than constraints, since development requires a prime mover. Without them, there can be no development. If the brakes are on, stagnation is unavoidable. Even the problem of nationalization or socialization can now be put in terms of the social or cultural output of the given organization, in connection with development criteria. This new attitude has important repercussions on ways of thinking. On the one hand, no *humanist* thought can, at the risk of verbiage and powerlessness, divorce itself from technical thought about the conditions of its implementation. On the other, humanism itself is condemned to remaining pure, in other words validity is now the object of scientific study.

Thinking over the probable effects of using certain resources in preference to others is made more difficult as the realization grows that these resources, on which the social subject can act, interact with situations on which he cannot act. It no longer suffices to assert like Sartre (who follows Marx in this) that history has its own laws, unamenable to the intentions of the historical subject (Sartre, 1960). The science of action has begun to study the features of the interaction in two cases; that in which the decision of the social subject comes up against odds and that in which it clashes with enemies. The former comes under programming theory, the latter under games theory. Even when these theories cannot be applied, due to the lack of pertinent data, they prompt a new way of conceiving the interaction between means and probable occurrences. A major point in the use of monetary, temporal, spatial, human or legal resources is the search for optimacy, i.e., the determination of maximum output (by reference to whatever preference criterion) at minimum cost (in money, men) in the economic, the social or the cultural sphere. The comparison between effect and need consists in an actual or hypothesized control of the results: R/B. The comparison between results and means applied to reach them leads to an efficiency study R/M. The search for efficiency is the search for maximum result at minimum cost $R+/M-$. This embodies a wider, changed concept of output. Instead of exhibiting a negative, resentful or indifferent reaction to economic productivity (whereas the majority of society benefit by it and are unprepared to give up that which allows for mass consumption), one is contrasting it with another positive output, social and cultural in character, which can also generate a developmental policy, with its investments, its production—creation and its consumption—participation. It is the specific productivity of cultural and social development: to produce more "human values" (cultural level) among a growing number of people (social level), and not only more goods for more consumers.

The sociologist should and can change to deal with new problems. In the past, entire areas of knowledge formerly amenable only to the introspective method and to philosophical discourse have been treated by objective methods borrowed from the physical sciences. These sectors of knowledge became autonomous disciplines: economics, biology, linguistics, and later, sociology and psychology. Far from having been checked, this evolution still goes on and the science of man is exploring a vast field which it had never entered before: theory of decision-making, cybernetics, operational research, praxeology, science of communication and control, model building, programming theory, games theory, mathematics of action, thinking machines etc. Some have believed that these were discoveries for specialists only. They have merely complained against the rise of the "technocrats" whose power derived from these new forms of knowledge. Yet, according to my hypothesis, this new progress of the scientific spirit may yield results which will affect the world more than its earlier advances. Most intellectuals have not yet understood that this is a new way of thinking applied to the operation most common to man: action. The frontiers of knowledge and of action are challenged thereby. The movement has started. Like that of the human sciences in the previous period, the advance of the social sciences of action strikes me as irreversible. Its consequences are beginning to be felt already in a growing number of areas, through studies and the consultation of technocrats, experts and development specialists of all kinds (Massé, 1965). A new approach is required from the four main partners in planning: the research worker asked to gather pertinent observations and to construct development models on their basis, the administrator who defines the means, the cultural expert who suggests cultural objectives and the elected politican who compares, integrates and, finally, makes a decision. This involves a change in mental attitudes for which none of them have been prepared.

The research worker, while his thought unfolds in his specific framework, should *integrate* all the problems of forecasting and planning cultural development in his research area. Sociology cannot substitute for the creative impact of values. Even if the sociologist is a humanist, sociology is not a form of humanism. It can provide answers to questions about "what is" and even about "what can be". If a social subject supplies values and value orientations it can work out both advisable and applicable criteria for a given period and study their implications. It can study the pre-requisites for more coherent or more effective action. To deal with forecasting and planning, it is not enough to apply sociological results to action: the conditions and processes of action must themselves become the subject of sociological research (Lanfant, 1972). Such a sociology needs precise rules, it rejects the study of "total social facts" (Touraine, 1965; Dumazedier, 1967b) to concentrate exclusively on all the facts pertinent to the action problems raised. Instead of first studying the social facts shaped by social determinism, it focuses on a social subject who is both determined and determining, acting with all the resources at his disposal and struggling against all the constraints of the situation, which limit his scope for creation or control. Instead of eliminating value judgements, it studies their objective implications. Instead of disregarding the means required for development, it includes them in its sphere of observation, turns them into alternatives for intervention and assesses their probable outcome. Instead of confining itself to direct comments on the past and the present of the studied unit, it concerns itself also with the past and the present of other units whose present situation makes it possible to foresee a more or less probable situation of the former unit. It accepts concentrating on the problems of reducing future uncertainty, which are most useful to the makers of history, rather than merely observing what has already occurred. In order to determine the best techniques for verification, observation, explanation and forecasting, the sociologist does not only rely on the resources of sociology, but on those of other sciences (economics, linguistics, psychology), despite the difficulties involved in borrowing them. In order to work out his hypotheses about possible interventions in relation to the criteria desired by the social subject studied, he accepts breaking out of his isolation and cooperating with the politician, the intellectual and the administrator (rather than merely consulting them). In field work, he associates the social subject with the analysis of his situation and his project to the full extent compatible with the rules of scientific objectivity: he does not merely let the social subjects in on the feedback of his enquiry, he associates them to all its phases. He thus contributes to the progress of rationality in the thought processes of men of action. He always tends to rely on various forms of participant observation (Lanfant, 1967—69). This is what is meant by *active sociology*.

The *cultural expert* is best qualified to propose the values a cultural policy should promote, with regard to creation, dissemination or the participation of the public. He too confronts new problems when he participates in the formulation of a place for cultural development.

He must begin by questioning the extent and the limits of his own "knowledge of the public". The direct experience which the creator, the informer or the group leader has of his audience is an unreplaceable source of insights. However his perception is selective. The subjective nearly always blends with the objective when the person involved draws his own balance sheet. The cultural expert should know how to use scientific analyses of his public's reactions. He must therefore open his field to the sociologist without construing the latter's questions as "spying".

The contribution of the social sciences is useful to accurately know the attitudes of the social categories which make up a public. It is indispensible to know the reactions of that part of the public which is not reached by the system of creation, dissemination or by the educational system. It is about the choice of values that the expert is more competent, but he cannot withdraw into splendid isolation in that capacity. Otherwise his output might not be welcomed by the public. At the start, the innovator is nearly always a loner who resists the dominant ways of conforming. However, his dialogue with politicians (who integrate his cultural values with a general ideology) and with research workers (who objectively confront possible models of communication with the expert's and the public's values) is necessary to the progress of cultural development in the various spheres of society.

The expert's change of attitude is equally important for programming and for the choice of means. If his aim is to reach the widest possible population by his prestige or his influence, owing to the best programming and with the most rational use of resources, his co-operation with the research worker and the administrator within the joint planning team becomes desirable and feasible. It in no way limits his inventive capacity and his creative freedom.

The administrator, whether in public or in private, in profit-making or in voluntary organizations, should also display a new attitude within the planning team. He will not restrict himself to the information supplied by administrative reports, for the data collected and processed by researchers in accordance with scientific procedure is equally useful to him in support of his proposals or his decisions. Decisions become hypotheses to meet needs.

With regard to the values by which his decisions are guided, the administrator within a planning team must not be a blinkered bureaucrat. He requires the assessments or the proposals made by cultural experts, for cultural ends to prevail over administrative ones. He should feel the need for a constant dialogue with the political representatives in power and in opposition, in order to confront cultural and political values and to analyse the ideological meanings, which — without him being always aware of them — may underpin cultural values. The assistance of the research worker may be indispensible to this analysis.

In the choice of ends and means, the administrator does not merely make "routine" decisions which more or less automatically prolong the past. He attempts to display inspiration and rigour in formulating alternatives and hypotheses about the likely outcome of each decision in given short or long term conjunctures.[47]

The politician himself, whatever his view of economy or society, should reform the dominant way of thinking in political life.

In the last resort, planning always implies a political choice. No research, no creation, no administration can substitute for it. This choice is the ultimate one. If research fosters the illusion that this can be dispensed with, it is only because it smuggles in criteria for decisions which are outside the range of its competence. If an administration gives the impression that the choice of priorities pertains to itself alone, it is an usurpatory bureaucracy or technocracy. In the planning of cultural development, the politician alone, as has already been said, should have the last word. But he ought to have a new type of approach. In the first place, he should know the limits of political competence, precisely to the extent that this consists in making the ultimate choice of objectives to be achieved to the exclusion of all others. He ought to seek prior information not only direct from the electorate, but indirectly by relying on scientific thought and by entrusting studies in depth to research groups and expert committees.

When he has to solve problems of creation, dissemination or organization, in the areas of technological, scientific, artistic or ethnical knowledge, the politician should surround himself with experts, know how to listen, and conduct a dialogue with them. Unless he is ready for this type of cooperation, he may, without even knowing it, make decisions which are conservative or retrograde in relation to living culture, under the cover of social or political values alien to cultural dynamics. When several alternatives possible in the short or the long term are submitted to him by the joint planning teams, the politician should, in so far as possible, ensure that their probable implications in situations which are not equally likely will be studied. He will have to be ready to cooperate with the administrator and the researcher in order to work out the likely results of each solution in relation to costs — economic, institutional or human.

These are the outlooks required from the four big partners within planning teams. General ideologies are very important because of their implications for final decisions, but these problems of new mental attitudes occur in all ideological circles when confronted with the new issues of cultural development planning.

What is the part played by social "movements" (in the sense of Touraine, 1965) in this process? I consider that, despite the need for small working parties in which the best qualified people challenge each other, the drawing up of a plan should involve the most diverse social movements to the fullest possible extent. Hence the greatest amount of information and training is required at all levels of national, regional and local life. The plan will be truly applied not only when the government grants the material means needed for its implementation, but when the approaches and the means selected are understood, discussed, revised or suggested by the interested parties themselves. Finally, the planning of cultural development should be flexible. It should leave room for the more or less freakish cultural developments which can emerge or explode at any time, to challenge its forecasts. The people must always remain ready to retain a part in a society where forecasting and planning are increasingly necessary and possible to avoid waste, absurdity and scandals (Willener, 1970). Mannheim had wisely suggested in his "planning for freedom" an unplanned sector to fill this function.

V.2. Adult Education: an Operation for Cultural Development

One of the most important forms of action intended to ensure that the whole adult population actively participates in cultural development is, in my view, adult education. Despite the efforts made by employers, this mainly takes place in leisure time (Leveugle, 1963; Johnstone and Rivera, 1963). I shall attempt to define the problem of adult, and that of continuing education in the light of my earlier comments on cultural development.

A cultural development operation

To define is, in the first place, to locate. The cultural needs of the new society have stimulated, particularly during the last score of years, a multiplicity of initiatives which have gone in France under many imprecise names: cultural dissemination, educational aspects of mass communication, propaganda or popular publicity, popular culture, self-tuition, and, in the last instance, continuing education. Can all these activities be regrouped in the category of adult education? This seems unlikely. It would involve mixing very different kinds and levels of operation, thereby depriving educational action of any precision. Which generic term could cover all these activities and among them, which would coincide with the specific criteria of adult education?

Adult education is a cultural development operation. Some (Verner et al., 1960) tend to reduce it to the action of external educational agents on a learner. Of course, this is very important, but too often the relationship between the educational agent and the learner may be trapped within a sub-culture, when it is not an open avenue of communication between the more elaborate culture of society and the culture experienced by the people, but a closed network of interchange between the educational agents and the learner's sub-cultures.

Hence the first step is to connect adult education with culture and with society. The first question to tackle is that of the interdependence between the educational agent's, the learner's, his milieu's and the whole society's culture. Adult education then appears as the establishment of communication between the cultural systems of diffusers (inventors, researchers, creators) and those of receivers (all the individuals for whom adult education is meant). It is one of the intermediary systems on the whole cycle of society's cultural development which links the producers of cultural symbols with cultural disseminators, disseminators with participants and participants with producers.

At the level of finality, adult education needs to be consciously and voluntarily oriented by continuous and coherent action towards the systematic acquisition of knowledge or towards the methodical development of new attitudes, by an active subject. This feature rules out any operation aiming only at the entertainment or the information of the subject, even on a theme at a very high cultural level, even through an educational programme or exhibition. From this viewpoint, to refer to cinema or TV films, to radio programmes or magazine reading as a "parallel education" may be very striking, but boils down to a misnomer. However, an organised series of shows or exhibitions, with a commentary intended to facilitate either the acquisition of structured knowledge about technique, art or science, or alternatively a change in depth of attitudes about work, politics or leisure, could be a form of adult education. Such an operation attempts to endow the subject with the opposite of that "mosaic-like culture" to which Moles rightly refers in connection with the messages generally issued by the mass media.

With regard to methods, adult education requires the use of social action external to the individual and characterised by continuity or repetition, so as to ensure effective learning. The discontinuity and dispersion of uncontrolled messages may, of course, achieve educational results, but they will be random ones.

Where can self-tuition be located? This can be defined as the adult's systematic self-education with the use of various material aids to learning. Its importance is considerable. In the previously quoted survey, among the 61% of adults who had received systematic tuition, 41% had participated in study groups, conferences, courses or correspondence courses, but 38% had applied systematic training programme without relying on any system of educational relationships. They had worked by themselves on a topic of their own choosing, with the instruments they had found for themselves, without the assistance of educational agents. In French social history, the importance of self-tuition as compensation for the absence, or inadequacy of school or university education is well known (see Duveau, Cacérès).

The needs of the self-taught led to the creation of many commercial establishments for adult education. Thus several authors consider self tuition as part of adult education. For them the educational agent is, so to speak, within the learner. This is the standpoint adopted by Johnstone and Rivera, who define adult education as follows: All the activities consciously and systematically organized to acquire new information, knowledge or "skill". This definition covers half of the problem, namely the ultimate ends of adult education which are to stimulate methodical and continuing self-tuition in the face of all present or future changes, but it leaves out the action of society to further this end.

This symbolic societal action represents a cultural intervention of society upon itself. It is an indication of an active society confronted with change; thus society, through the classes, categories and groups which comprise it, endeavours to reduce the cultural laws and inequalities which might prevent the population from gaining mastery over economic, social and personal development.

Finally, it shows that society endeavours to make this cultural development operation most efficient in order to provide the best conditions for voluntary self-tuition. Thus any system of adult education reflects a major requirement of what might be called an educational society. This point strikes me as fundamental.

Thus adult education can be sociologically defined as a cultural development operation of society or of its component groups, consciously aimed at economic, social and personal development, through a continuous or repeated learning process which connects the social subject's culture with cultural kinds and levels best suited to the promotion of this development. Such a definition makes it possible to tackle the three main problems raised by adult education in modern societies.

1) How to promote genuine mutual communication between the creators' and the public's cultural level through a learning process? This conditions the permanent elaboration of cultural democracy mid-way between the esoteric and the mediocre.

2) How to strike a balance between adult education and other means of cultural development, especially in the mass media? Machlup (1963) reckons that in the United States expenditure on entertainment for advertising purposes equals the sum total of the amounts spent on secondary and higher education for teenagers and for adults.

3) How to balance the time spent on entertainment and on voluntary self-tuition, on recreation and on the continuing re-creation of the self, within the cultural development of a society characterised by increase in leisure time and leisure values?

Ends and means

Functions
On the assumption which has just been outlined, the functions of general adult education should first be defined in relation to school and university education. From this angle, it is a way of catching up: it provides a substitute for those who have not been able to reach in the secondary and higher system, the level to which they aspire. It is also a way of effecting change: it caters for those who have completed some studies in a given field and who wish to undergo another course in a different one. It is also a way of receiving in-service training or retraining: it is meant for those who want to supplement or rectify their education which is no longer up to date.

Adult education should also always be defined by direct reference to the evolution of knowledge. Indeed its functions should increasingly and at all levels of instruction relate to the trend towards the constant renewal of knowledge, particularly in connection with labour requirements; otherwise much waste of time, money and energy will follow for society and for the individual. When creative imagination and scientific accuracy are displayed in reviewing the approach, the content and the means of adult education for catching up or retraining, they are not only capable of efficacy, but also of providing an innovatory cultural pattern which may be useful for the reform of the educational system itself, in a fast–moving society where culture is being continuously reassessed.

Finally, as has been said above, an essential function of continuing education is to help the whole population remain capable of playing a part in the cultural development of society.

The public
A major problem arises: it is the individuals with the highest educational attainments who make most use of the adult education network. In France, where the working class make up about one-third of the active population, it is unusual to find more than 5% of them among those involved in adult education. In the United States while 30% of the active population are working class (NORC 1963), only 20% of them engage in adult education in the

widest sense, including cookery, gardening and bridge classes. This rule applies even in socialist countries, despite the scope and quality of some working class achievements.

Yet, despite "social romanticism" (in Bourdieu's terms) about popular education and consequent illusions about its ability to replace the school, the history of this education shows that in the past it has ensured the promotion of individuals deprived of grammar school and university training. No educational system has satisfactorily solved the problem of giving to socially and intellectually marginal individuals in an advanced industrial society the best means of access to highbrow culture.

Programme

The problems of work are dominant in adult education. At Annecy, 67% of the heads of household who systematically seek information during leisure time do so on scientific and technical subjects, and 60% on topics connected with their occupation. In the United States, about 33% of those who register for an adult education course (either to study alone or in a group), i.e. 9,020,000 people, are studying subjects directly connected with their job (Johnstone and Rivera, 1965). Both surveys also point to the importance of practical interests relevant to family life (cookery, nursing, sewing, decorating, gardening, child care, etc.). In the United States 3,440,000 people enrol for these activities. On the other hand, studies relating to religious and ethnic problems only take fourteenth place at Annecy and only attract 3,820,000 people in the United States.

The low level of interest in political and economic problems is equally striking: third place at Annecy, 1,080,000 people involved in the United States.

However, if all adult education courses aimed at the individual as an end in himself, either for entertainment or for personal development (physical training, speed reading) are considered together, they include seven million people, i.e. seven times as many. The question asked at Annecy makes it impossible to draw any parallels, but the trend seems to be the same. This has also been observed in the socialist societies which have reached a more advanced stage of development (Strumilin, 1964).

This evolution raises an important problem. For the first time, advanced industrial societies have to programme studies for a growing number of adults who "volunteer" to devote part of their leisure time to a systematic effort of intellectual and social apprenticeship. There is a conflict between the values of pleasure and of effort, between those of leisure and of basic commitment to the creation and the organisation of the family and the political community. How can adult education in advanced industrial societies spread the awareness of world social problems in a society where growing and widespread wealth is accompanied by a valorisation of enjoyment, both of money and time? Riesman's question "Abundance for what?" (Riesman, 1954), is echoed by Liveright's "Adult education for what?" (Liveright, 1968).

From adult to continuing education

Cultural obsolescence occurs so quickly in the new society, despite educational reforms, and adult education seems so fragile unless it is linked with the schooling of children, that the concept of continuing education gradually gained ground in the fifties on both sides of the Atlantic. A longer period of compulsory school attendance would not suffice, despite educational reform, to ensure the population's cultural development in the new society; an expanded adult education, regardless of improvements, would be equally inadequate, unless the very foundations of the educational system were changed. Hence the idea to spread a new kind of education over a lifetime rather than to merely lengthen schooling, and to seek for each individual, each milieu, each subject, the period best suited to systematic learning, whether compulsory, optional or voluntary. Each advanced society seeks new coherent and graded systems of pre-training, in-service training or re-training for children, youngsters and adults. This is called continuing education. Although longer school attendance is currently popular, the end of the present school and university system may be in sight. This demise may be more clearly announced by the recent student and pupil revolts throughout the world than many other widely desired outcomes.

In a society where innovatory knowledge is increasingly required at work and in all daily activities, the need for self-tuition grows and will be more keenly felt at all ages, despite unfavourable socio-cultural conditions.

Citizens are compelled by the new role performed by experts and technocrats to continuously increase their knowledge in order not to be forgotten, manipulated and alienated. Under these conditions, a renewal of tomorrow's school and university system may be initiated by the first types of adult education, centering on individual *freedom of choice* in new situations. In the past, pedagogical renewal started in nursery schools, in the future, it may start in adult education. School and university education would then gradually be reduced to a basic instruction preparatory to the other education, received throughout life. The point would not only be learning how to learn, but turning continuing education into a need, making it second nature, basing a life style on it and, to this end, reorganising the structure of society to fit this target. In a society better adapted to the requirements of human development, it may become possible to provide at any time programmed instruction on request. Recent discoveries (electro-video-recording) announce the time when educational tapes may be used with ordinary TV sets, like mini-cassettes are with tape-recorders.

Thus new resources may be put at the disposal of the 60% who have felt the urge to study again in later life. Could it be the start of an educational revolution which would make the home a center of continuing education, as was the case for two years during the Teveq (Educational Television of Quebec, 1967–69) experiment, when the conventional school only provided backing on Saturday? The cultural functions of the family, of the mass media and of the educational system, as well as the networks of relationships within them would be deeply altered.

Beyond the decline of the "Gutenberg galaxy" and the rise of the "Marconi galaxy", it becomes conceivable in a mass society that culture as such fertilised by learning culture, will be continuously created and recreated. The emergence of this continuing education system, which society needs, implies changes in outlook and structure. Such changes will probably take a very long time, they may be uncertain and dramatic. They are an aspect of the cultural revolution we are facing in our attempt to confront the still obscure problems raised by an emerging new society.

V.3. Towards an Active Sociology: Social Determinants, Forecasting, Decision-Making

I have endeavoured to show the need for cultural planning and for adopting the new viewpoints required for its formulation. These viewpoints should apply to the study of present and future cultural needs, to the choice of development criteria, to the determination of targets and to the selection of means.

I have tried to stress that their adoption implies a complete change in outlook among the various participants in cultural planning; the researcher, the administrator, the politician and the population as a whole.

Finally, I have given the example of continuing education as an incentive to the whole population's active participation in cultural planning.

I shall now attempt to outline the principles of an active sociology, which provide a *methodological* framework where, in my view, all the observations made above fit.

A new type of sociology is required by the problems of cultural development, action and planning. Although I am aware of this fact, I find it difficult, as I have already said, to conceive of such a sociology and to apply it. I query this uncomfortable situation in which sociological work makes slow progress. Having participated in the foundation of a national movement for popular education in 1945, I have had little success in integrating its main trends with an empirical research capable of changing its membership's outlook and ways of acting. Their decisions have seldom been considered as assumptions about probable outcomes.

Even the assessment of past results never managed to increase rationality in future action. Moreover, it is equally difficult to integrate the problems of action with research as it is to integrate research results with action, even when those responsible for both share the same general ideas and work in cooperation. A later experience was no more conclusive. Having accepted to work as a sociologist with a group of economists convened by Massé to study action, (1965) I was struck by the need for outlining the dynamics of socio-cultural development and for confronting them with the dynamics of socio-economic development, but also by the dearth of pertinent sociological data. Theoretical studies are not very useful and current empirical research yields little relevant information to reduce future uncertainty and thus to enable the taking of calculated risks. Gruson writes "economic analysis guided by the requirements of action is constantly beset by sociological problems which it is unable to tackle." It should at least attempt to put them clearly so that the sociologist, in turn, lets his research be guided. Is it merely a matter of letting research be guided? (Gruson, 1968).

In a sort of sociological confession, Touraine confronted similar problems to those I have raised (Touraine, 1965). "Most of those who undertook the study of sociology a few years after the war, as I did, have been dominated rather than guided by a double situation: a scientific dependence on American sociology which brought us not only research techniques, but new ways of thought, and participation in the hopes, the disappointments and the crises of French society, which, in the wake of the Liberation, was more concerned with its own transformation than with its workings. No sociologist of my vintage can claim to have overcome this contradiction." I have experienced the same malaise. However, when Touraine refers to the need for sociological thought to reach the level of the great social theories of the past, I wonder whether the sociology of action possesses the necessary methods to do so.

A new "positive" sociology is needed. Obviously it would not be positive in the sense of adhering to the scientific thesis of neo-positivism; the reverse will be shown to be true. It is positive in that it needs to study all the relationships involved in a system of action geared to changing a situation A into B, considered by a social subject to be preferable by reference to a criterion of development C. If sociology is confined to the study of the determination whereby a social fact is shaped like a thing, it is not relevant to the problem raised here. Indeed, it considers the human intervention opposing these blind forces as a negligible or exogenous variable. Nor is it relevant if, within this general perspective, it merely studies the dysfunctional gap between an actual situation and an ideal one, within a system assumed to be steady. For the system itself may be changed by innovatory action (Touraine, 1965). Therefore, the conditions in which a social subject faces social determination and the process whereby a voluntary change is affected become objects of knowledge. Sociology will be relevant to the problem I have outlined if it focuses on a social subject treated as an active being, and not on a social fact treated as a thing. Its main object will be the social subject, both *guided* by a plan for a possible intervention in a probable situation in relation to desirable criteria and also *determined* by all the social determinants which either directly or indirectly play the part of inputs or constraints on this project, and by *no others*. Indeed, in each situation, the number and intensity of relevant variables, positively or negatively linked with the subject's plan, do not remain constant. They always make up a "concrete whole", or rather, so to speak, a concrete sub-set, but its size and its content vary with the system of action considered. Thus, for each problem of intervention which he investigates, the sociologist will attempt to list all relevant variables in order to treat it as a system and, if possible, as an ideal type.

This might seem reminiscent of Comte's famous eulogy of the positive spirit, but the parallel would be misleading. For he allocated the need to entrust the positive scientists with the theoretical work of "social re-organization". In an empirical sociology which completely separates the formulation of a hypothesis from its corroboration, as it does analysis from application, no confusion may be allowed between the sociologist who observes and the man of action who makes decisions. The sociologist does not decide – he merely observes a system of action shaped by a social subject. In turn, he analyses this system from the inside (analysis of the subject's plans) and from the outside (analysis of results, of their implementation). He uses the indicative, or the conditional, never the imperative. His observations can never yield any conclusions unless they are mediated through a system of explicit or implicit values. The sociologist will reason in the following way:

1) If the preference criteria of a given social subject are adopted as a vantage point.

2) If such and such resources and constraints are available for the social subject's intervention in a situation.

3) Taking into account the probable results of the interaction between a possible system comprising $A_1 A_2 \ldots A_n$ interventions, and probable situations $S_1 S_2 \ldots S_n$.

4) From among all possible systems of intervention, $I_1 I_2 \ldots I_n$, it is then e.g. I_2 which is most likely to yield the result best suited to the preference criterion of the social subject.

The concepts of *future uncertainty* and of its probabilistic reduction could neither be included in Comte's positive sociology nor in Marx's dialectical sociology. Comte did not grasp what Laplace's probabilistic thought could contribute to sociology, while Marx never mentioned it at all. The sciences of rational forecasting and decision-making were not yet developed at the time. Their growth among the social sciences is merely some twenty-five years old. Yet they are basic to my forecasting sociology, underpinned by hypotheses about action. While it relies on Marxist, positivistic or other assumptions, depending on the requirements of the studies situation, my sociological method fits into the historico-empirical frame of reference of post-1920 modern sociology but is mainly based on the result contributions of decision-making and forecasting theory. I suggest that this sociology of forecasting and decision-making be called *active sociology*.

It may consist in basic research if it primarily follows the internal laws regulating the development of knowledge. It may consist in applied research if it is predominantly subordinated to the external requirements of progress in action. In active research the two imperatives may both apply, without merging. Indeed they seldom tally with regard to the degree of accuracy expected from research results and to the duration of the research work.

Thus, it is neither its "fundamental" nor its "applied" characteristics which distinguish active sociology, but the problems it selects and the system of relevant variables it devises, from the viewpoint of a social subject. Linguists call active the mode which indicates that the subject undertakes the action rather than undergoes it (passive mode). Active sociology mainly studies the possible action of the subject on the situation by which he is determined. Its field is a sub-set of variables referring to a *system of action* and its relationships of relative dependence on, or independence from, the set of other variables making up the global situation.

Active sociology thus seeks, for a given situation and time, to foresee the probable results of interaction between probable determinants and the possible interventions of a social subject guided by the development criteria of a social situation which, in turn, determines him.

Any active sociology begins by selecting and ordering all relevant positive or negative elements in a research area. Relevance is defined by the choice of desirable and possible criteria for the given social subject's intervention on a probable process of short or long term evolution in a situation. It is possible, by defining the area in advance, to secure the historical and empirical data most pertinent to the problems of rational decision-making.

At this initial stage, the basic procedure of active sociology does not differ from that of operational research. At a more advanced stage of the subject matter, the initially selected information might provide for an operational research entirely devised from what Chernoff calls "betterment criteria" (Lasswell, 1963).

However, in operational research, the initial situation is considered as known, and so are the desired targets for its transformation. Such is not the case in active sociology. The conditions and processes of change for a given period must be investigated. The initial situation and the "ranges" of probable change in the following period are then defined. This is not a conventional historical study, but an attempt to choose, from among all the processes of change those which correspond to such explicit developmental criteria and to assess the limits of their likely short or long term extension, in connection with one or several possible interventions in the immediate or more remote future. "Known factors are only used by the mind as raw material for the assessment of the future" (Lasswell, 1963). Observations as well as surmising are involved in the study of these past and future processes, hence the possibility of simulation. Such processes roughly correspond to what Lasswell calls "development constructs" (de Jouvenel, 1964). Active research at this level rests on an analysis of a *double conditional probability*. Future uncertainty is to be reduced by a double prognosis about the probability a) of a situation, and b) of the results yielded by the interaction between an intervention and this situation.

Active sociology may apply to all levels of actual or potential action; by reference to a given criterion, it will be centered on needs, targets, means (resources and constraints), actual or probable results. For instance in my research on the cultural development of a town (Annecy), I have mainly concentrated on studying the possible objectives of cultural plans (kinds or levels aimed at) and of social plans (numbers and categories of population), as well as their implications.

In active research, statistical data is mainly used to build development models including both teleological (aims) and instrumental (means) variables. The purpose is neither to replace the analysis of the global society's social framework nor to continue prophetic thinking about the "laws" of evolution: e.g. Comte's "law" of three stages, Marx's "law" of the emergence of socialism from capitalism, Rostow's "law" of the dispelling of social conflicts by mass consumption. The sociology of decision-making does not attempt to provide a new general theory of historical praxis. More modestly, it merely endeavours to assess the likely success of fragmentary development models for a social unit, in a situation and a period defined in relation to a probable change, involving possible interventions guided by the desideratum of a given social subject.

1. Thus this sociology is *subject oriented*. It is centered on a social subject (organization, class, social category), which it does not consider as a "thing". The subject is active in the field of action considered, it supports the centres of decision-making by development agents etc. Its involvement in the field of research is desirable, up to a point.

2. This sociology is *relativistic:* it is clearly defined by reference to development criteria, resulting both from the value system selected by the social subject and from the determining situation. Hence a double source of research problems. On this basis the researcher can, with the man of action's critical cooperation, construct a coherent set of research hypotheses corresponding to all the operations actually taking place in the sphere of action: realization of needs, choice of targets, quest for means, forecasting of situations and of their interaction with results. This coordinated set of hypotheses will lead to the selection of the concepts, dimensions and indicators required to process the relevant variables. The hypothesis becomes a hypothetical synthesis. It becomes a coherent set of relationships required by the system of action and susceptible of investigation. Touraine has aptly shown that in the

sociology of action the major problem consists in the relationship between the historical subject's normative leanings and the determinating factors inherent in his situation. What value will the observer ascribe to this relationship with values, which is a major component of the historical subject's social dynamics? Touraine rightly attacks philosophies of history and their illusory confusions between the subjective and the objective, the desirable and the probable. However, to undertake the study of a social subject as fighter and as creator, entails adopting a viewpoint. The sociology of action must be relativistic.

3. Lastly, this is a *forecasting* sociology. Touraine refers to the social movements which challenge the dominant norms of the economic, social, political or cultural system, or are preparing to do so... Yet how can their chances of success or failure in the short or long term future be assessed? This problem is crucial. The sociologist cannot merely describe the social subject's innovations; he must stand back and, taking account of changing situations, resources and constraints, make a *forecast* about them, after having attempted to both observe and explain. From the creator's point of view, the past is the sphere of powerlessness. The die is cast. It is only in the future, either short or long term, that intervention is possible. Among today's social movements, how can one distinguish those whose trends are highly likely or unlikely to be implemented tomorrow? The researcher is bound to think in probabilistic terms, if a scientific approach is not to become impossible (Bourdieu and Reynaud). Yet Touraine has not made a single attempt to think about the future of social movements in such terms. When he alludes to it, he displays an enduring social romanticism whereby the historical subject proceeds in the future as if that very future could not be an object of knowledge. To my mind, this attitude is already superseded. Today's science begins to explore a new area: the future or rather a certain future. I shall clarify this point and shall not shrink from repetition in an attempt at clarity about an approach which is unfamiliar to the dominant school of sociology.

V.4. Forecasting, Decision-making. The Comparative Method

In sociological circles, serious objections, which are not only methodological, but also epistemological and even ethical, are levelled at the notion of a forecasting sociology. Some prefer to limit sociology to the study of present day issues, fearing that a probabilistic study of problems in becoming might prove an opportunity for shelving the former. Others prefer to confine themselves to a purely negative critical sociology, lest a sociology concerned with the probable evolution of contemporary society be bound by a conservative ideology. Yet others prefer to focus on the mental picture of an ideal society, whose prerequisites are never the subject of a probabilistic study, and to derive from it a frame of reference for a static analysis of society.

Finally other sociologists merely study change as it occurs, since to them the probabilistic analysis of future trends and of the results possible interventions may yield, pertain to the sphere of action rather than to sociology.

These objections represent major obstacles to the development of forecasting sociology. The analyses required to refute them would go beyond the scope of the present study. I shall outline instead the main epistemological and methodological hypotheses which underpin my comparative study of seven advanced industrial and post-industrial societies.

V.4.1. Is sociological forecasting possible?

What is meant by sociological forecasting must be clarified first. It is not imagining a future world, as Huxley or Orwell imagined an industrial or post-industrial society. This approach to the future is the artist's means of expressing his own joys or, more frequently, his own fears, through the medium of fiction. We have no way of distinguishing between the subjective and the objective, between what is probable and what is either desired or feared.

Nor is forecasting to be confused with utopia, the product of philosophical thought on "the ideal state".

It is not prophecy either. When Victor Hugo foresees the Universal Republic of the future, he may be creating one of the great inspirational myths which mankind strives for despite all vicissitudes and catastrophes, but his is not a forecast, it is the product of mystical thinking.

Forecasting is a scientific approach with a more modest objective, it does not embrace all it would be desirable to foresee, but only a limited set of events whose occurrence can be probabilistically assessed.

It is made specific by reasoning based on the systematic observation of invariants in analogical models.[48] Hence forecasting reasoning would be impossible without:

a) the choice of analogical models related to probable future models, since the direct observation of the future is obviously impossible.

b) the search for invariants within analogical models. It is those invariants which will permit forecasting. If they don't exist, no forecasting is possible.

More accurately, forecasting reasoning based on invariants in analogical models rests on a double hypothesis:

a) The relationship between the explicandum e.g. (leisure X) and the explicans (post-industrial characteristics, Y,Z) is held to be constant in analogical models, whatever the values of Y or Z; (Y) corresponds to the variables on which a given social subject may act and (Z) corresponds to those which determine him without him being able to have any influence.

$X = F(Y, Z)$

b) This relationship will remain constant between X and Y,Z, regardless of the other variables (e) in the probable models of the future situation. The impact of other variables (e) is held to be negligible.

It is only within these limits and under these *conditions* that forecasting in sociology, as in economics, becomes possible. Indeed scientific forecasting can never aim at certainty. It merely attempts to minimise uncertainty by outlining conditional probabilities. It follows a path, that of probabilistic science (Matalon, 1967; Bell, 1960) which is neither reducible to the knowledge of the determined nor to the ignorance of randomness.

V.4.2. What are the degrees of forecasting?

The sociologist who undertakes forecasting observation and reasoning is often discouraged because he bears in mind the quantitative form of forecasting in econometrics. In that science, amounts are often measurable and are part of models which are often extremely simplified. In sociology, measurable quantities are often less important than other factors and the complexity of socio-cultured facts prohibits oversimplified models which would be nonsensical. However, forecasting differs from measuring and corresponds to amounts whose precision varies. Moreover, it covers more or less definite periods of time. In some cases, forecasting may yield both a date and a quantity, e.g., taking account of the trend of cinema attendance in France over the last five years and explanatory factors (increase in TV viewing etc.) and, if a given hypothesis is made about the probable evolution of these factors and possible interventions on them during the next three years, according to the experience of countries which have experienced a cinema crisis before (U.S.A., Canada), one may foresee a decrease or an increase of $X\%$ in attendance.

However, one should not expect sociological forecasting to be always quantified and dated. Probability does not require measurement. A forecast may be approximately dated (e.g. a range between 1970 and 1975) or undated. When it is impossible to specify dates, forecasting may be limited to the indication that change will probably occur in a given direction rather than in another, within an indeterminate future. Whether dated or undated, a forecast may be expressed either as a measurement (e.g. a percentage) or as a sequence (e.g. this before that) or as an attribute (e.g. this or that). Thus, a forecasting problem may be given at least six alternative replies depending on the type of forecast.

	Measurement	Sequence	Attribute
Dated	1	2	3
Undated	4	5	6

V.4.3. What are the sociological methods available for forecasting?

This is tantamount to asking: among sociological methods of observation, which are those whereby analogical models can be discovered and invariants needed for forecasting found? In the light of recent attempts at forecasting sociology, these methods may be roughly assigned to three categories, depending on the type of information on which forecasting reasoning rests.

a) Conditional extrapolation (or temporal elasticity).

b) The comparative observation of behaviour patterns in reference categories corresponding to the wishes or projects of members in groups (social elasticity).

c) The comparative study[49] in a contemporary society of phenomena expected in a future society (spatial elasticity). My comments will be mainly devoted to this approach, because an on-going comparative study on changing leisure patterns in seven advanced industrial societies led me to put greater stress on this method.

The application of the comparative method to forecasting is fairly common in economics. The attraction of this method largely accounts for the interest in the American economy displayed by all analysts of economic development. Many missions from industrial societies based on private ownership have gone to the United States to carry out comparative studies. In industrial societies based on public ownership, comparative studies of the American economy are becoming more and more frequent. Socialist economists implicitly accept the value for forecasting purposes of American production and consumption in sectors where the target they assigned themselves in the sixties was to catch up with the United States within the next ten or twenty years.

In sociology, the situation is not the same. It is rare for the comparative method to be associated, at least explicitly, with forecasting. In the past, the forerunners or founders of scientific sociology, Montesquieu, de Toqueville, Durkheim or Marx, often relied on comparisons with foreign countries to raise the general problems linked with the quest for the ideal society, for the best political system or for the fairest economic organization. The comparative method was bound with the illustration of philosophical thought rather than with the probabilistic checking of forecasts. Durkheim is known to have considered this method as the only possible one in sociology (Durkheim, 1927), but never contemplated applying it to forecasting. Comte explicitly assigned to sociology the task of foreseeing, in addition to observing and explaining. But he failed to grasp the contribution which the probability calculus advocated by Laplace could make to forecasting thought in sociology, and indeed condemned it on sociological grounds.

We have made little progress until now. In 1960, assessing the new trends of the comparative method in anthropology since Tylor. Within pointed to the regression of comparisons between the cultures of entire societies and the progress of comparisons between more limited and better sampled cultural areas in which systematic observation is guided by a few well defined assumptions whose corroboration is sought in several different contexts. However, he does not mention any trend towards forecasting (Lindzey, 1968).

After a long period during which national or local surveys on limited samples were almost totally dominant in quantitative research, the sociology of the sixties re-introduced the use of the comparative method. Yet, to my knowledge, no round-table addressed itself to the problem of applying the comparative method to sociological forecasting before 1972.[50]

I intend to show that the use of the comparative method is more and more necessary in relation to the new problems already faced by sociology and which will become more numerous (see Seventh Congress of the International Sociological Association at Varna in 1970: Report on "Sociology, forecasting and planning"). I also mean to show that this use will become increasingly possible due to the general progress of forecasting thought in analogical models originating from cybernetics and of the probabilistic methods generated by them (Bross, 1961). It is in this spirit that I undertook a forecasting study of leisure patterns by attempting to apply the comparative method. I have endeavoured to outline a forecast of the problems raised by the social and cultural uncertainties surrounding the leisure of men and women at the time when a technological society moves from the industrial to the post-industrial stage. This study covers the United States, French-speaking Canada, Quebec, Sweden, Romance Switzerland, France, West Germany and Czechoslovakia. It is progressing slowly, both because financial resources are slow to secure ... and because I am forced to tackle new epistemological and methodological problems as I go along. The first phase of this group work has prompted the following preliminary thoughts.

a) How can the comparative method be used to overcome the limitations of other methods?

b) What are the specific characteristics of the comparative method which result in maximum relevance to forecasting thought?

V.4.4. The comparative method and other methods of sociological forecasting.

I shall attempt to show how the observation of elasticity may be used as a method for overcoming the limitations inherent in each of the other methods, namely the observation of temporal elasticity and that of social elasticity (the various concepts of elasticity being borrowed from a joint study with the economist Piatier).

a) Observation of temporal elasticity (or conditional extrapolation)

This forecasting method is well known in economics. Though its past has often been disappointing (in that it failed to forecast crises), its techniques have been perfected since. It is currently relied on to tackle not only short, but long-term forecasting problems. It rests on the hypothesis that, even in the case of revolutionary innovation, change is never wholly discontinuous. This has often been corroborated. The "voluntaristic" revolutionaries who disregard it get or may get results wholly inimical to their intentions. In situations where no historical breaks occur (though change is rapid), the assumption whereby the future is always, up to a point and for a time, a continuation of the past, is in the main acceptable. This kind of situation has been predominant until now in the first post-industrial societies, despite some recurrent social upheavals (student revolts, black power etc. . . .). Forecasting thought has also made considerable progress for the last few years in the technical sphere where discoveries may have repercussions, often difficult to foresee, on social outlooks and relationships. Models have thus been discovered and perfected, allowing conditional extrapolation to be used with fewer risks of error than in the past (Jantsch, 1968).

This method is suited to many social problems, closely related to economic phenomena, e.g. the growth rate of skiing holidays and even their social class distribution in the next ten or twenty years, as a function of some likely hypotheses (Dumazedier, 1968/9). However, it has obvious limitations, since it is impossible to foresee whether, after twenty years, a new technical discovery which may not yet have been glimpsed in research laboratories, will not upset one's present forecasts by its economic and social implications (Jantsch, 1968; de Jouvenel, 1964). Moreover, the method of conditional extrapolation is often incapable of forecasting saturation points or reversed trends (e.g. the onset of the rush to the suburbs after the trend towards city dwelling in the United States at the beginning of the 20th century).

It is in such cases that extrapolation must be supplemented by the comparative method. Observations in space may rectify observations made over time. Indeed, new factors likely to emerge in the future of society (B), may already be present in a society (A) whose economic and social evolution is more advanced in some respects than $(B$'s$)$. Their effects may be observed at present and may be hypothesized to occur in society (B), when the new factors themselves have appeared. The possible resistance of historical specificities to change must of course be assessed, but this method frees forecasting thought from the "historical illusion" increasingly generated by a fast changing society. Despite the mistakes it has constantly prompted in the last twenty years in European, African, Asian or Latin-American societies confronted with the models generated by post-industrial America, the illustion dies hard. It consists in the too easy belief that cultural traditions, national character etc. ... would provide sufficient obstacles to the diffusion of the so-called "American" models. Yet, from year to year, despite countless hostile statements, mores, ideas and tastes, born in the post-industrial context of the United States, have been seen to spread in various circles of different societies as production, consumption, urbanisation, industrialisation, education, communication and/or trade grew in the respective countries. Thus tomorrow's history may, under some conditions, be deduced not from yesterday's, but from the contemporary history of another society. If forecasting history existed, as Marc Bloch wished, it would not be able to forego the use of the comparative method.

b) Observation of social elasticity

A different method is used in forecasting, which consists in observing an analogical model in the behaviour patterns of reference categories (social elasticity). These are known to often correspond to the projects or wishes of membership groups. This relationship between the behaviour patterns of the former and the projects of the latter may be hypothesized as comparatively constant, at least over a given period. When a change occurs in the environment (better living conditions, higher educational levels), the behaviour patterns of membership categories will be most likely to be analogous to the present patterns of those whose norms guided their conduct. Those who "prepare for the future" have often been misled by their ignorance of such facts. Thus in industrial society, many intellectuals were mistaken in expressing the belief that the workers would create an original culture, a "working class culture" with living conditions, longer leisure time, improved education etc. Reality turned out to be quite different, both under socialism (Filipcova, 1966) and under capitalism (Kaes, 1962). In France, a national survey on a big sample drawn from various kinds of enterprises throughout the country has clearly shown that the workers' cultural frame of reference was not an ideal culture, specific to their background, but the culture of those whom the wider society considers as most cultured. The idea of a distinct working class culture is rejected by 80% of respondents (Kaes, 1962), although the persistance of a sub-culture among manual workers is confirmed by recent surveys (Dumazedier and Ripert, 1966; Hoggart, 1958; Goldthorpe, 1969).

Yet this method has limitations which must be fully known. To what extent will what one might call social imitation affect the formation of future behaviour patterns? How will the cultural values and social norms specific to an environment resist the adoption of new values and norms? How will the two sets combine? Such unknowns cannot be explored by the method of reference groups.

The comparative method can again give invaluable assistance. Indeed it enables one to observe today and *elsewhere* the evolution undergone by a subculture similar to that which one is attempted to forecast here for tomorrow. Obviously in any given industrial society, the working class has norms which cannot be wholly identified with those of its counterparts in more advanced industrial societies, such as the United States, Sweden, English-and French–speaking Canada, but empirical sociology has shown e.g. that its relationships with other social classes have many similar characteristics (Wilensky, 1964). Moreover, many common specific characteristics have been identified once the material and cultural conditions of post-industrial society emerged. How have these relationships and norms of the working class changed in relation to the norms of other classes in society? Owing to such observations on change in society (A), the simple comparison between the behaviour patterns of reference categories and the projects of membership categories in society (B), to which forecasting thought is applied, become less akin to mere conjecture.

V.4.5. Characteristics of the method of comparative spatial elasticity as applied to forecasting.

A knowledge of the most advanced post industrial society, i.e. of *American society* (Riesman, 1950; Lipset, 1963; Marcuse, 1964) strikes me as being a prerequisite for the study of the social and cultural problems accompanying the transition from industrial to post-industrial stage. Such a choice does not imply preference for any form of ownership either of the means of production or of distribution. Nor does it imply any positive or negative feeling towards the so-called "American civilisation," as it has been somewhat vaguely called. It is neither a political nor an ethical choice, but a scientific necessity. I quite understand the repulsion towards this kind of study experienced by many researchers, e.g. South Americans, who are aware of their country's dependent position in the context of a certain Yankee economic and political imperialism.

I understand that the same attitude may be exhibited by many researchers in Quebec, where in some key industries up to 90% of the capital is owned by the giant neighbour and where economic, social and cultural life is still under the burdensome influence of Anglo-Canadian tutelage. Similarly, research workers from socialist industrial societies find it easier to issue blanket condemnations of "American capitalism" than to objectively investigate the first problems of post-industrial society in the light of the American capitalist experiment. Yet such approaches to the questions I have raised seem detrimental to scientific knowledge. They leave out the main area of post-industrial experience. They involve the risk of formulating future problems in abstract terms or, even worse, of borrowing from the conceptual frameworks of yesterday's society analytical tools ill-suited to understanding a society in the making. They may shackle the sociological imagination with outdated ideologies. Indeed it is primarily the scientific observation of post-industrial characteristics in American society which gives the best chances of locating the true problems raised by the advent of mass production, distribution and consumption connected with the new problems of social relationships and cultural values through mass organisations or techno-bureaucracies and through the symbolic systems of mass education, leisure, information and culture. All those who are engaged in comparative studies of the social and cultural uncertainties surrounding mass leisure in post-industrial society agree on this premise, whether their general perspective is a liberal or a socialist one. This analysis of post-industrial American society is to them no less indispensible as a prerequisite for the knowledge of future capitalist or socialist post-industrial societies, than that of the first industrial society, the British, was to Marx and Engels for studying the problems of industrialization and socialism.

However, such an analysis of American society is full of snares. The subject is distorted by emotional incoherence. It is easy enough to generalize about "American": essays, novels, films etc. are much more common than scientific studies. What does this conglomeration of signs called "America" mean and what does each of its components mean? At some stages in the development of a science, we know that general ideas may be positive, help formulate problems and even sometimes highlight a scientific problem. At other stages, these ideas become an obstacle to the growth of scientific knowledge (Bachelard, 1957). But I feel that in the second half of the 20th century, the proliferation of general outlines, of brilliant, but fragmentary or unclear, judgements on "America", hinder the progress of the historico-empirical comparative sociology needed to formulate and to corroborate a body of hypotheses on the characteristics of post-industrial society. The initial task consists therefore in rejecting all these general and abstract representations prior to attempting an analysis of the concrete components which make up "America". This is by no means easy. It entails at least two operations:

a) *To demarcate* from each other coherent sub-sets corresponding either to a specific cultural tradition, or to a system of economic organization, or to a system of characteristics pertaining to post-industrial society etc.

b) To analyse the degree of mutual *interdependence* characterizing these sub-sets of homogeneous elements. It may then prove possible perhaps to treat such sub-sets as complex variables, more or less clearly demarcated from others. At the end of the research project, the assertion that a sub-set named "characteristics of post-industrial society" exists, may be corroborated.

The first systematic observations on post-industrial society have been attempted by American researchers studying the United States and virtually excluding other societies from their analyses. Hence their general conclusions are open to doubt. Their studies may suffer from a somewhat socially and ideologically ethnocentric approach, whereby the American capitalist solution to the problems of post-industrial society often appears as *the* solution which will, sooner or later, prevail in any society. This is a possible bias of which the researcher himself may be unaware.

For example, let us consider one of the best studies devoted to the socio-culture implications of the new society, Riesman's *The Lonely Crowd*.

I have already outlined my views on this book, published in *1948;* I admire its penetrating observations, even when they are unsystematic, and its intuitive insights, even when they have not been given the form of hypotheses amenable to corroboration (Dumazedier, 1965).

The main thesis, which has been quoted earlier, is that mankind has experienced two genuine revolutions: one put an end to traditional society and gave birth, after two centuries, to industrial society while the other is occurring under our very eyes, primarily in the United States, and will give birth to the post-industrial society. According to Riesman the most far-reaching social and cultural changes are generated, in actual life, by mass consumption and mass leisure. In his view the same changes may be foreseen in all types of future post-industrial society. Yet can the questions arising from the American experience of the forties be a basis for generalisations?

a) Will the function and the structure of mass leisure consumption be similar to the patterns characteristic of the early American post-industrial stage?

b) Can the interaction between, on the one hand, these post-industrial patterns and, on the other, national traditions, ownership of the means of production, and educational systems (including continuing education), be held to be insignificant?

To analyse the situation of the United States alone does not seem to offer adequate answers to these questions. Which method would yield the best results? In my view, American society ought to be compared with others which have reached at least in part, the post-industrial stage or which are about to get there, whilst pertaining to different cultural and social contexts.[51]

From this angle, one society is of great strategic interest, despite the neglect of most American sociologists investigating post-industrial problems: I refer to Canada and especially *Quebec*. Since 1959–60, it has been experiencing a renewal. Initially impelled by a conservative ideology, then bent on catching up, it is increasingly prompted by projects or collective dreams of autonomous development.

After the United States and like English-speaking Canada, it is already confronting some problems of post-industrial society (Bergeron, 1967; Rioux, 1969; Laplante, 1969), despite being economically dependent on the States, despite the issues of biculturalism, despite its economic retardation in relation to Ontario and its internal inequalities (Gaspésie, St. Jerôme etc.).

The structure of its active population and its production level already conform to the post-industrial type. Its per capita income is the third in the world and in 1967 out of one hundred workers, 8.4 are employed in agriculture, 30.3 in industry and the majority i.e. 61.3 in the service sector (as against 40% in France). By observing the Quebec society, one can ascertain how post-industrial characteristics evolve in the context of a French-speaking culture, of North American "Frenchness" (Carisse and Dumazedier); hence the Anglo-Saxon factor characteristic of the United States can be eliminated as far as possible. This (relative) exclusion

199

is made easier by the intensification of the struggle waged by most Montreal and Quebec elites for the economic, cultural and linguistic autonomy of their society.[52]

Another problem arises. How to get rid of American (Anglo-Saxon or French) variables from the investigated area? To this end, the same phenomena should be investigated in a European context. From this viewpoint, I would consider the study of two advanced industrial societies, the *Swedish* and the *Swiss* (both French- and German-speaking) as particularly relevant. I have also included Federal Germany and France; the former because it is the most advanced industrial society in the European Common Market (11% of workers employed in agriculture, 48% in industry, 41% in the services as of 1964), the latter because its economic evolution closely follows that of the Federal Republic within a different cultural context (14% in agriculture, 39.5% in industry and 44% in the services, as of 1968). In these societies, post-industrial characteristics are developing within the framework of European cultures. Are these features analogous or likely to become analogous to those of English or French-speaking America?

It may also be asked whether the common features of post-industrial society in these various countries do not derive from an economic and social structure dominated by capitalist initiative at the levels of production and distribution. Their economic system is undeniably a capitalist one, despite various ratios of privately owned capitalist firms to non-capitalist private sectors (e.g. Swedish cooperatives) and to publicly owned enterprises (about 30% of the national income in French society). How can this variable be abstracted to check whether post-industrial characteristics remain constant? The difficulty is almost insuperable since no post-industrial society exists as yet outside the orbit of capitalism. Yet I thought it might prove useful to study new trends in the sixties in the socialist industrial society most advanced on the dimensions of industrialization, urbanization, education and popular culture: *Czechoslovakia.* It is in that society that the first social and cultural changes announcing the advent of post-industrial characteristics have begun to appear. Russian society has, of course, been able to develop some industrial sectors to reach a high level of efficiency and spectacular results. Yet it is Czechoslovak society which seems to be the socialist society closest to the post-industrial stage (especially if the artificial retardation of productive forces imposed for twenty years by the Comecon discipline, instigated by the USSR is borne in mind). Despite the current crisis of its economy and the straitjacket in which it has been forced, Czechoslovakia achieves the highest per capita levels of all socialist countries both with regard to output and to the structure of the active population. Out of one hundred Czechoslovak workers, 22 are employed in agriculture (as against 30% in the USSR), 46 in industry and 32 in the services (i.e. the highest rate of all socialist industrial societies, except East Germany) (Richta, 1969).

By applying the method of concomittant variations to these various contexts in order to complement or rectify the study of American society, a better knowledge of the specificity pertaining to the general features of post–industrial society and an understanding of its various possible types will be achieved.

V.4.6. How to conduct the comparative observation of those various areas to find out whether invariants enable one to assert:

a) The permanance of variable (x): e.g. cultural and social content of mass leisure and its implications for other occupational, family etc. activities.

b) The constant correlation between this content (x) and the specific characteristics of post-industrial society $(y.z)$.

I shall not attempt to compare global societies. In a first stage I shall not investigate the variations in the socio-cultural implications of post-industrial society in relation to the different systems of ownership of the means of production. I shall merely ascertain whether in these societies common characteristics in the evolution of the leisure variable (x) may exist in connection with common characteristics in the evolution of post-industrial variables, including those on which the social subject can have an impact (y) and those on which he can have none, but which affect him (z).

This approach will be vindicated if three hypotheses can be corroborated in turn.

Hypothesis A:

These two intercorrelated sub-sets of variables (x and y,z) are relatively independent from the other variables specific to each type of society (culture, economic and political system). They would make up a set quasi-independent from the rest of society. It is this set common to the most advanced industrial societies which might be called post-industrial variables. I must begin by corroborating the hypothesis of quasi-independence which recalls the so-called quasi-closed systems of analogical models in cybernetics. This initial check implies the exclusion of two comparative approaches:

a) That which arbitrarily links one feature with another without ascertaining how likely this connection is, as against other possible ones in the same or in different contexts. For instance a poet and a social prophet like MacLuhan posits a "causal" relationship between some features of the mass media and other pairs of features characterising the societies of the "electronic" age. This anomaly in MacLuhan's scientific thought in no way detracts from the interest afforded by his insights into the mass media, some of which may serve as original assumptions for researchers to study. However, such analytical unproven connections cannot serve as evidence (MacLuhan, 1964: Cazeneuve, 1970).

b) The opposition attitude must also be rejected. It consists in a refusal to distinguish sub-sets within a "whole", whose structure is considered as specific and distinct from the sum of its parts. I do not deny that this may be an interesting point of view, but everything depends on the problem raised. To deal with mine, I need to empirically check the degree to which a sub-set of relevant (post-industrial) variables is dependent on, or independent from the set constituted by each society and to establish intercorrelations (x and y,z) within this sub-set of relevant variables. The a priori holistic attitude is not suited to my comparative work which must ascertain whether the relationships making up a structure exist or not.[53]

Hypothesis B:

If the former hypothesis about quasi-independent relevant sub-sets is corroborated, it is useful to formulate a second assumption about the evolution of these sub-sets: given variables x, y, z, characteristic of today's more advanced society (A), how have these variables evolved? What has the evolutionary process from X_o to X_1 been and what were its dynamics: $Y_o Z_o \ldots Y_1 Z_1$? Did variable X_o in society (A) have, in its time a value similar to that of variable X_o which can be observed today in a society moving towards the post-industrial stage (society B)? If this is the case, hypotheses might be made about process $X_o \ldots X$ on the basis of process $x_o \ldots x$ and about the dynamics $Y_o, Z_o \ldots Y_1 - Z_1$ (Society B) on the basis of the already known dynamics $Y_o - Z_o \ldots y_1\ z_1$ (in society A). In other words, it is advisable to associate the historical and the comparative methods: thus the study of contemporary differences between two societies, A (more advanced) and B (less advanced), should be supplemented by the study of the evolution undergone by these differences, through the investigation of the more advanced society's (A's) past.

Hypothesis C:
The study of an advanced society (A) may also serve forecasting in another way. Indeed the influence of reference categories on the dynamics of evolution in that society may be reconstructed. Social elasticity, analysed in society (A) may stimulate hypotheses on the possible influence of reference categories in society (B), which is being observed at present. For instance, being already acquainted with the impact made in the past by the travelling habits of the wealthiest categories of the United States population on the increased interest in tourism on the part of other classes in that society, one can hazard hypotheses about the growth of tourism in Quebec, despite cultural differences. I shall start from an investigation of the current behaviour patterns and interests of the wealthiest groups in that country.

The uncertainty of the forecast is reduced to the extent that comparison can corroborate all three hypotheses in the same study. The information used may originate from various sources. It need not be taken from the same level of social reality. Some may be local in origin, some national. Some may be composed of survey results, some of aggregates. This variety of the material matters little. The pertinence of the information consists only in the opportunity it affords of comparing two values in the same kind of units, so as to reckon temporal, social or spatial elasticities. In fact, the greatest variety in the type of relevant information used is advisable in order to ascertain the permanence of similar trends or disparities by cross reference. Hence both those who stress the limitations of using aggregates in the search for correlations (Robinson's Ecological Fallacy) and those who stress with equal pertinence the limitations of using survey results, which are prey to subjective errors (Individualistic Fallacy) (Scheuch, 1968, p.176–210) can be dismissed. Forecasting thought should be able to rely on the greatest possible number of comparable trends and disparities, despite the variety of kinds of information available.

In conclusion, it seems useful to stress the difficulty involved in compiling the information relevant to forecasting in a given society. This data is often scattered. Its collation takes a lot of work, in several stages:

a) gathering all available data on each country investigated and attempt at initial comparative treatment.

b) harmonisation of the collected data in order to make up comparable sets for secondary analyses.

c) preparation for the comparative observation of samples selected by reference to the same principles and investigated by the same methods in the light of the same hypotheses.

The first stage is all too often underestimated by sociologists accustomed to the special requirements of sample surveys. In fact, it is absolutely fundamental. Its results may exceed expectations, even when secondary analyses prove difficult. This is a lengthy task and the outcome is not always proportioned to the efforts made. Hence it would be desirable for sociological research institutes to put more emphasis on the mechanical storage of local, national and international data.

Notes to Chapter V

[45] It should be noted that Meyersohn, a co-author of the second anthology, gradually rejected this viewpoint, which was discussed in seminars of the ISA Executive. The new anthology he collaborated in no longer embodies this distinction (Meyersohn, 1972).

[46] In France as in the US half the people accept advertising, a quarter are

indifferent and a quarter object to it (Steiner, 1963).

[47] The operation of the bureaucracy, as described by Michel Crozier is far from resembling this pattern.

[48] In cybernetics, analogical models are ... sets of delineated and structured variables representing a situation which does not exist with a sufficient degree of approximation or a degree deemed sufficient.

[49] By comparative method is meant a comparison drawn between different societies, i.e. what is conveyed by the English term "cross-cultural studies."

[50] International Round Table of the French National Centre for Scientific Research organized in October 1972 by the Committee on Leisure of the International Sociological Association, the European Centre for Leisure and Education, and the International Centre of Social Gerontology.

[51] It should be noted that Lipset studies other nations to pinpoint differences with the First New Nation. Yet the task of distinguishing the (probable) universal characteristics of post-industrial society from specifically American features has received little attention from major American sociologists to date.

[52] Between late August 1968 and late January 1969, some 40 bombs were planted in Montreal, probably by the FLQ (Front for the Liberation of Quebec) or by others.

[53] In the same vein, see the criticism made by Levi-Strauss (defended by G. Gurvitch (1958) in *Anthropologie Structurale*, Paris: Plon) of global concepts and a priori of the "structure" of societies.

Conclusion

Individual and group thinking, based on the results achieved and the questions raised by empirical sociology, led up to a few propositions which will be summarised below. In the post-industrial development of technological societies, spare time, leisure activities and values have not only been generated by the reduction in working hours due to advanced technology. This factor accounts only for the increase in available time, but does not explain why leisure should generally have been promoted in the time thus freed from work. The promotion of leisure does not make sense unless one posits a gradual reduction in the scope of the control which the basic social institutions exert over individuals and an unprecedented aspiration towards self-expression. Both phenomena are the outcome of social movements in which not only workers, but women, teenagers, old-age pensioners, etc. play an active part in their own right. I hope to have highlighted this treble process which has been all too often ignored by the sociology of leisure, hampered by its derivation from the sociology of work.

This is not to say that everybody's life is (or soon will be) dominated by leisure values. Among workers and women, among the young and the old, minority groups which are often considerable remain unaffected by these new values. Their lives are almost exclusively regulated by the values of work or study, of family duty, of socio-spiritual or socio-political commitment. This may be due to the pressure of necessity, to a keen sense of duty or to a personal definition of pleasure. In consequence, leisure is only perceived by such minority groups as a way of getting occasional rest or recreation, whereas for the majority, leisure activities increasingly tend to take up most of the time spent away from the job and stimulate a growing concern for self-fulfillment, at whatever level.

In order to analyse such complex phenomena, the sociology of leisure should concentrate on a rigorous definition of its specific subject matter. Leisure is not idleness, since it presupposes a job as its polar opposite, whereas idleness negates employment. The confusion between leisure and idleness, for which Veblen is responsible in part, dies hard. Yet leisure cannot be equated with time free from paid work. It corresponds only to one part of this time, the rest being taken up by housework and family duties, which the sociologists of leisure have tended to overlook. However, leisure ought now to be defined as freedom from household tasks as well as from work. The sociology of leisure should also distinguish between leisure and spare time. The latter encompasses socio-spiritual and socio-political activities, as well as the activities primarily aimed at achieving personal satisfaction. The social meaning of these two types of activities is clearly different. Leisure ought to be unambiguously differentiated from socio-spiritual and socio-political commitment, which pertain respectively to the sphere of religious and of political sociology. It is only the activities primarily aimed at self-expression – no matter how much the individual has been socially conditioned – which constitute leisure and which warrant the distinctiveness of a special branch of sociology: the sociology of leisure. Obviously, related concepts overlap to some extent and their mutual relationships are often close. Yet the facts they span do not have the same meaning for society. Moreover any science must define its specific object at the risk of remaining bogged down in approximations or phraseology.

My present viewpoint on the relationship of leisure and work diverges from the ideas which have been dominant since the origins of the subject matter. Empirical sociology has shown beyond doubt that the impact of work, of the divison of labour and of the resultant class stratification on differential leisure behaviour patterns and values is obvious and lasting. The ideas put forward by some ideologists of post-industrial society on the "*embourgeoisement*" and on the "integration" of the working class into the middle classes should be heavily qualified and toned down. It has been shown, however, that cultural and social discrepancies between the leisure patterns of factory workers and those of other urban wage-earners are subject to great variations. Provided the indicators used in this study are retained, they can never be reduced to dichotomous contrasts, such as those which used to exist in the days of Marx and Zola.

Yet this is not the main feature of my approach. To my mind, the labour/leisure dichotomy which has for forty years (from Elton Mayo to Georges Friedmann) contributed to progress in the observation and in the interpretation of leisure, is now more likely to lead to stagnation. It prompts increasingly stereotyped statements. It detracts from research designs. It conceals the development of mutual relationships whereby leisure is increasingly affected by *all* institutional commitments and/or influences them in turn, often as a challenge to obligations. These are the main unknowns which, I believe, should now be unravelled. In a novel type of society, dominated by the tertiary sector, freeing and allocating time and space sets a major social problem. The quality of individual and group life is at stake, not only in leisure activities and at work, but in schools and in the home, in the fulfillment of socio-spiritual and socio-political commitments. To my mind, this is the task to which the sociology of leisure should address itself in forthcoming years, with the cooperation of other sociological specialisms and, if possible, in an interdisciplinary context.

However, the evolution of leisure is anything but simple. Its expansion is hampered or negated by many economic and social obstacles and by deep-rooted prejudice. It is certainly true that the production of goods and services in an affluent society generates pressures which tend to subordinate the chances of self-fulfillment available to the mass of consumers to the laws of standardisation and of maximum profits. Empirical sociology should spare no efforts in ascertaining the exact scope of this economic conditioning. Furthermore political propaganda threatens to reduce leisure to an electoral or ideological slogan, especially as both leisure and the democratisation of culture set problems out of which political capital can be made. Yet an apolitical approach tends to turn leisure into child's play which might produce apathetic and unenterprising citizens. How can leisure, for adults, tap the marvellous sources of inspiration which flow during childhood without lapsing into childishness?

Confronted with these manifold dangers, leisure organizations are scattered. As a rule they lack the necessary political awareness. When they engage in political activities, they echo the party dissensions rooted in other spheres, but fail to bring forth a coherent and lasting social movement aimed at the implementation of an innovatory and democratic cultural policy, to match the scale of the new problems set by mass leisure. Can sociology help unearth the facts which would contribute to the solution of these problems both in theory and in practice? I hope to have shown that this is a challenge to the future orientation of sociology. Two conditions will have to be met for this discipline to effectively contribute to the study of the major unknowns connected with the development of leisure:

a) it will have to elaborate, in conjunction with 'development' economists, a valid operational framework by reference to which the trends of wealth and spare time development can be assessed; this would be a challenge to the cultural development — in and out of school — of a group, a class or a whole society over a given period of time, rather than to "culture" in general.

b) it should become capable of encompassing both the study of trends and the reduction of future uncertainty, as well as the analysis of a social subject's intervention and of its interaction with the various influences by which it is determined. Hence it should increasingly deal with forecasting and with decision-making.

Unless these two changes occur, I fear that sociology will make but a modest contribution to the analysis of the conditions and processes amounting to what I had ventured in 1962 to call a "leisure civilisation" in the making.

I hope to have made it clear how various individual and collective research projects led me to conceive the complex dynamics whereby leisure is created and developed, its specific characteristics, its new values, their determinants and their implications for the utilisation of time and space, as well as for cultural and social problems. In my view, they are at the very heart of the uncertainties which beset the industrial age.

For sociology to be capable of more efficiently dealing with these problems, a new framework for cultural development and new methods of active sociology for forecasting and decision-making must be devised. Unless these epistemological and methodological instruments are perfected, I fear that the contribution sociology can make to a knowledge of the conditions and mechanisms I have called "a leisure civilisation" will remain slight.

Can one speak of leisure civilisation as looming on the horizon of advanced industrial societies? Some greet this hypothesis with scepticism, many deride it as naive. Nearly all sociologists ignore it or reject it.

It is obviously an unacceptable expression in many respects. Firstly it is arbitrary to characterize a society, a culture or a civilisation, by reference to one single feature. The type of civilisation which emerges with the predominance of the tertiary sector in the economy may be characterised in various ways, by reference to its causes and its effects, or their dialectical relationship. I have already said so. It is equally legitimate to speak of a neo-technical, an atomic, an electronic or a cybernetic civilisation . . . or to single out mass consumption, the sexual revolution, the generational conflict etc. as major features. Yet, in sociology, to conceptualise is often to fight false ideas and myths. The state of thought at a given time cannot be disregarded in this process. When thought seems to lag behind the situation, sociologists must put forward a new conceptualization of this situation which although it is experienced, is not taken into account in the dominant collective representations.

This struck me as necessary in the second half of the fifties. At the time, the problem of leisure was not yet raised before public opinions. Researchers were still dominated by outdated representations of work and of politics, very close to the 19th century. Under such circumstances, it seemed legitimate to conjure up the idea of a possible leisure civilization, which prompted the gathering together of many scattered facts in order to raise a *general* problem. It was therefore an attempt to remove leisure from the residual position it occupied in collective representation, so as to grant it the same degree of importance as to other allegedly more serious, social facts. Have I succeeded? Although the term I used met with some journalistic and educational success, I doubt it.

From another point of view, some detractors of the leisure civilisation may I fear, be confusing the descriptive and the normative approach. If "civilisation" were understood in the normative sense, by reference to criteria for the cultural and social development of mass society, the term would not be justified in my view. In a society like ours, where market laws tend to standardise leisure goods and services, where the educational system is wholly unfitted to the general culture experienced through leisure by the young and by adults, popular leisure as a whole is clearly not dominated by invention of creation. It is the product of an interaction between the si...e of productive forces, of social institutions and of basic personality. I hope to have shown that as the post-industrial age dawns, leisure produced by the progress of productive forces, by the regressing control of basic social institutions and by the promotion of new personal aspirations, tends to exert a growing influence on the whole way of life. Increasingly, even in the industrial societies guided by an official philosophy of work, it benefits from the time freed from work and housework, much more than voluntary social work, socio-spiritual or socio-political commitment does. More and more, family life is changing, duties are differentiated from leisure or semi-leisure: the former tend to shrink, the latter to increase, while the style of leisure tends to change the performance and even the interpretation of obligations. Workers spend most of their free time in leisure pursuits, except for the privileged few for whom work is a major source of creation or responsibility and for an important minority who need to supplement insufficient wages. The same point applies to the retired. All the unions are now claiming for a new decrease in the duration of work. While it is shaped by working conditions, leisure is less and less regulated by the law of work. Leisure time is less and less spent in restoring the force to work, despite some growth in nervous fatigue. Even in the Soviet Union, a new approach has been observed.

Leisure is more and more conceived for its own sake, to satisfy new personality needs at whatever cultural level. Everywhere a dwindling of work values and a development of leisure values has been observed, especially among the young. A new aspiration tends to seek some properties of leisure in work itself. As C.

Wright Mills wrote: "today work tends to be assessed by the criteria of leisure" (Mills, 1966). Similar comments have been made about schoolwork. The level of education received certainly affects the content of leisure. However, this influence is lesser than it seemed when an attempt is made to ascertain the number of individuals to whom positive or negative correlations between education and leisure apply. In addition, a major aspect of the educational crisis consists in the refusal to do part of the compulsory school work. Such a refusal is linked with a claim for voluntary self-selected learning, inseparable from a new style of leisure for the young. Initially run by the churches, leisure activities were gradually freed from their control. It is the leisure patterns of parishioners which prompted the clergy to change the timing, the location and the style of religious services. Though influenced by the cultural policy (or its lack) in the enterprise, the city or the State, the leisure of the people remains part of private life. Resistance to any authoritarian organization of leisure, by whatever institution, whether syndical or political, remains very strong, despite constant attempts to use it for propaganda purposes. Market laws mould leisure, but increasingly diverse social movements protest against this debasement. My observations and forecasts show that, at the risk of failing, no reform of work or education, of the family or of socio-spiritual and socio-political life, can ignore the scope, the structures and the values of leisure for all social classes, age groups and for both sexes. Any overall policy aimed at enhancing the *quality of life* by a new allocation of time and space ought to begin by reassessing the implications of leisure for all areas of social and personal life. It is these facts which prompted me to speak of the possible advent of a leisure civilisation. This civilisation is not a golden age starting tomorrow. It is a set of new social and cultural problems which, to be solved *tomorrow,* must be seriously considered *today.*

Among the reservations or criticisms stimulated by this approach of the sociology of leisure, I attach special importance to the recent thoughts voiced by Georges Friedmann. His view of leisure within his analysis of the technological civilisation has changed considerably. He first envisaged leisure as an entertainment or as a compensation for work. Then he sought to ascertain to what extent free time is truly freed from constraints and conditioning. Many facts which spring to mind dictate pessimistic replies to his queries. He has never been very interested in the category of facts which show the growing, though often hidden, impact of leisure values on work and on all the other activities which simultaneously condition leisure. As from 1970, he wholly rejected the prospect of a possible leisure civilisation. "It is henceforth clear that the technological civilisation cannot be a leisure civilisation" (Friedmann, 1970).

Let us examine his arguments and the facts on which he may have relied. Friedmann himself grouped and outlined them in a few pages:

a) The introduction of the shorter working week does not suffice to effect major changes. It is a failure.

b) Leisure has not succeeded in compensating for the dehumanising effects of disintegrated work for most workers. Managers have no time for leisure, a majority of workers don't know how to use it. They are bored, they take up another job or they potter.

c) Leisure has become a mere commodity. The Hippies are rebelling against it, and not only against work.

d) Lastly, leisure is accompanied by a psychological devaluation of work. Even when it is a success, it channels the main interest away from work. This is a "pathological" situation.

Empirical sociology could supply facts to support certain of these ideas, but other facts reveal a more complex situation. Some of the latter have already been outlined, especially in Chapter Two, and will not be repeated. Georges Friedmann warned that his book was not scientific, "though based on experience and observation." I would have wished his statements to fit in better with all the facts available in today's empirical sociology of work or of leisure.

On the other hand, I think that I grasp the general theme of the book in which this assessment of leisure appears. In technological civilisation, Friedmann denounces a growing imbalance between the power of man and his wisdom. This is what he calls the great imbalance, often described as "hallucinating" or "terrifying". He goes against the tide when he calls on men to make an inner effort capable of matching their outer power over things. We are quite ready to hear this call. But how can such an inner effort be made?

By a "genuine education," but in a constantly changing society this education cannot be restricted to children. It must be continuing, and consequently affect part of leisure. Besides, given the present crisis of schooling and the new claims of youth for freedom of choice, how can it consist only in compulsory studies? At the risk of failing if this were not the case, it would have to impinge also on the leisure of the young.

Considering the strength of the dynamics generating free time and leisure within this free time, a sustained, though moderate, expansion of leisure may be expected. It is hard to conceive how the genuine education of which Friedmann speaks could remain alien to the developmental function of leisure. I feel, on the contrary, that a new social policy towards this function is a condition for the upsurge of "genuine education". In my view, Friedmann's thoughts on this theme are based on an outdated notion of the educational system, despite its reforms, and on a concept of relationships between compulsory schoolwork and voluntary studies during leisure, which no longer reflects the aspirations of the young generation.

Finally, a methodological issue arises; I wonder how Friedmann relates the negative statements in his work to the sociological method. He writes: "whatever the documentary value of specialised research on the temporal, cultural, and functional dimensions of leisure, they show that they do not go deeper, further they demonstrate the impossibility of understanding the facts they supply without making a general reference to the whole condition of man in the technological civilisation." It is difficult to grasp what exact meaning is given by Friedmann to the term "demonstrate". Is this a scientific demonstration? I don't see what system of evidence it is based on. I fear that there is a certain confusion between two kinds of knowledge. Empirical sociology can only deal with the problems it is capable of solving. It does not pretend to solve all the problems which the philosopher can and should raise about "the whole condition of man." However, to establish social facts or to predict their evolution under the label of leisure civilisation, reliance on sociological observation and forecasting is a prerequisite for any "demonstration".

If one wants, like Friedmann, to stimulate an inner effort in order to solve or to reduce the great imbalance, one may either preach some values disregarding the conditions and processes of their implementation or apply the rules of sociology on forecasting and decision-making to the relevant interventions. Yet Friedmann, in a recent debate with Fourastié, only sees new delusions of scientism in the science of forecasting and planning (Friedmann, 1970). Under these conditions, on what scientific method is the tenet that technological civilisation is not evolving into a leisure civilisation, based?

Even if an attempt is made to compare all available facts in a systematic approach to social reality, certainty always eludes one. All that can be attempted is to reduce the uncertainty surrounding a future which is initiated in the present. Can sociology do more without self-betrayal?

References

AFC-CIO, Eighth Annual Conference on Community Services (1964) "How do people feel about free time? " New York.

Ahtik, V. (1960), "Les conditions d'une planification sociale du loisir," *International Social Science Review,* 12, 623–630.

Andrée, J.M. (1966), *L'Otium dans la Vie Morale et Intellectuelle des Romains, des Origines à l'Epoque Augustéenne,* Paris: PUF.

Aron, R. (1962), *Dix-huit Leçons sur la Société Industrielle,* Paris: Gallimard, p.377.

Bachelard, G. (1957), *Formation de l'Esprit Scientifique,* p.257, Paris: Vrin.

Barrett, D.N. (ed.) (1961), *Values in America,* p.182, Notre Dame, Ill.: University of Notre Dame Press.

Baudrillart, J. (1968), *Le Système des Objets,* p.288, Paris: Gallimard.

Beljaev, V. and Vodzinskaya, V.V. (1961), "The study of workers' time-budgets as a method of concrete sociological observation," *Vestnik L.G.U.,* 23.

Bell, D. (1960), *The End of Ideology,* p.416, Glencoe, Ill.: Free Press.

Bergeron, G. (1967), *Le Québec après Deux Siècles de Patience,* Paris: Seuil.

Bize, Dr. (1961), *Le Surmenage des Dirigeants,* p.170, Paris: Entreprises Modernes.

Bossermann, P. and Kaplan, M. (eds) (1971), *Technology, Human Values and Leisure,* p.256, New York: Abingdon Press.

Bourdieu, P. and Passeron, J.C. (1964), *Les Héritiers – les Etudiants et la Culture,* p.180, Paris: Minuit.

Bourdieu, P. and Reynaud, J.D. (1966), "Une sociologie de l'action est-elle possible?" *Revue Française de Sociologie,* Vol.7, No.4, pp.508–517.

Bross, I.D.D. (1961), *Prévisions et Décisions Rationnelles,* p.266, Paris: Dunod.

Busch, C. (1973), *Problèmes et Perspectives de la Sociologie du Temps Libre. Contribution à une Définition du Champ d'Etude*, p.390, The Hague: Mouton.

Caisse Interprofessionnelle de Prévoyance pour les Cadres (1965), "Les cadres retraités vus par eux-mêmes."
Cazeneuve, J. (1952), *Psychologie de la Joie*, p.86, Paris: Presses Littéraires de France.
Cazeneuve, J. (1961), *La Mentalité Archaique*, p.205, Paris: A. Colin.
Cazeneuve, J. (1970), *Les Pouvoirs de la Télévision*, p.385, Paris: Gallimard.
Cazeneuve, J. and Oulif, J. (1963), *La Grande Chance de la Télévision*, p.242, Paris: Calmann-Lévy.
Charpentreau, A. (1967), *Pour une Politique Culturelle*, p.228.
Chombart de Lauwe, M.J. and P.H. et al., (1963), *La Femme dans la Société*, p.441, Paris: CNRS.
Clawson, M. and Knetsch, J.L. (1966), *Economics of Outdoor Recreation*, p.348, New York: JMP.
CNRO (1968) *Réalités du Troisième Age*, p.223, Paris: Dunod.
CNRS (1969) "Attitudes, comportements, opinions des personnes âgées dans le cadre de la famille moderne," Paris.
Commissariat au Plan, Groupe 1985 (1964), "Réflexions pour 1985", p.156, Paris: Documentation Française.
Cooms, P.H., *La Crise Mondiale de l'Education*, p.322, Paris: PUF.
Cox, H. (1971), *La Fête des Fous*, p.240, Paris: Seuil.
Crémieux Brilhac, J.L. (1965), "Objectifs et propositions du Colloque de Bourges," *Expansion de la Recherche Scientifique*, 22, 5–6.
Cros, L. (1961), *L'Explosion Scolaire*, Paris: Sevpen.
Cuisenier, J. (1964), "L'ordre des choix dans une planification indicative," *Revue philosophique*.

Donfut, C. (1972), "Les vacances: loisir du troisième âge? Ouvriers retraités face à une nouvelle réalisation de vacances," p.236 (thesis summarized in *Gérontologie*, 20, 194).
Dumazedier, J. (1954), "Les loisirs dans la vie quotidienne," *Encyclopédie Française*, vol.14, section G, p.33.
Dumazedier, J. (1960), "Ambiguité du loisir et travail industriel," *Cahiers Internationaux de Sociologie*, 27, 89–112.
Dumazedier, J. (1962), *Vers une Civilisation du Loisir*, p.318, Paris: Seuil.
Dumazedier, J. (1963), "Contenu culturel du loisir ouvrier dans six villes d'Europe," *Revue Française de Sociologie*, 1, 12–21.
Dumazedier, J. (1964), "Structures lexicales et significations complexes," *Revue Française de Sociologie*, 1, 12–26.
Dumazedier, J. (1965), "David Riesman et la France, 1963–85," *Revue Française de Sociologie*, 6, 379–382.
Dumazedier, J. (1967a), "Marxisme et Sociologie," *Socialisme: Revue du socialisme international et québecois*, 1.

Dumazedier, J. (1967b), "Les confessions sociologiques d'un enfant du siècle," *Esprit*, 4, 701–715.
Dumazedier, J. (1968–9), "20,000 lits à la neige," *Economie et perspective de la montagne*, 12–13–14.
Dumazedier, J. (1969), "Education Permanente," Encyclopedia Universalis, 8, t.5.
Dumazedier, J. Baquet, M. and Magnane, J. (1950), *Regard Neuf sur le Sport*, p.244, Paris: Seuil.
Dumazedier, J., Carré, R. and Guinchat, G. (1966), *Le Loisir en France*, p.1052, Paris: Centre de Recherches d'Urbanisme.
Dumazedier, J. and Guinchat, C. (1969), *La Sociologie du Loisir*, p.128, The Hague: Mouton.
Dumazedier, J. and Markiewicz-Lagneu, J. (1970), "Société soviétique, temps libre et loisir," *Sociologie*, 11/2, 211–229.
Dumazedier, J. and Ripert, A. (1966), *Loisir et Culture*, p.398, Paris, Seuil.
Dumazedier, J. and Samuel, N. (1969), Post-industrial societies and leisure time," *Society and Leisure*, 1, 15–25.
Dumazedier, J. and Suffert, A. (1962), "Fonction sociale et culturelle des cafés dans une ville," *Année Sociologique*, 197–249.
Dunn, D. (1971), *Report on Voluntary Work in the USA*, Washington: US Dept. of Parks and Recreation.
Durkheim, E. (1927), *Les Règles de la Méthode Sociologique*, p.186, Paris: Alcan.

Faure, H. (1963), "Une enquête par sondage sur l'utilisation des voitures particulières et commerciales," *Consommation: Annales du CREDOC*, 1, 1–81.
Faure, H. and Bracke, J.C. (1971), "Enquête sur les loisirs et le mode de vie du personnel de la RNUR," *Consommation: Annales du CREDOC*, 2, 3–35.
Filipcova, B. (1966), *Man, Work and Leisure*, p.156, Prague: Svoboda.
Filipcova, B. (1966), "Some Sociological Aspects of Cultural Development in Czechoslovakia," unpublished.
Foote, N.N. and Cottrel, L.S. (1955), *Identity and Interpersonal Competition. A New Direction in Family Research*, p.308, Chicago: University of Chicago Press.
Fortin, G., Tremblay, M.-A. and Laplante, M. *Les Comportements Economiques de la Famille Salariée du Québec*, p.407, Quebec: Laval Univ. Press.
Foskett, J.M. (1955), "Social structure and social participation," *American Sociological Review*, 20, 431–438.
Fourastié, J. (1962), "Prévision et évolution," *La Table Ronde*, 10, 9–19.
Fourastié, J. and F. (1962), *Histoire du Confort*, p.128, Paris: PUF.
Fourastié, J. (1966), *Les 40,000 heures*, Paris: Gauthier-Laffont.
Friedan, B. (1965), *The Feminine Mystique*, p.367, London: Penguin.
Friedmann, G. (1946), *Problèmes Humains du Machinisme Industriel*, p.389, Paris: Gallimard.

Friedmann, G. (1950), *Où va le Travail Humain?* p.391, Paris: Gallimard.
Friedmann, G. (1956), *Le Travail en Miettes*, p.347, Paris: Gallimard.
Friedmann, G. (1959), "Etude et pratique de la planification," (Introduction), *International Social Science Review*, special 3, 337–352.
Friedmann, G. (1970), *La Puissance et la Sagesse*, p.507, Paris: Gallimard.
Friedmann, J. (1965), "Réflexions finales", *Communications*, 5 ("Culture supérieure et culture de masse"), 42–52.

Galbraith, J.K. (1967), *The New Industrial State*, p.422, London: Penguin.
Gans, H.T. (1962), *The Urban Villagers*, p.367, New York: Free Press.
Gans, H.T. (1967), *The Levittowners; Ways of Life and Politics in a Suburban Community*, p.474, New York, Pantheon Books.
Girard, A. (1964), "La fin de l'ère des goûts et des couleurs," *Expansion de la Recherche Scientifique*, 21, 3–6.
Girod, R. (1972), "Sociologie du temps libre," mimeographed (Introduction to World Congress on Childhood and Free Time).
Goguel, C. (1965), "Les vacances des Français en 1964," *Etudes et Conjecture*, 65–102.
Goldthorpe, J.H., Lockwood, D. et al, (1959), *The Affluent Worker*, Cambridge: CUP.
Goode, W. (1959), "The sociology of the family," in Martin, R.K., Broom, L. and Cottrell, L.S. (eds), *Sociology Today*, p.623, New York: Basic Books.
Gordon, L., Voek, V.J., Genkin, S.E., Klopov, E.V. and Sokolova, S.N., "The typology of complex social phenomena," *Voprosy Filosofii*, 7, 52–64.
Govaerts, F. (1969), *Loisir des Femmes et Temps Libre*, p.312, Brussels, Institut de Sociologie.
Grazia, S. de (1962), *Of Time, Work and Leisure*, p.559, New York: 20th Century Fund.
Grossin, W. (1969), *Le travail et le temps: horaires, durées, rythmes*, p.250, Paris: Anthropos.
Grushin, B. (1966), *Free Time: Duration, Structure, Problems, Perspectives*, p.155, Moscow: Pravda.
Gruson, G. (1968), *Origine et Espoir de la Planification Française*, p.438, Paris: Dunod.
Gurvitch, G. (1958), *Anthropologie structurelle*, p.450, Paris: Plon.

Harrington, M. (1962), *The Other America*, p.186, London: Penguin.
Hassenforder, J. (1965), "Le retard des bibliothèques françaises," *Expansion de la recherche scientifique*, 22, 46–48.
Hausknecht, M. (1962), *The Joiners*, p.141, New York: Badminster Press.
Havighurst, R.J. and Feigenbaum, K. (1959), "Leisure and Life Style," *American Journal of Sociology*, 145–404.
Henle, P. (1966), "Leisure and long work week," *Monthly Labor Review*, 7, 721–728.
Hoggart, R. (1958), *The Uses of Literacy*, p.384, London: Penguin.
Huizinga, J. (1970), *Homo Ludens*, p.251, Paladin.

Husén, T. (1968), "L'éducation permanente," *Convergence,* 4.

IFOP (1964) "Réduction du temps de travail et aménagement des congés," *Sondages,* 2, 63–75.

IFOP (1967), "Sondage réalisé à la demande du Commissariat général au Tourisme et de la DATAR," *Revue 2000,* 6.

Illich, I.D. (1971), *Deschooling Society,* London: Calder and Boyars.

INSEE (1962), "Recensement de 1962". Paris: INSEE.

ISA (1970), "Proceedings of the Sixth World Congress of Sociology", vol. 3, Louvain.

Jantsch, E. (1968), *La Prévision Technologique.* Paris: OECD.

Jeannière, A. et al. (1963), *Démocratie d'Aujourd'hui,* p.191, Paris: Spes.

Johnstone, J.W.C. and Rivera, R.J. (1965), *Volunteers for Learning,* Chicago: Chicago City Press.

de Jouvenel, B. (1964), *L'Art et la Conjecture,* p.369, Paris: Plon.

de Jouvenel, B. (1972), "Le langage des heures," *Analyse et Prévision,* 13, 347–461.

Kaes, R. (1962), *Les Ouvriers Français et la Culture,* p.592, Paris: Droz.

Kahn, H. and Wiener, A. (1967), *The Year 2000,* New York: Macmillan.

Kaplan, M. (1960), *Leisure in America,* p.350, New York: Wiley.

Katz, E. and Lazarsfeld, P. (1955), *Personal Influence,* p.400, New York: Free Press.

Kerr, W. (1965), *The Decline of Pleasure,* p.319, New York: Macmillan.

Kinsey, A. et al. (1948), *Sexual Behaviour in the Human Male,* p.804, Philadelphia: Saunders.

Kinsey, A. et al. (1953), *Sexual Behaviour in the Human Female,* p.842, Philadelphia: Saunders.

Kolpakov, B. and Volgov, V. (1968), "Studies on budgets in the USSR", *Vestnik statistikii,* 12, 20–27.

Lafargue, P. (1965), *Le Droit à la Paresse,* p.80, Paris: Maspéro.

Lancelot, A. (1968), *L'Abstentionnisme Electoral en France,* p.290, Paris: A. Colin.

Lanfant, M.F. (1967–1969), *Ensemble de Rapports sur l'Animation Socio-Culturelle,* Paris.

Lanfant, M.F. (1972), *Les Théories du Loisir,* p.254, Paris: PUF.

Laplante, M. (1969), *Le Développement Culturel de la Pensée Québecoise,* p.363, Paris.

Larrabee, E. and Meyersohn (eds.) (1958), *Mass Leisure,* Glencoe, Ill.: Free Press.

Larrue, J. (1965), *Loisirs Ouvriers chez les Métallurgistes Toulousains,* The Hague: Mouton.

Lasswell, H. (1963), *The Future of Political Science,* p.256, New York: Atherton Press.

Laurent, J. (1955), *La République et les Beaux-Arts*, p.227, Paris: Julliard.
Ledermann, S. (1956), "Alcool, Alcoolisation; Données scientifiques de caractère psychologique, economique et social," *Cahiers de l'INED*, p.315, Paris, PUF.
Lefebvre, H. (1958), *Critique de la Vie Quotidienne*, p.272, Paris: Arche.
Le Roux, P. (1968), "Les vacances des Français en 1967," *Etudes et Conjectures*, suppl. 6, 1–12.
Le Roux, P. (1970), *Les Comportements de Loisir des Français*, p.62, Paris: INSEE, Ménages, série M.
Lestavel, J. (1964), "La mutation des associations culturelles," *Expansion de la Recherche Scientifique*, 21, 7–9.
Leveugle, J. (1968), *L'Education Permanente*, p.225, Paris: Privat.
Lévi-Strauss, C. (1962), *La Pensée Sauvage*, p.397, Paris: Plon.
Linden, S.B. (1970), *The Harried Leisure Class*, p.183, New York: Columbia Univ. Press.
Lindzey, G. (1970), *Handbook of Social Psychology*, p. 249, Reading, Mass.: Addison Wesley.
Lipset, S. (1960), *Political Man*, p.432, New York: Doubleday.
Lipset, S. (1963), *The First New Nation. The United States in Comparative and Historical Perspective*, p.260, New York: Basic Books.
Littunen, M. (1960), *The Social Functions of Holidays*, Turku Research Institute of the School of Social Science.
Liveright, A.A. (1968), *A Study of Adult Education in the United States*, p.138, Cleveland: Center for Study of Adult Education.
Luchini, A. (1999), La Fréquentation des équipments religieux, étude rétrospective sur le comportement des Francais, Paris: Comité National des Constructions d'Eglises, 63p.
Lynd, R.S. and H.M. (1937), *Middletown in Transition*, p.604, New York: Harcourt.

MacLuhan, M. (1964), *Understanding the Media: The Extensions of Man*, p.366, New York: McGraw Hill.
Mandel, E. (1961), "Socialist Economy," in Heilbronner, R.L. and Fords, A.M., (eds), *Is Economics Relevant?*, p. 315, Pacific Palisades, Calif: Goodyear.
Mannheim, K. (1936), *Ideology and Utopia*, p.318, London: Routledge.
Mannheim, K. (1950), *Freedom, Power and Democratic Planning*, p.384, London: Routledge.
Marcuse, H. (1964), *One Dimensional Man. Studies in the Ideology of Advanced Industrial Society*, p.260, Boston: Beacon Press.
Martinet, A. (1960), *Eléments de Linguistique Structurale*, p.223, Paris: A. Colin.
Marx, K. (1963–67), *Oeuvres: Economie* (Rubel, M., ed.), vol.I, p.1819, vol.II, p.1970, Paris: Gallimard.
Maslov, P.P. and Pisarev, I.S.V. (1965), *Sociology in the USSR*, vol.I, p.533, vol.II, p.504, Moscow: Mysl.

Massé, P. (1965), *Le Plan ou l'Anti-Hasard,* Paris: Gallimard.
Matalon, B. (1967), *Les Raisonnements Prévisionnels,* CREDOC et Groupe d'Etude du Loisir, p.25, mimeographed.
McKain, W.C. (1947), "The social participation of old people in a California retirement community," unpublished, Harvard University.
Mead, M. (1971), *Le fossé des Générations,* Paris: Denoël/Gonthier, 160p.
Mendras, H. (1961), "L'agriculture et l'avenir de la société rurale," *Bulletins SEDEIS Futuribles,* 20.12.1964, suppl. no.2, p.22.
Mendras, H. (1967), *La Fin des Paysans,* p.358, Paris: SEDEIS.
Meyerson, I. (1948), *Les Fonctions Psychologiques et les Oeuvres,* p.223, Paris: Vrin.
Mihovilovitch, M. (1969), *Leisure of the Citizens of Zagreb,* p.85, Zagreb: Institute for Social Research.
Mills, C.W. (1956), *White Collar, the American Middle Classes,* p.378, New York: OUP.
Moles, A. (1967), *Sociodynamique de la Culture,* p.342, The Hauge: Mouton.
Morin, F. (1970), *Le Journal de Californie,* p.269, Paris: Seuil.
Morris, E. (1955), *Utopia 1976,* New York: Reinhard & Cine.

Naville, P. (1967), *Le Nouveau Léviathan,* p.515, vol.I, Paris: Anthropos.

Opinion Research Corporation (1957), *The Public Appraises Movies,* vol.II, Princeton, N.J.
Outdoor Recreation Resources Review Centre (1966), "Outdoor Recreation," 27 vols., Washington.

Paillat, P. and Wibaux, C. (1999), "Les citadins âgés," *Cahiers de l'INED* no.52, p.292, Paris, PUF.
Parker, S. (1971), *The Future of Work and Leisure,* p.161, London: McGibbon & Kee.
Patrusev, V.D. (1966), "Time as an economic category," *Mysl,* 1, Moscow.
Pergeaud, Y. (1968) — see CNRO (1968).
Petrosjan, G.S. (1965), *The Non-Work Time of Workers in the USSR,* p.193, Moscow: Ekonomizdat.
Peuple et Culture (1960), "Planification et Education Populaire."
Piatier, A. (1963) — see SOFRES (1963).
Piatier, A. (1964), "Economie et Culture," *Expansion de la Recherche Scientifique,* 21, 12–17.
Pieper, D. (1958), *Leisure, the Basis of Culture,* London: Faber & Faber.
Prudenski, G.A. (1964), *Time and Work,* p.350, Moscow: Mysl.

Reich, C. (1970), *The Greening of America,* p.294, New York: Random House.
Reich, W. (1971), *What is Class Consciousness?,* p.76, Socialist Reproduction.
Richta, R. (1969), *La Civilisation au Carrefour,* p.468, Paris: Anthropos.

Riesman, D., Glazer, N. and Denney, R. (1950), *The Lonely Crowd*, p.386, New Haven, Conn.: Yale Univ. Press.
Riesman, D. (1954), *Individualism Reconsidered and Other Essays*, p.529, Glencoe, Ill.: Free Press.
Riley, M.A. and Foner, A. (1968), *Aging and Society; an Inventory of Research Findings*, New York: Russell Sage Foundation.
Riva Poor, I. de (1970), *4 Days, 40 Hours*, Cambridge, Mass.: Bursk & Poor.
Rosenberg, A. and White, L. (eds.) (1957), *Mass Culture. The Popular Arts in America*, p.561, Glencoe, Ill.: Free Press.
Rosensthiel, H. and Mothes, J. (1965), *Mathématiques de l'Action. Langage des Symboles, des Statistiques et des Aléas*, p.483, Paris: Dunod.
Rowntree, B.S. and Lovers, G.R. (1951), *English Life and Leisure*, p.482, New York: Longmans Green.

Sartre, J.-P. (1960), *Critique de la Raison Dialectique*, p.951, Paris: Gallimard.
Scheuch, E.K., (1960), "Leisure time activities and family cohesion," *Sociological Review*, 8.
Scheuch, E.K. and Meyersohn, R. (eds.), (1972), *Soziologie der Freizeit*, p.352, Cologne: Kiepenheur Witch.
SEMA (1965), "Perspectives du cinéma français," *Bulletin d'Information du Centre National de la Cinématographie*, 91.
Shanas, E. et al. (1963), "Panel on Social Attitudes towards Retirement and Support of Older People," in Orbach, H.L. and Tibbits, C. (eds.), *Aging and the Economy*, p.237, Ann Arbor: Univ. of Michigan Press.
Shanas, E. et al., (1963), *Old People in Three Industrial Societies*, p.478, New York: Atherton.
Skorzynski, Z. (1962), "The main daily activities of Warsaw inhabitants," *Zdrowie publiczne*, 1, 35–50.
SOFRES (1963), "221,750,000 consommateurs," p.250, Paris, Sélection du Reader's Digest.
Steiner, G. (1963), *The People Look at Television*, p.422, New York: A. Knopf.
Strumilin, S.G. (1959), *The Work Day and Communism. The Problems of Socialism and Communism in the USSR*, Moscow.
Strumilin, S.G. (1964), *On Problems of Labour Economics*, vol.III, Moscow.
Swados, H. (1958), "Less work, less leisure," E. Larrabee and R.B. Meyersohn, (eds), *Mass Leisure*, Glencoe, Ill.: Free Press.
Syndicat National des Editeurs (1965), "Monographie de l'édition," p.160, Paris: Cercle de la Librairie.
Szalai, S., et al., (1973), *The Use of Time*, The Hague: Mouton.
Szczepanski, J. (1969), *Problèmes Sociologiques de l'Enseignement Supèrieur en Pologne*, p.330, Paris: Anthropos.

Taietz, P. et al. (1956), *Adjustment to Retirement in Rural New York*, n.p.
Touraine, A. (1965), *Sociologie de l'Action*, p.509, Paris: Seuil.
Touraine, A. (1969), *La Société Post-Industrielle*, p.319, Paris: Denoël.

Tyriakan, E.A. (1970), "Remarques sur une sociologie du changement qualitatif," in Balandier, G., *Sociologie des Mutations*, 83–94, Paris: Anthropos.

U.S. Department of Commerce, Bureau of the Census (1967), "Historical statistics of the USA," p.154, Washington.

Varagnac, A. (1948), *Civilisation Traditionnelle et Genre de Vie*, p.404, Paris: Albin Michel.

Vauban, S. de (1872), *La Dîme Royale*, p.190, Paris: Bureaux de la Publication.

Veblen, T. (1957), *The Theory of the Leisure Class. An Economic Study of Institutions*, p.414, London: Allen & Unwin.

Verner, C., Nelson, L. and Ramsey, C.E. (1960), *Community Structure and Change*, p.464, New York: Macmillan.

Villadary, A. (1968), *Fête et Vie Quotidienne*, p.242, Paris: Ed.ouvrières.

Villeneuve, A. (1970), "Les déplacements domicile-travail," *Economie et Statistiques*, 17, 3–17.

Ward, J.A. (1961), "A nationwide study of living habits," unpubl. quoted in Kleemeier, R.W. (ed.), *Aging and Leisure. A Research into the Meaningful Use of Time*, New York: OUP, 125.

White House Conference on Aging (1971), "Retirement roles and activities," Washington.

Wilensky, H. (1960), "Travail, carrière et intégration sociale," *Revue internationale*, 4, 587–607.

Wilensky, H. (1961), "Aging and leisure."

Wilensky, H. (1961), "The uneven distribution of leisure. The impact of economic growth on 'free time'," *Social problems*, 9, 32–56.

Wilensky, H. (1964), Mass society and mass culture, *American Sociological Review*, 29(1) April.

Willener, A. (1970), *L'Image-Action de la Société ou la Politisation de la Culture*, p.291, Paris: Seuil.

Within, J.W.M. (1968), "Methods and problems in cross-cultural research," in Lindzey, G. (ed.), *Handbook of Social Psychology*, London, 5 vols., vol.II, 693–728.

Wogensky, A. (1964), "L'urbanisme," *Education Nationale*, 2, 6.

Yankelovich, D. (1969), "A study of the generation gap conducted for CBS," New York: CBS.

Youmans, E. (1961), "Economic status and attitudes of older men in selected rural and urban areas of Kentucky," p. 43, Univ. of Kentucky Agricultural Experimental Station.

Zdravomyslov, A.G., Rogin, V.P. and Siadov, V.A. (1967), *Man and his Work*, p.130, Moscow.

Zetterberg, R.G. (1971), "Survey of a representative sample of the city of Stockholm," *Look*, 7.

Zygulski, K. (1972), *Introduction to the Problems of Culture*, p.380, Warsaw: Wydawnickycrzz.

Author Index

Ahtick, V., 12, 77, 78
Anderson, A., 25
Andrée, J.M., 9
Aragon, 61
Aristotle, 15
Aron, R., 160

Bachelard, G., 4, 197
Barrett, D.N., 124
Baudrillart, J., 40
Beljaev, V., 26
Bell, D., 34, 113, 122, 189
Bergeron, G., 199
Bize, R., 24
Bosserman, P., 12
Bourdieu, P., 161, 178, 187
Bracke, J-C., 19
Bross, I.D.J., 164, 192
Busch, C., 12, 39, 104

Cacérès, B., 175
Cain, J., 98
Carisse, C., 199
Cazeneuve, J., 13, 34, 58, 75, 104, 154, 163, 202
Charpentreau, J., 158
Chombart de Lauwe, M.J. and P.H., 27
Clawson, M., 19, 20
Comte, A., 9, 183, 186
Cottrell, L.S., 79
Cox, H., 12
Cros, L., 55, 161

Crozier, M., 205
Cuisenier, J., 164

Daric, J., 131
Davis, G., 103
Debeauvais, M., 159
Destouches, 29
Dommanget, M., 33
Donfut, C., 99
Dumazedier, J.J., 18, 37, 44, 45, 47, 54, 57, 63, 84, 85, 94, 97, 108, 113, 120, 123, 128, 131, 133, 134, 146, 162, 169, 194, 195, 198, 199
Duminy, J., 141
Dunn, D., 35
Durkheim, E., 191
Duveau, G., 175

Engels, F., 33, 36

Faure, H., 19, 55
Feigenbaum, K., 11
Filipcova, B., 12, 122, 195
Foner, A., 95, 96, 97, 98, 100, 101
Foote, N.N., 79
Fords, A.M., 16
Foskett, D.J., 96
Fourastié, J., 16, 38, 144, 148, 216
Fourier, C., 148
Freud, S., 148
Friedan, B., 64
Friedmann, G., 11, 22, 122, 155, 156, 209, 213, 214, 215, 216

Galbraith, J.K., 17
Gans, H.T., 43, 144
Girard, A., 158
Girod, R., 3
Glazer, N., 114
Godard, J-L., 160
Goguel, C., 56
Goldthorpe, J.H., 37, 124, 195
Gordon, L., 12
Govaerts, F., 12
de Grazier, S., 12, 13, 15, 122
Grossin, W., 26
Grushin, B., 12, 23, 45, 46, 47, 48, 49, 51, 52, 65, 71, 122
Gruson, G., 182
Guinchat, C., 45
Gurvitch, G., 5, 157, 205

Hansen, B., 99
Harrington, M., 129
Hassenforder, J., 66
Hausknecht, M., 35
Havighurst, R.J., 11, 78, 99, 121
Heilbroner, R.L., 16
Henle, P., 19, 20, 38
Hoggart, R., 195
Hugo, V., 188
Huizinga, J., 145
Husén, T., 112
Huxley, A., 188

Illich, I., 132

Jakobson, 78
Jantsch, E., 193, 194
Jean, G., 159
Jeannière, A., 28
Johnstone, J.W.C., 34, 134, 173, 175, 178
de Jouvenel, B., 92, 185, 194

Kaes, R., 195
Kahn, H., 16, 18
Kaplan, M., 12, 68, 79
Katz, E., 89, 154
Kerr, W., 64
Kinsey, A., 28
Kirovsky, 26
Knetsch, J.L., 20
Kolpakov, B., 45
Komarovsky, M., 10, 46

Lafargue, P., 10, 59, 107
Lancelot, A., 34
Lanfant, M.F., 3, 12, 64, 169, 170
Laplace, 184, 192
Laplante, M., 127, 199
Larrabee, E., 11
Larrue, J., 23
Lasswell, H., 185
Laurent, J., 162
Lazarsfeld, P., 89, 154
Ledermann, S., 85
Lefebvre, H., 12
Le Roux, P., 100, 101, 102
Lestavel, J., 158
Leveugle, J., 173
Levi-Strauss, C., 57, 78
Linden, S.B., 65
Lindzey, G., 192
Lipset, S.M., 12, 196, 205
Littunen, Y., 12
Liveright, A.A., 179
Lockwood, 37
Lovers, G.R., 11
Luccini, A., 32
Lundberg, G., 10, 11
Lynd, R.S. and H.M., 10, 77

Machlup, F., 176
Mannheim, K., 148, 156, 157, 173
Mandel, E., 16
Marcuse, H., 72, 196
Martinet, A., 77
Marx, K., 9, 10, 69, 107, 147, 184, 186, 191, 197, 209
Maslov, P.P., 45
Massé, P., 169, 181
Matalon, B., 189
Mayo, E., 122, 209
McKain, W.C., 95
McLuhan, M., 146, 154, 202
Mead, M., 41
Mendras, H., 16, 55
Meyersohn, R., 11, 22, 205
Meyerson, I., 42, 69
Michel, 124
Mihovilovitch, M., 12
Miller, S., 103
Mills, C.W., 213
Montesquieu, 191
Moreno, J.L., 147

Morin, E., 31, 146
Morris, E., 138
Morse, N., 122
Mothes, J., 164

Naville, P., 25, 64

Olzewska, A., 12
Orwell, L., 188
Oulif, J., 58, 163

Paillat, S., 95, 100, 102, 103, 104
Parker, S., 12, 69, 122
Passeron, J.C., 161
Patrushev, V.D., 12
Pergeaud, Y., 95
Petrosjan, G., 12
Pfeiffer, E., 103
Piatier, A., 57, 100, 159, 166, 193
Pieper, J., 12, 30, 33
Pisarev, I.S.V., 45
Proudhon, C., 9
Prudenski, G., 12, 30, 45, 46, 51, 65, 71

Rabelais, 148
Reich, W., 37
Reynaud, J.D., 187
Richta, R., 18, 36, 37, 40, 47, 107, 113
Riesman, D., 11, 12, 27, 34, 43, 54, 62, 114, 179, 196, 198
Riley, M., 95, 96, 97, 98, 100, 101
Rimbaud, A., 148
Rioux, M., 199
Ripert, A., 37, 57, 108, 113, 120, 162, 195
Riviera, R.I., 34, 134, 173, 175, 178
de Riva Poor, I., 23, 24, 26
Rosenberg, A., 11
Rosensthiel, H., 164
Rostow, 186
Rowntree, B.S., 11
Rubel, M., 104

Samuel, N., 18
Sartre, J.P., 167
Scheler, M., 4
Scheuch, E.K., 12, 25, 204

Shanas, E., 93, 95, 98
Skorzynski, Z., 12
Smith, A., 146
Steiner, G., 154, 155, 204
Strumilin, S.G., 10, 12, 35, 45, 46, 49, 51, 65, 178
Suffert, A., 85
Sullerot, E., 27, 28, 29
Swados, H., 22
Szalai, A., 12, 36, 65, 70, 72
Szcrepanski, J., 47

Taietz, P., 96
Taves, M.J., 99
de Toqueville, A., 191
Touraine, A., 18, 54, 110, 113, 159, 169, 173, 182, 187
Tylor, E.J., 192
Tyriakian, E.A., 31

Varagnac, A., 14, 32
Vauban, S. de, 14
Veblen, T., 10, 12, 14
Verner, C., 174
Vilar, J., 159
Villadary, A., 12
Villeneuve, A., 129
Vodzinskaya, V.V., 26
Volgov, V., 45

Weber, M., 151
Wibaux, C., 95, 100, 102, 103
Wiener, A., 16, 18
Wilensky, H., 11, 12, 19, 68, 122, 153
Willener, A., 173
Within, J.W.M., 192
White, L., 11
Wogensky, A., 143
Wolfenstein, M., 75

Yankelovich, D., 27, 34, 35

Zdravomyslov, A.G., 21, 23
Zetterberg, R.G., 28
Zola, E., 61, 209
Zvorikin, 50
Zygulski, K., 12

Subject Index

Active sociology, 164–170, 181–186
Adult education, 2, 52, 173–180
Associations, 88

Continuing education, 2, 131–132, 179–180
Cultural action, 59–62, 162
Cultural development, 5–6, 173–176
Cultural expert, 170–171
Cultural planning, 156–173
Cultural policy, 36–38, 155, 210
Cultural inequality, 51–53
Culture, 59–61, 149
    mass, 6, 11, 139–140, 153–158, 174–180

Evolution of leisure,
    in France, 19, 27, 29, 34–36, 53–64, 84–102, 177
    in USA, 10, 19–21, 23–25, 28, 34, 95–96. 102–104. 134, 178–179, 196–200
    in USSR, 12, 23, 26, 29, 35–36, 43–52, 200–201

Family pursuits, 25–30, 97–99
Free time/time freed from work, 16–22, 24–25, 38–39, 47–49, 52, 55, 69–71, 94, 129–131, 212

Games, 89–90, *see also* Interests, physical
Gardening, 56–57, 101–102

Hedonism, 75–76
Holidays, 20, 26, 55, 71–72

Ideology, 4–6, 33, 163–169
Idleness, 10, 15, 208
Individual, social value of the rights of, 41–43, 71–72, 76, 146–149
Interests
    artistic, 57–59, 101
    intellectual, 50–59, 102–103
    physical, 99–101
    practical, 101–102
    social, 85–91, 103–104

Leisure
    classification of, 72–73, 77–83
    definitions of, 67–76, 104, 208
    ethics of, 145–150
    facilities for, 55–59, 138–145
    factory workers', 52–53, 86, 114–115, 177, 193
    managers', 23–25
    mass, 11, 199
    studies, 12
    young people's, 27, 34–35, 55

Mass media, 153–154
    radio, 50, 58, 90–91
    television, 50, 57–58, 90, 180
Methods, 4–7, 46–47, 153–205, 215
Moonlighting, 22–25

Obligations
    family, 25–30, 97–99
    institutional, 73–74, 148
    socio-political, 30, 33–38. 69–70. 96–97
    socio-spiritual, 33, 95

Productivity, 45, 54, 125–126, 167–168

Reading, 58–59, 102
Religion, 14, 31–33
Retirement, 72, 92–105, 135–136

Self-tuition, 175
Social classes, 6
Social dynamics, 38–43
Social indicators, 51, 181–187
Society
    industrial, 15, 17, 31, 36–37, 178–179, 197–198
    post-industrial, 15, 18, 20–21, 65, 147–148, 193, 196–201
    pre-industrial, 14, 15, 126, 128, 130, 134, 163

Sociology of leisure
    empirical, 11, 22, 207
    comparative, 12
    historical, 12, 13, 14, 18–22

Time-budgets, 10, 20, 26–27, 35–36, 45, 71, 94, 129

Urbanism, 138, 145

Values, 4, 6, 123–125, 149–150, 207, 213

Weekends, 19, 21, 24, 25, 55, 56, 57, 72
Women's liberation, 26, 28, 29, 69, 129–131
Work
    duration of, 19, 25, 29, 94, 109, 111, 115, 127
    professional, 48–49, 109–112, 115–119, 127–138
    school, 131–132, 213
    versus free time, 107–150, 157, 208–209

LIBRARY OF DAVIDSON COLLEGE